MW00619187

TO BATAAN AND BACK

*This book's publication is generously sponsored
by the C. C. Taylor '51 Texas A&M University
Corps of Cadets Publishing Fund.*

Miscellaneous
Excerpt from W. Churchill's "A Roving Commission"
July issue of Reader's Digest – 1940

   Prisoner of War! It is a melancholy state. You are in the power of your enemy. You owe your life to his humanity, your daily bread to his compassion. You must obey his orders, await his pleasure, possess your soul in patience. The days are very long. Hours crawl like paralytic centipedes.

   Moreover, the whole atmosphere of prison, even the most easy and best regulated prison, is odious. Companions quarrel about trifles and get the least possible pleasure from each other's society. You feel a constant humiliation in being fenced by railings and wire, watched by armed men, and webbed about with a tangle of regulations and restrictions.

In Tom Dooley's canvas journal.

TO BATAAN AND BACK

THE WORLD WAR II DIARY OF
MAJOR THOMAS DOOLEY

★ ★ ★ ★ ★ ★ ★ ★ ★ ★ ★ ★

Edited and Transcribed by
JERRY C. COOPER

With **JOHN A. ADAMS JR.** *and* **HENRY C. DETHLOFF**
Foreword by COL. JAMES EDWIN RAY

Texas A&M University Press
College Station

This paper meets the requirements of ANSI/NISO Z39.48–1992 (Permanence of Paper).
Binding materials have been chosen for durability.
Manufactured in the United States of America

LIBRARY OF CONGRESS CATALOGING-IN-PUBLICATION DATA
Names: Cooper, Jerry C., 1941– editor. | Adams, John A., Jr., 1951– editor. |
Dethloff, Henry C., editor.
Title: To Bataan and back : the World War II diary of Major Thomas Dooley /
edited and transcribed by Jerry C. Cooper with John A. Adams Jr. and
Henry C. Dethloff.
Description: First edition. | College Station : Texas A&M University Press,
[2016] | Includes bibliographical references and index.
Identifiers: LCCN 2016034103| ISBN 9781623494339 (book/cloth : alk. paper) |
ISBN 9781623494346 (book/paper : alk. paper) | ISBN 9781623494353 (e-book)
Subjects: LCSH: World War, 1939–1945—Personal narratives, American. |
Dooley, Thomas, 1913–2006—Diaries. | World War,
1939–1945—Campaigns—Pacific Ocean. | World War,
1939–1945—Philippines—Bataan (Province). | World War,
1939–1945—Philippines—Corregidor Island.
Classification: LCC D811.A2 T6 2016 | DDC 940.54/7252092 [B]—dc23 LC
record available at https://lccn.loc.gov/2016034103

"It's not what you have been thru,
but the way in which what you have been thru
has affected you."

—*miscellaneous note near the end of
Tom Dooley's sixth (canvas-covered) journal.*

⌒

This book is dedicated my father, Francis C. Cooper '30,
whose wars were fought on the home front,

and to my cousin, Col. Earl Owen Cullum '35,
a classmate of Tom Dooley and a hero of the war in Burma.

CONTENTS

The World War II journals of fellow Texas Aggie Tom Dooley '35 reveal many facets of the relationships he had with family, schoolmates, friends, and fellow servicemen in his life and military career. Although I never met him, I almost feel a kinship. The young cavalry lieutenant, from his perspective as aide to a key general leading an impossible campaign, chronicles the effort to defend the Philippine Islands in the months following Japan's almost simultaneous attacks there and at Pearl Harbor, December 7th, 1941. His accounts bring us increased awareness and a heightened appreciation of an assembly of heroes and their heroic actions that helped inspire a nation to return from defeat to success and victory . . . not unlike an earlier campaign that inspired victory for Texans at San Jacinto, following a valiant, but failed defense at the Alamo.

Common to both campaigns, the defeats were not a failure of will; nor of commitment; nor of skill; nor of effort. At the Alamo and Bataan/ Corregidor, our compatriots were too far from home and were blocked from supplies and reinforcements sufficient to meet the capabilities of their adversaries. Nevertheless, in both cases, they did the best they could with what they had. Their heroic spirit and effort, along with a growing outrage at the subsequent barbaric treatment of the vanquished by their victors, inspired and fueled the determination to avenge them by our commitment to pursue each conflict to ultimate victory.

It's easy for me to relate, vicariously, to Tom Dooley. We're both native-born Texans; both young officers commissioned from our Texas A&M Cadet Corps training; both fought alongside allies in Southeast Asia, some of whose culture, military training, and experience left them, at times, less than competent and reliable (though many of them, too, fought doggedly and with heroism). Both Tom Dooley's and my Western Pacific service started and ended near Clark Air Base. Lieutenant Dooley ran a gauntlet through the first Japanese air raid on Clark AB in order to link up with his boss, Major General Jonathan Wainwright. After three years and four months as POWs, Dooley and Wainwright returned to participate in the formal surrender of the Japanese forces in the Philippines, before returning home. I attended jungle survival school at Clark AB prior to my duty in the Vietnam War. Following my six years, nine months as a POW in North Vietnam, I and all American POWs went to Clark AB Hospital for medical checkups and intelligence debriefings before returning to the USA.

Similarities in our shared experiences don't end there. As prisoners of war, we and our fellow captives were all denied humane treatment required by international law. In WWII, POWs faced periodic brutality (beatings and starvation). In North Vietnam rope tortures were used to extract "war crimes confessions," apologies, and anti-USA, anti-war statements. Captives in both wars were subject to humiliating and demeaning acts, like being forced to bow to all enemy personnel, even the lowest ranking guard, cook, or turnkey (jailer). In WWII, officers were coerced into doing manual labor while senior officers and weaker, ill, or injured officers were made to herd sheep or goats, or tend other farm animals. The North Vietnamese communists staked out many POWs at military targets, attempting to deter attacks. (One personally memorable example: in October 1967, John McCain's US Navy A-4 aircraft was brought down while attacking the Hanoi Thermal Power Plant, where I had been among the hostages.) For POWs in both WWII and Southeast Asia, inadequate medical care led to preventable deaths and permanently crippling injuries (but my instinct is that the WWII POWs of the Japanese fared worse). In both wars, acknowledgement of the status of missing men was poor to nonexistent, leaving survivors in tormenting doubt for weeks, months, and years. (Here, I feel that we in North Vietnam fared worse.) Further, mail was not permitted initially and for long periods, sometimes being used for coercive leverage and unjustified punishment.

When under extreme duress during interrogations, both Tom Dooley and I played "dumb" (like a fox), or too ill or too stressed (like a possum) to respond as our captors demanded. Most POWs, when coerced or tortured to answer sensitive questions, would obfuscate, filibuster, and mislead (like a momma bird faking a "broken" wing, leading predators away from the "targeted babies"). I especially identified with Dooley when he quoted his interrogator as growling in frustration, "Dooley, you're too stupid to be an aide to a General." In that situation, you know, for the moment, that you've won an infrequent victory; but you have to keep a poker face, or you blow it. I wondered if Dooley could hear the same warning, from the recesses of his Aggie fish-year (freshman) memory, as I did, when that oppressive "wethead" (sophomore), about two inches from my face, yelled something like "Fish Ray, keep that buzz (smile) off your face!" (My interrogator just yelled at me, "Ray, you have bad asstitude!")

There is nothing inherently heroic about being a prisoner of war. POWs contribute little, if anything, to the success of their nation's goals and objectives. Some circumstances of capture could even be judged "less than" honorable. Most attributable valor or heroism is in leadership, behavior, contributions, and achievements prior to being captured. And yet, even while in captivity, some extraordinary actions can be recognized as worthy of commendation. Dooley notes some instances but, for obvious reasons, could not include others. To facilitate later recall of details, Dooley records cryptic, benign events, which, if discovered, would not give captors cause to seize and destroy his notes, or punish, injure, or kill any POWs in retaliation. But these entries would establish timelines and memory joggers for eventual unrepressed publication of the inhumane, brutal, and barbaric reality.

[In this regard, I must caution against reading Dooley's diary entries after the fall of Bataan and Corregidor in isolation. As noted, they couldn't tell the whole story. Many relevant details came later in the 22-part series of *Dallas News* articles based on Dooley's journals in 1945. I also recommend reading the 52-part series THIS IS MY STORY by General Jonathan M. Wainwright in the *St. Joseph* (Missouri) *Gazette* and newspapers across the nation in 1945, later published as *General Wainwright's Story* in 1946.]

Even among the differences between Tom Dooley's experiences and mine, I could find common threads. He was much older than I, but almost the same age as my dad, who was also a Texas Aggie, Class of '38, and a science and vocational agriculture teacher. Tom Dooley was a cavalry officer, while I was an F-105D fighter/bomber pilot; but, when I was young, my dad usually had one or two horses for us to ride. One of Tom's closest contemporaries was Lt. Thomas Patrick Gerrity, an Army

Air Corps pilot. Tom Gerrity became the Air Corps liaison officer with General Wainwright while his hand and arm were healing from injuries inflicted during a Japanese air raid. I empathized with him, as he ached to heal and return to flying, as well as with all their efforts to keep the dwindling fleet of airplanes operational with no resupply of planes, fuel, and spare parts. Again and again, Dooley records examples of contemporaries doing the best they could when confronted with meager and disappearing resources.

Let me conclude with two benefits I had, that Tom Dooley didn't, and why I feel that is important. First, while I was in Jr. High School, there was an English teacher whose husband, James E. "Red" Reynolds, had been an enlisted Navy man in the Pacific and a prisoner of the Japanese. "Red" and Edith Welch Reynolds had compiled a manuscript from periodic diary notes he had made, kept hidden, and carried home. When I showed an interest in his experiences, they loaned me their manuscript. As I now recall, it was similar in many respects to Tom Dooley's, except that as an enlisted man, Reynolds and his fellow POWs were worked in factories and mines. In addition to the brutality and near starvation, the freezing cold itself was often life threatening in Japan and Manchuria (something we Vietnam POWs rarely felt). So, while I was a POW, whenever I did feel painfully chilled, or a bit down (depressed), I'd eventually remind myself, "If "Red" Reynolds could endure and survive, in an overall experience as bad as or worse than mine, so should I." Having been forewarned, I was forearmed.

Second, while at Texas A&M, I often had upperclassmen who, rather than harass us with frivolous trivia, made us read and memorize biographical sketches of Aggie high achievers, such as the Texas A&M awardees of the Medal of Honor: Carswell '38, Fowler '43, Harrell '43, Hughes '43, Keathley '37, Leonard '42, and Whiteley '41. We actually met and heard personal talks from Harrell and Whiteley. The other five had left their "last full measure" of devotion to duty on the fields of battle. So I had the additional benefit of their heroic and sacrificial examples. However, Dooley's motivation and attitude, as gleaned from his notations and his list of books he read and discussed with friends, indicates to me that he had similar stimulating role models from his education, training, and service experience, two prime examples being his boss, General Wainwright, and, up the chain, General Douglas MacArthur.

In any generation, that which we promote and encourage our fellow citizens, and all human beings, especially our young people, to read, study, treasure, and revere will influence and likely determine the values, the capability, and the motivation they will need to sustain and improve future human civilization.

—Col. James Edwin Ray, US Air Force, Texas A&M Class of 1963
Prisoner of War, North Vietnam, May 1966–February 1973

It is with great pride that we introduce the very personal record of one who experienced the horror of surprise bombing attacks on the Philippine Islands at the outset of World War II. Lt. Thomas Dooley's six journals (comprising more than five hundred handwritten pages) begin shortly after the attack on Pearl Harbor, Hawaii, cover the struggle against mounting odds, and continue through more than three years as a prisoner of war.

For most of the past seven decades those who viewed Dooley's record included only his family and close friends.

In the summer of 2005, when I was seeking permission to include Tom Dooley's 1978 Texas A&M campus Muster address in a book of Aggie Muster speeches, I asked his wife, Catherine "Kitty" Dooley, "Are you having any luck convincing the children that Colonel Dooley's diaries should be placed in the A&M archives for proper preservation? If they insist on keeping the originals, I hope we could borrow them just long enough to have copies made for the archives."

A few months later Kitty's daughter, Mary Randolph "Randy" Dooley Peters, sent me copies of the journals, prompting me to seek permission to transcribe and possibly publish them. On December 20 she wished me Merry Christmas and stated, "Would be fine for you to transcribe them." And she added, "I don't know about you, but I'll be able emotionally to relinquish the diaries pretty soon, because I know A&M will be able to preserve and protect them, and they are invaluable to me."

After I sent Kitty and Randy the unedited transcript of the first journal (Pearl Harbor to mid-April 1942), Randy wrote that her father had had a mild heart attack. A month later she notified me that Tom Dooley had died on the 26th of March 2006, at the age of 92. Texas A&M Singing Cadets Director David Kipp furnished sheet music and CDs so that A&M music would be used at his memorial service.

Tom Dooley's six World War II journals arrived in College Station in mid-May 2009, and on May 18 they were turned over to the Texas A&M University Archives.

Right after this my wife, Carole, showed me that Tom Dooley's diaries were referenced in a special twenty-two-part series published in the *Dallas Morning News* in October 1945. While researching this series, I found a six-part series, published by the *Chicago Times*, based on the diary of Lt. Thomas Patrick Gerrity, who had worked closely with Dooley and Maj. Gen. Jonathan Mayhew Wainwright at Bataan and Corregidor before escaping to Australia and eventually flying forty-nine combat missions. Gerrity's diary parallels Dooley's first journal from the day after the Pearl Harbor attack until shortly before the surrender of Bataan and Corregidor, in April/May 1942.

Dooley's journals chronicle the stand against a superior force that gave the United States and its allies time to develop a plan and marshal the forces necessary to defeat Japanese attempts to dominate Southeast Asia and the Pacific. Often compared to the 1836 stand of the Texians at the Alamo, Bataan and Corregidor occupy a vital place in the history of warfare.

I owe a debt of gratitude to John N. Drayton, for not only his masterful editing of the manuscript, but his countless contributions in fleshing out names and ranks as well as pointing me to important sources of clarifying information. His interest in the subject matter constantly buoyed my spirits and helped me complete the book. Texas A&M University press director Shannon Davies, editor-in-chief Jay Dew, associate editor Patricia Clabaugh, and others at the Press have turned what could have been a difficult chore into a pleasurable experience. Anne Boykin's excellent maps help readers relate to Tom Dooley's story.

I would like to say a heartfelt "Thank You" to C. C. Taylor '51, whose support and encouragement not only initiated efforts to produce this book, but made its publication possible. He is an Aggies' Aggie in every sense of the phrase. In addition to funding numerous scholarships and program endowments, he made it his life goal to tell the world about Texas A&M's contributions in times of war and peace. The university is a richer place because of Aggies like C. C. Taylor. I also want to express my appreciation to John A. Adams Jr. '73 and Texas A&M emeritus history professor Henry C. Dethloff. Their personal prodding, understanding, and advice has made this a real labor of love.

—Jerry C. Cooper '63
Editor, *The Texas Aggie* magazine 1971–2002

The wartime journals of lst Lt. Thomas Dooley, a Texas Aggie, class of 1935, and aide-de-camp to Maj. Gen. Jonathan Wainwright in the Philippines, comprise six small notebooks and ledgers carefully inscribed with penciled daily notes commencing on Monday, 8 December 1941, at Clark Field, Philippines. The journals are distinctive historic documents. They are among very few personal daily diaries that cover World War II from beginning to end. Moreover, they provide a portrait of the war in the Philippines and the South Pacific from the perspective of an aide to General Wainwright. Dooley was acquainted both with the key officers and officials heading America's military forces and with some officers heading the Japanese armed forces. He is an observer of American defensive positions, military resources, strategies, and expectations in the Philippines.

In addition to chronicling the brilliant maneuvers and skilled deployment of extremely limited resources that delayed and often repelled the landings of large Japanese forces on Luzon, Dooley describes the personal relationships he had with those he met. His concern for their welfare and for his family back home is apparent. He collected the recipes that POWs often discussed to take their minds off of the privations of captivity; he wrote down songs they composed; he kept track of his weight and his inoculations; and he created a detailed record of American officers in Karenko POW camp.

Dooley's story begins when a perceived time of "peace and quiet" is disrupted by the Japanese attack on Pearl Harbor and the almost simultaneous invasion of the Philippines. On 15 December 1941, Dooley wrote his own "foreword," recapping the first week of the conflict.

The story begins as expectations of reinforcements and supplies are transformed into desperate retreat and resistance on Bataan and Corregidor. Relief never comes, and the defense ceases when American forces surrender in the Philippines on 5 and 6 May 1942. Dooley begins his imprisonment in company with General Wainwright and other American officers and military personnel in a variety of Japanese POW encampments in the Philippines, Taiwan, and Manchuria.

The end of Dooley's ordeal was foreshadowed by events in early August 1945. Lt. Charles "Chili" McClintick '40, a Texas Aggie from San Antonio, was returning from a mission over Honshu, Japan, on August 6 when he saw a "dark mushroom cloud" off to the left of his aircraft. The crewmembers were later informed that an atomic bomb had been dropped over Hiroshima. A few days later, on August 9, another Texas Aggie, flight leader Lt. Richard Collins '45, reported seeing "an extremely bright flashing fireball, rising up through a cloud cover, rapidly growing in size," which changed in a matter of moments into "a tall, irregular stovepipe shape" that reached to the heavens. A second atomic bomb had fallen, this time on Nagasaki. At noon on August 15, Emperor Hirohito accepted the American terms of surrender.

On August 16 Dooley noted that the Japanese guards were acting differently and that a number of "parachutists" had dropped into the compound. At first the POWs thought the parachutists were "Japs on maneuvers," but in fact they were American soldiers wearing sidearms. Soon after that, Dooley reported, "Pfc. Griff" asked a Japanese guard if the war was over, and the guard said, "Yes—tomorrow you will understand." Then, on August 17, Dooley noted that General Parker, Air Vice-Marshal Paul Maltby, and several other ranking officers were called to the prison-camp headquarters. When they returned, General Parker assembled the Americans and announced that an armistice had been signed. That evening Red Cross food was issued and the place was "gay with plenty of food, coffee, and cigarettes."

Following Dooley's return to Texas, the *Dallas News* ran a series of celebratory stories based on his experiences and the American relief and recovery from war. The newspaper announced the series 19 September 1945:

Voices from Bataan

The story of Bataan and Corregidor, the Greatest Heartache America ever suffered will never die. The heroic, gangling figure of Gen. Jonathan (Skinny) Wainwright shepherding a tattered band of Americans through the war's darkest moments.

Now it comes to life in a warm and human narration carved from the diary of young Texas Lt. Col. Tom Dooley of McKinney, the man who stood by General Wainwright's side on Bataan and Corregidor as his aide. He knows the story of Bataan, Corregidor, and Skinny Wainwright; he saw every moment of it.

Then he lived through three years, three months and twenty-one days of Japanese-made hell in prison camps before liberation came. With General Wainwright, weak and gaunt from imprisonment, he proudly witnessed the surrender aboard the USS *Missouri*. Then they flew home together to the nation's acclaim.

Gen. Jonathan M. Wainwright's Post-War Service

On 5 September 1945, three days following the Japanese surrender, General Wainwright received his fourth star. Five days later he arrived in Washington DC, where he visited the Pentagon (which had been constructed during the war) and the capitol, where he addressed the House of Representatives and the Senate. Then, at the White House, he walked into the rose garden, where President Harry S. Truman surprised him with the Medal of Honor. After brief service as commander of Second Service Command and the Eastern Defense Command at Fort Jay, Governors Island, New York, he became the commander of the Fourth Army at Fort Sam Houston, Texas, where he served a year and a half before retiring in August 1947.

On 17 April 1947, he led Fourth Army troops into Texas City, Texas, following disastrous explosions there. According to Bill Minutaglio, author of *City on Fire*, Wainwright arrived at city hall and told Mayor Curtis Trahan's liaison, John Hill, "I'm General Jonathan Wainwright. Mr. Hill, the Fourth Army is here, and we are ready to take over." When Hill informed him the governor had not declared martial law, Wainwright responded, "Mr. Hill, you are absolutely right. What do you want the Fourth Army to do?"

Gen. Wainwright's syndicated 1945 newspaper series, "This Is My Story," was expanded in a book, *General Wainwright's Story*, published in 1946. He added two chapters: "Conclusions," in which he analyzed the steps required to prevent another major conflict, and "Commendations," in which he saluted all the units under his command for their delaying actions and heroic performance against overwhelming odds.

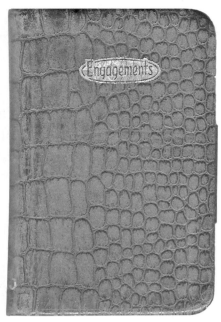

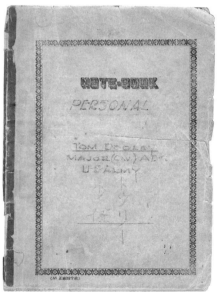

Left to right, top to bottom:

First Journal ("Personal Record")
December 1941–April 1942.

Second Journal ("Engagements")
May–December 1942.

Third Journal ("Note-Book Personal"
Red Band); 1 January 1943–7 October
1944; 25–27 April 1945. POW camp pay
account; inoculations; list of American
officer POWs; Camp #4; list of books.

Journal photos courtesy the Tom
Dooley Family.

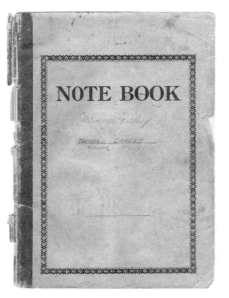

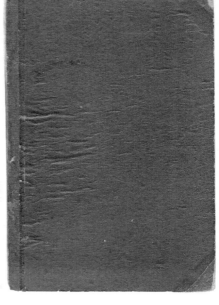

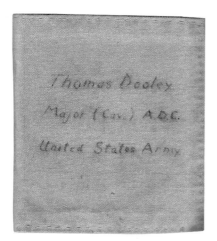

Left to right, top to bottom:

Fourth Journal ("Note Book" Black Band) Lists of books and songs, and prisoner-treatment comparisons, copies of letters, signatures·of POWs.

Fifth Journal (Black Cover) 16 August–6 September 1945. List of flight crew, Manila to Washington DC.

Sixth Journal (Canvas Cover) Lists of personal belongings and books; reminders; recipes; timelines; odd notes; excerpts from books; Gen. Wainwright's Song; inoculations; weight record; addresses.

Journal photos courtesy the Tom Dooley Family.

TO BATAAN AND BACK

ONE

Duty Calls

World War II began 7 December 1941 with a surprise attack on Pearl Harbor by 360 Japanese fighter planes, bombers, and torpedo planes that crippled the US Pacific Fleet, sinking or damaging nineteen warships and crippling 188 aircraft. Two thousand four hundred three men died, and 1,178 more were wounded. Word of the attack reached American forces in the Philippines later that same day (already December 8). Major LeGrande A. "Pick" Diller, aide-de-camp to Gen. Douglas MacArthur, commander of American forces in the Philippines, issued a press release at about 8:00 A.M. stating, "There is a morning paper out and the Japs have started it." Dooley, aide-de-camp to Maj. Gen. Jonathan Mayhew Wainwright, heard about the press release from Col. Frank Nelson, and Dooley's first reaction was that Nelson must be dreaming or "had a hangover." But it was true. Confirmation came soon. A radiogram signed by General MacArthur read simply, "A state of war exists between the US and the government of Germany, Japan and Italy."

More definitive confirmation followed. As Dooley drove from Ft. Stotsenburg to Manila on an errand for General Wainwright, he saw smoke. His first thought was that the local "Baluga" tribesmen were setting fire to the brush in their hunt for game. But when he saw that the smoke was mixed with high-flying dust, he realized that the "Japs were bombing the Hell out of Clark Field!" The war had come to the Philippines. Lt. Tom Dooley was in a unique position to observe and witness the war from its beginning in the Philippines, on 8 December 1941, until its close, with the Japanese surrender aboard the battleship USS Missouri in Tokyo Bay on 2 September 1945. He was there from the beginning to the end. And as aide-de-camp to General Wainwright he was in touch with American and Philippine field commanders, acquainted with many, and present when many critical combat decisions were made.

Tom Dooley's Senior Class Photo. From *1935 Long Horn* (Texas A&M Yearbook).

Generals Jonathan M. Wainwright and Douglas MacArthur in the Philippines before the war. From Wainwright, *General Wainwright's Story*. Photo courtesy John A. Adams, Jr.

What follows is the story of war, surrender, imprisonment, and peace as recorded in the journals of Thomas Dooley, a 1935 graduate of the Agricultural & Mechanical College of Texas—which contributed many of its graduates to military service in the Philippines. When Commandant and Professor of Military Science and Tactics Col. George F. Moore '08 received orders assigning him to duty in the Philippines, he reportedly selected almost thirty graduating Aggies to precede him to his new post.

Tom Dooley was born and reared in McKinney, Texas, a small farming community of about 7,500 that, over the next century, would mushroom into a Dallas suburb of about 150,000. By the standard of those days, he was a "city" boy, driving an ice wagon while in grade school and high school and playing some football at Boyd High School, where he was "engaging and friendly." He aspired to go to college and work in the booming Texas oil business. Accepted into A&M, he studied engineering and was (as required) a member of the Corps of Cadets. During his senior year he was elected Head Yell Leader.

1934–35 Texas A&M Yell Staff: L. M. "Jocko" Roberts '36; Tom Dooley '35, chief yell leader; Roland "PeeWee" Burks '35; and "Yannie" Schott '36. From *1935 Long Horn* (Texas A&M Yearbook).

The five most popular members of the Texas A&M Class of 1935 were W. E. Fitzgerald, circulation manager of *The Battalion*; F. W. H. Wehner, Senior Class president; J. C. McHaney, cadet colonel; Ed Mears, Senior Class VP; and Tom Dooley, chief yell leader. From *1935 Long Horn* (Texas A&M Yearbook).

Jobs were scarce in Texas when he graduated in 1935, and life could be pretty turbulent. And so it was with Tom Dooley. Six months after graduating he landed a two-month job as superintendent with the New Deal's Works Progress Administration in Plano and McAllen. Going on active duty as a second lieutenant with the US Army on 15 January 1936, he headed a Civilian Conservation Corps (CCC) camp in Bonham for six months. On 5 July he signed up for one year of duty with the 2nd Squadron of the 12th Cavalry at Ft. Ringgold (near Rio Grande City), after which he found himself again unemployed until September 1937, when he went to work for Sun Oil and then Halliburton in south and southeast Texas.

In July 1940 he was reactivated for duty with Headquarters 1st Cavalry Brigade at Ft. Clark and Ft. Bliss, in West Texas, where he received orders to join the 26th Cavalry in the Philippines.

He sailed from San Francisco aboard the SS Washington *and arrived 8 May 1941. He would be at Ft. Stotsenburg, north of Manila, until 8 September, when he was assigned as aide-de-camp to Maj. Gen. Jonathan M. Wainwright, commander of the Philippine Division at Ft. William McKinley, south of Manila. On 27 November, Wainwright was named commander of the North Luzon Force, and he moved his headquarters staff, including Dooley, to Ft. Stotsenburg. On 8 December 1941—7 December Hawaii time—Dooley's life and that of every American changed forever.*

On that date Tom Dooley began keeping a daily journal recording the flow of events that changed war from a far-off "fracas" to a horrifying reality—death, destruction, imprisonment, and starvation—followed by freedom and a return home. His journal is a unique on-site record of war and the conduct of war by senior officers and personnel in the Philippines.

12-15-41

My intentions are to keep some sort of running account of what goes on in this fracas. Not a diary nor a memorandum, but a cross between the two. I am one week late in getting this poop on the go—that is, it will be one week old in about four hours. My turn came up as Duty Officer from 12:00 midnight to 8:00 a.m. and the routine being very quiet tonight I can get this under way. Corporal Molina, Battery A, 24th Field Artillery (Philippine Scouts) is the Non-Commissioned Officer on duty and he has just shown me a copy of the radiogram signed by General MacArthur saying "a state of war exists between the US and the government of Germany, Japan and Italy".

Opposite, above: Map of Philippine Islands showing Tom Dooley's path as a prisoner of war. Map by Anne Boykin.

Opposite, below: Map of Luzon showing US military installations and key towns. Map by Anne Boykin.

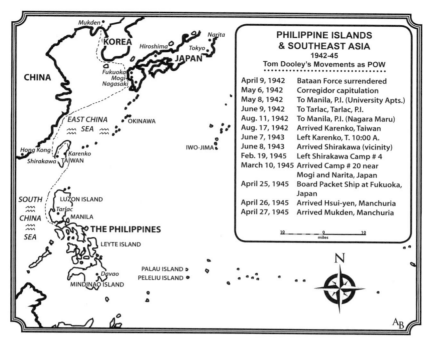

PHILIPPINE ISLANDS & SOUTHEAST ASIA
1942-45
Tom Dooley's Movements as POW

April 9, 1942	Bataan Force surrendered
May 6, 1942	Corregidor capitulation
May 8, 1942	To Manila, P.I. (University Apts.)
June 9, 1942	To Tarlac, Tarlac, P.I.
Aug. 11, 1942	To Manila, P.I. (Nagara Maru)
Aug. 17, 1942	Arrived Karenko, Taiwan
June 7, 1943	Left Karenko, T. 10:00 A.
June 8, 1943	Arrived Shirakawa (vicinity)
Feb. 19, 1945	Left Shirakawa Camp # 4
March 10, 1945	Arrived Camp # 20 near Mogi and Narita, Japan
April 25, 1945	Board Packet Ship at Fukuoka, Japan
April 26, 1945	Arrived Hsui-yen, Manchuria
April 27, 1945	Arrived Mukden, Manchuria

5

As said, I am one week late in getting started and am trusting that I can jot down from memory the points I want. I'll start from Monday morn. 12-8-41. That day began quietly and peacefully . . .

With this and the following entries, Lt. Thomas Dooley, Texas A&M Class of 1935, began an amazing series of six journals, in which he recorded his personal activities and those of his friends and fellow soldiers stationed in the Philippine Islands before, during, and after the Japanese attack on Pearl Harbor in December 1941. As an aide-de-camp to Maj. Gen. Jonathan M. Wainwright, commander of the forces on Bataan and Corregidor, he was uniquely positioned for regular contact with the various commands and to personally witness the opening conflicts of World War II—as well as the final moment, the surrender of Japan aboard the USS Missouri, on 2 September 1945.

Monday Dec. 8, 1941—Manila

Started very quietly with no thought of impending confusion. Was staying at Army-Navy Club in Manila and got up about 7:30 a.m. after putting Gerry MacPherson on the *"Taiping"* at 3:00. Had breakfast and read routine talk in "Bulletin," then took a book, "GWTW" [*Gone with the Wind*], to 915 Belen St. to Mrs. H.F. Williams for Gerry. When I got back to the ANC saw Col. Frank Nelson, who has shared my room and he said "There is another morning paper out and the Japs have started it. They bombed Hawaii." I really gave this little thought due to my belief that the Col. was a bit hazy from a hangover, but soon found he was quite right. Had an appointment with General Jonathan M. Wainwright at US Army Forces Far East Headquarters at 10:00 a.m. and got there about 9:45 a.m. The Gen. is usually about 15 min. early and I was surprised not to find him there. While sitting in the waiting room I heard Major LeGrande A. "Pick" Diller, MacArthur's aide-de-camp, give out a press release to the effect that Davao + Baguio had been bombed. About that time Capt. [*John R.*] "Johnny" Pugh came out of [*Lt.*] Gen. [*Richard K.*] Sutherland's office and said all this unbelievable talk was quite true. I stayed around long enough to get some dope from Johnny to go back to Stotsenburg and checked out of Army-Navy Club about 11:15 a.m. [*Johnny R. Pugh, General Wainwright's senior aide-de-camp, was commissioned in the US Cavalry from the US Military*

Haruki Iki, *Repulse* and the *Prince of Wales* © 1980, Keith Ferris '50. Japanese Betty Bombers like this one flew out of Saigon on 8 December 1941 to attack Malaysia and the Philippine Islands. Used by permission of the artist.

"Too Little, Too Late" © 1991, Keith Ferris '50. 20th Pursuit Squadron Commander 1st Lt. Joseph H. Moore in his P-40B engages Japanese Zeros during 8 December 1941 bombing of devastated Clark Field below. Used by permission of the artist.

Academy in 1932. He also served at G-2 for I Corps in the Philippines.
After commanding the 82nd Airborne Division's 325th Airborne Regi-
ment and 2nd Squadron of the 3rd Armored Cavalry Regiment, he served
on the Army G-3 staff, with the CIA, as Chief of Staff of the Berlin Com-
mand, and G-3 of the 8th Army in Korea. He then became Chief of Staff
of Second Army, Commander of the 3rd Armored Division, and Com-
mander of VI Corps. His awards would include three Silver Stars, the
Distinguished Service Medal, the Legion of Merit, and the Bronze Star.
He retired as a Major General and died on 2 March, 1994.]

Manila was just hearing all the news and traffic was getting more
difficult than usual (if possible). The only change I could notice on the
Highway on the way up was the friendly attitude of all the natives. They
had the news and my being in uniform brought a "Hello Joe" and wave
all along the drive. I turned off as usual at Dau and got across the RR
and into Camp Del Pilar before I noticed anything wrong. I glanced up
and saw smoke, thinking first of the story the Gen. tells about Balugas
setting fire to the brush to aid in the hunt for game, but soon realized
that the smoke was mixed with high flying dust and that the Japs were
bombing Hell out of Clark Field. I had wondered how I would react
to first duty under fire and thinking back on my reactions, I am quite
proud, for the idea didn't enter my mind to turn back. I did stop the
car long enough to look up (the top was down) and count the enemy
planes. Later found that I only counted one flight of 27. They really were
a beautiful sight in close formation. Hard to detect for they were silver
against a clear sky and flying very high (between 10,000 + 20,000 feet).
I'm glad now that they had German tutors and organization in this
first day for the line on the bombs across Clark Field, had it continued,
would have caught me at Del Pilar.

I drove faster then, up the bad road into Stotsenburg with one
thought in mind.—To get to Gen. Wainwright—I did, but at one time
I didn't know whether I'd make it or not. Natives (civilian workers)
were streaming out of the post. First thought—like rats from a sinking ship, but later actions of the Filipinos show that the family tie was
strong and their only thought was to get their families to the hills.

When I got in the vicinity of Margot station (an Angeles barrio) all
Hell popped loose and it proved to be the 200th Coast Artillery area
and they were fighting off dive-bombers and ground-strafing planes.

I got on a deadend road due to new construction and, as I was coming out of that, one Jap attack plane came quite near. Machine gun fire broke out in front of me and the din was terrific. I could plainly see the markings on the Jap plane. Kept on thru the general maintenance area and got to Headquarters building and about that time the Gen. drove up from his quarters and nonchalantly said, "Hello Tom, how was your courting." I said I was well up on it and it looked like it was a good thing. He asked if I was nervous and I said certainly, but always was even when going to a dance. My "mañana" attitude had caught up again, because here a war had opened up and caught me without even a pistol. I borrowed one from the Gen. and returned it later in the day, when I drew some equipment from Headquarters Troop of the 26th Cavalry. [*General Wainwright wrote of this incident in* General Wainwright's Story: *"While this was happening, Tom Dooley drove up with a screeching of brakes and jumped out of his car. I saw from the direction in which he came that he must have driven right past Clark Field. 'Tom, you damned fool, you didn't drive past Clark during this bombing, did you?' I shouted at him angrily. 'Sure, sir,' he said. 'You sent me orders to report to you as fast as I could, and I was worse afraid of you than I was of those bombs.' I stalked inside my headquarters, with Tom at my heels and quietly wrote out the order which gave him, and the young gunner (who had just been wounded), Silver Stars. I guess they were the first decorations of the Pacific war."*]

Soon after the raid subsided I went with the Gen. and Col. [*Clinton A.*] Pierce, Commanding Officer of the 26th Cavalry, on an inspection of Clark Field. The damage was terrific. It was terrible to see all of that wonderful Air Corps equipment burned or still in flames. The B-17's were the main object of their raid and they certainly did a job on them. Final count—13. Went from Clark Field to the Hospital where they were bringing in casualties in all conditions and by all transportation at hand. People were quite jittery, even medicos, which I had not expected to see. (If I forget on tomorrow's notes, I want to comment on [*Maj. James A.*] Jim McCloskey's behavior—he came thru as expected. He's a man and a prince of a fellow.) [*McCloskey was the first regular US Army doctor to lose his life in World War II on Bataan, 26 March 1942.*]

While at hospital, one Air Corps bomb truck drove up with 3 dead. They took off the blanket and you could tell from across the street that they were dead by the color, so pale it seemed yellow. Spent the rest of the p.m. getting some equipment together and doing odd turns for the General. Johnny came in about 6:00 PM and was quite perturbed which was only natural. Of course a blackout had been ordered and I got to bed very early. Johnny was mulling about the quarters, as usual and couldn't get to sleep, but I fell asleep as I hit the pillow.

Tuesday 12-9-41—Stotsenburg

Not quite so hectic, this date. Troops digging more "fox holes" and staff sections getting better organized. Johnny and [*Maj. Joseph Ludger*] Chabot moved into my office and I sort of attached myself to G-2 section. Numerous reports coming in. Some now seem absurd, but everyone felt that each should be checked. An American woman, Mrs. Neckes, who was caught at Stotsenburg in the raid, spent last night at the General's and he sent her to join her husband in Manila today. No trains running so she went in the General's car. Mr. Neckes is manager of Mackay Radio, so we sent radiograms by her. Mine to mother saying, "Everything alright, don't worry." I know she will, though. That's the worst about this war—of course besides the death of a lot of wonderful people—the worry I know that Mother, Dad + Cissy are going thru. I wonder if they called Margaret [*Boyd*] when they got my radiogram. Thought also about the Xmas gifts that I got off on the 25th of Nov. Have heard today that the *Hugh L. Scott* was sunk. I believe the Xmas presents were on that boat. Had sent Margaret a nice Chinese house coat with Chinese shoes to match. Hope by some chance they get thru. Won't be able to send the money I had intended to Mom and Dad in addition to some bits of linen I had sent on the boat. Am sure they will understand. If I am in Manila around Xmas I am going to call home.

Wednesday 12-10-41—Stotsenburg

Francisco (our cook) came back today. He was not alarmed for himself, only for his family. He got them fixed comfortably in the mountains and now he is back to work. George, the houseboy at McKinley reported today, too. The 2nd Squadron of the 26th Cav. was sent to vicinity of Arrayat today under Major Thomas J. H. Trapnell to find and destroy paratroops. [*The supposed Japanese paratroopers were later thought to be pilots parachuting from damaged aircraft, descending bursts of antiaircraft fire, or jettisoned spare gas tanks.*] He had 2 Troop Cavalry, one battalion of Field artillery (self propelled) and one battery of tanks. Trap is a grand fellow, one of the best liked people I have ever seen. No one dislikes him. "He is not shooting cats now." Routine most of the day.

Visited hospital, talked with Jim McCloskey. He said Jack Kelly was OK. Hasn't seen him, but had heard from him. Suppose our tennis will have to wait until this war gets more routine. General Wainwright plans trip to Lingayen area tomorrow. Reports have come in that Japs have landed at Vigan and Aparri. Trust we can work on them enough to keep out their land-based aviation. On as duty officer at North Luzon Force Headquarters 'til midnight. Kept quite busy for a while, but so sleepy at 11:00 that I could hardly make it. Think when I get back to the States that I'll get M. S. M. [*an unidentified friend*] to let me spend a week on his farm if he doesn't have a telephone there. Johnny has come around now and can sleep nights. I can too.

Thursday 12-11-41—Stotsenburg

Another air raid today. No casualties and little damage done. Casualties on Monday's raid have been totaled—82 dead and about 110 wounded. 29 dead were civilians—poor little Carenderas that worked near Batchelors Building. We are getting Jap planes down though. Lots of them are being hit and the Japs toss out equipment to lighten the load so they can get as far back toward their base as possible. Quite a few have been brought down near here though. One plane shot down near Mabalacat (east of Stotsenburg) and Chaplain [*Maj. John E.*] Duffy brought a gun from it to G-2 section. Workmanship crude but they still fire. He reported that natives had buried the pilot and said he was man of larger size than the Chaplain which indicates he was a German. Planes in today's raid carried Swastika markings. The Nazis have planned and directed the execution of all this. It (especially Monday) was too methodical and timely. My appetite has doubled. For breakfast, even, which prior to "this" consisted of coffee and toast—now consists of fruit, coffee, toast, bacon + eggs and anything else within reach. Am still sleeping like a log when I hit the bunk.

Friday 12-12-41—Stotsenburg

Left about 9:00 a.m. this morning with the Gen. and made inspections of 3 Divisions in north. One of them had reported time of passing over and return of Jap bombers and by figuring the time I said "Gen., they hit Stotsenburg again." He said, "No, Manila." Also on the way in I saw grass fire which I remarked was set by falling plane. He said it was by Balugas. Upon return to Stotsenburg my statements proved sound and even correct. They had had a raid—26th Cav. 2 dead—5 wounded. 200th Coast Artillery 6 dead—7 wounded. The Japs had been after the 200th Coast Artillery area to try and knock out the antiaircraft guns. Their raid was unsuccessful. The fire (grass) I mentioned above had been caused by a Jap plane and the Jap crew of three had been captured by natives, trussed up and brought into the post. G-2 (Johnny and Joe) had been unsuccessful in their investigation. The Japs were tight mouthed and showed no change of expression except a thankful one when they were given water to drink. One eager Filipino trooper from Field artillery tried to kill one of the prisoners. He started in with his gun and was stopped. One trooper had a scalp wound from machine gun strafing fire in the raid previous. The Japs were sent to Manila. An Army Corps, which ours is, has no set-up for concentrating prisoners. That is usually done by Army Headquarters. Manila has had raids, the worst being today on Cavite, the naval base. Casualties were high. Everyone loves to hear what an Air Corps Squadron commander did today. His name—Lt. Boyd D. "Buzz" Wagner—took a P-40 north on a reconnaissance mission and found the Japs are using a small field at Aparri for basing attack and pursuit planes. "Buzz" was attacked by three Jap planes and he out-maneuvered them and shot down two of them. The other flier and Wagner proceeded to strafe the field. He set fire to five (5) planes on the ground and machine-gunned 7 more—accounting for loss of 7 planes and damage to 7. Nice work. [*Lt. Boyd "Buzz" Wagner was reportedly the first USAAF ace of WWII and earned a DSC.*]

Saturday 12-13-41—Stotsenburg

I am still driving the Buick convertible touring car with the top down that Dave Cook left with me. I do so much gadding about for the Gen. that I need the car. I was out with the Gen. but there is one machine gun bullet hole in one fender gotten during yesterday's raid. Headquarters moved their command post today to the field. Heavy foliage all about but it will not be satisfactory. Probably be moved soon. Wanted the Gen. to send me to Manila today, but he wouldn't. Planes came over a great many times today but no raid. They are probably taking photographs. Still eating like a bird (vulture). Am quite concerned about the *Taiping*, Gerry MacPherson's boat. She sailed at 4:00 a.m. the morning war broke out. Trust she is OK. A grand person. May get some information from Peggy McAvoy if I get to Manila. Col. MacPherson is in Hong Kong. Trust he is weathering the Jap storm.

Sunday 12-14-41—Stotsenburg + Bamban

No raids today. The alarm sounded once but the bombers kept on. I suppose they were headed for Manila, but have had no reports from there as yet. Still the Japs fly their bombers in a tight formation, very high, and the silver paint makes them hard to spot. They, for the present, have air superiority and know it. They seem to bomb at will, but I know what our air corps has at the time. It will be quite different soon. The Japs will rue the day they started this fracas. The bad part is that after we knock them down we will probably have to stay over here and do occupation duty, as in Germany after the last war. Morale is very high among both military and civilian personnel. On the way up here today—I can't disclose the location now—the Filipino brats on the road would greet you by holding up two fingers and form the Vee. Everyone you pass gives the V for Victory sign. Heartening to see. Parachute troops will catch more Hell than a little from natives. All weapons have been brought out and the Filipino Bolo (a big knife) is evident every place you see a native.

We have heard that the "linking islands"—Guam, Midway + Wake are still held by our Marines. Of course, Air Mail is out now and I don't know when we will get other mail thru, but I will try radiograms each chance I get to let Mom, Dad + Cissy know I am OK. Am sure they will let Margaret B. know when they hear. Radiograms are expensive, you know.

Monday 12-15-41—Bamban

My turn as Duty Officer has come up as mentioned in "Foreword" (Sounds like I should be in tweeds and smoke a pipe) and I got this thing up to date. (Suppose the main reason for this is I can go over it later and remember all this and the other thing is I can just hand it to Cissy when I get home. She can read it and I won't have to talk so much.) Col. [*Frank*] Nelson (G-3) came in just now to check up on things and he has just told me that the Gen. has made it of record to entitle me to a silver star citation. I asked what for and it seems the General was impressed by my driving thru the air raid to report to him. If I do get that it will be a terrific injustice to all those poor devils actually on Clark Field that were firing away. It means nothing really. Main things they (citations) are for is to build up morale and mine doesn't need it.

After breakfast. A dull day—few reports coming in. I have delayed writing this up again and we have moved so I can tell of our wonderful set-up here in the North Luzon Force Command post. We moved into the Bamban Sugar Central offices in the "Union Bar." The sugar people met us with open arms and gave the place over. Johnny, Joe Chabot, and I went up to the resident manager's home and had a beer with his Superintendent. The home is a delightful spot—like you see in the movies. Later came back for a shave and bath. Bathrooms—tile with sunken tile tub and showers—with hot water. Doesn't sound like we are in the field. Still eating like a vulture. To bed quite early, too.

Tuesday 12-16-41—Bamban

Went into Stotsenburg quite early on errands for Gen. Wainwright and various other staff officers and for myself. Got pay vouchers fixed up. Drew various equipment from Quartermaster. Stopped by Hospital and saw Jim McCloskey. He's still OK, then down to see Jack Kelly. He is standing pat with what remains of his outfit. They are among the few left at Clark Field. He wrote out a radio message to Elizabeth for me to send if I get to Manila. Back to the Command post and routine.

Wednesday 12-17-41—Alcala

Off quite early on trip alone. First to Stotsenburg to return pay vouchers and then on to Manila. Cashed checks for several people

and then went out to see Peggy McAvoy. She seemed delighted to
see someone and I was certainly so to see her. She was in the yard
supervising the digging of an air raid shelter. She told me of the first
raid in Manila. One bomb hit in the corner of the yard and Peggy's
maid, "Belini" was struck by shrapnel and killed instantly. Throughout
p.m. Denis and "Modesta" (the cook) searched the various morgues
and saw that she had a decent funeral. Had lunch with Peggy and
then went to McKinley to do my chores. Saw General Clagett and
Nick (aide-de-camp). Gen. C. in good shape. Nick seemed a bit jittery.
Paid mess bills to Nick. To Manila again. Went by Asiatic Petroleum
to see Denis. Gave him a note to Gerry to deliver if possible. Sent
radiogram to Mother and sent others for Johnny, Gen. Wainwright
and Jim Blanning. Earlier in p.m. had been on my way to "Tabacalera"
[*old Spanish tobacco company*] to pay for some cigars the Gen. had
bought and as I stopped at Red Light on corner of Isaac Peral + Taft
Ave. I looked into the car opposite a model A Ford—quite dilapidated
with some private (in coveralls) driving and the passenger was Matilda
Zobel. I had just stopped by her home and she was not there so left
note with Simplicio. Told her I would see her at Red Cross Canteen
(Elks Club) before 5:00 p.m.. Picked her up there. Went to Army-Navy
Club, had a drink, then took her home. Had to rush to beat blackout.
I drove very fast and it was getting dark fast. As I was just leaving
San Fernando, Pampanga, it was too dark and I was going about 65
m.p.h. and all of a sudden a railroad barricade loomed up in front.
Couldn't stop so I ducked my head and blasted thru. Barricade took off
the windshield, but I was unhurt and kept going. Looked back and a
train whipped across the road. As mother used to say, "What fools ye
mortals be." Got into Command post at Bamban O.K. and got to bed.

Thursday 12-18-41—Alcala

My birthday and uneventful. Sorry this war is on because I usually
get a note from Mother on this date. In fact, the last mail from States
was post marked Nov. 7. Went into Stotsenburg and first got myself a
pistol and tin hat because I gave my tin hat and gas mask to Peggy and
the pistol to Denis. They really need them around Pusay. Back in Bamban and the General standing waiting to move out to new Command
post (up North). Got into new campus about 11:30 a.m. and had lunch.

For his birthday on 18 December 1941, Tom Dooley was presented an American half-dollar by fellow aide-de-camp Johnny Pugh, and General Wainwright gave him the lucky commemorative coin he had received at the 82nd (All-American) Division convention in Atlanta, Georgia, in 1930. Photo courtesy the Tom Dooley Family.

Johnny came in about 4:00 and said Happy Birthday. He gave me an American half-dollar. He has had three of them since arriving in P.I. Gave Gen. one, me one and kept one. Lucky pieces. The General felt he must give me something and he reached in his pocket and gave me a lucky piece from a convention he attended in Atlanta, Ga. in 1930 of the 82nd Div. (All-American Div. in France). He had carried the piece in his pocket since that time (11 years) and was quite fond of it so it is a nice gift.

Friday 12-19-41—Alcala

Made a trip with Gen. Wainwright this date. First to 26th Cavalry Command post and then up to 71st Div. (Col. Selleck) and then to 11th Div. (Col. Brougher). Nothing much happened today. Routine. George (Private Simmons)—the McKinley houseboy and now orderly (Bull in china closet) with my help + instruction built a bamboo and cocoanut leaf shack outside our tent. George reported once at McKinley that he was an American Indian—his mother Filipino—his father—10th Cavalry soldier (Negro). He has applied for American citizenship. Johnny took him down to State Dept. George quite annoyed at being inducted into Philippine Army. Said he wanted to serve in US Army. Took a bit of explaining.

Saturday 12-20-41—Alcala

Off on another trip—alone—in a taxicab impressed in service at start of war and driven by a Manila taxi driver. Kept me scared to death. Went first to Bataan and saw Command post Philippine Division. Nice to see all of them. Gen. Lough's aide Joe Sallee was to have gotten married this date and to make it worse, he hasn't even heard from the bride-to-be since war broke out. He was quite low. Went on to McKinley from there and to Finance office + Post Exchange (PX) and then to Air Force Headquarters. Ben Clagett + Nick not there. Talked with Col. George over situation in North and later with Col. Grady + Capt. Hipps (G-3). On to Manila then and checked in at Army-Navy Club. Called Matilda Zobel and we went dancing at "Winter Garden" of Manila Hotel. Much fun, place quite crowded. No evidence of war except officers in uniform with pistols.

Sunday 12-21-41—Alcala

To USAFFE office quite early + found that Lt. General MacArthur is now a full General. Brigadier Generals Edward P. King, George Parker, George F. Moore, + Richard Kerens Sutherland promoted to Major General. Division Commanders [*Col. William E.*] Brougher, [*Col. Clyde A.*] Selleck, [*Col. Clifford*] Bluemel, and others were made Brigadier Generals. Oh, yes. Last Friday I received copies of General Order #5. North Luzon Force and I was first man awarded Silver Star Citation. Will send Mother + Dad copy. Went then to Air Force Headquarters and picked up an Air Corps Liaison Officer for North Luzon Force. His name, Thomas Patrick Gerrity. ("Wish my hair was green.") [*Gerrity's left hand was injured when a Japanese Zero attack on Nichols Field on 10 December destroyed his B-18 bomber. A week later he appears in Tom Dooley's journal when he was assigned as liaison to General Wainwright's headquarters. On Christmas Day he flew Johnny Pugh to Manila and four days later flew Dooley to Corregidor. Both trips came perilously close to ending the war for all three of them. Gerrity was made an unofficial aide-de-camp to General Wainwright on 6 Jan. He remained with Wainwright's Headquarters for three months until, following the advice of Edwin Dyess, he left for Australia by way of Mindanao on 2 April in an old Navy duck amphibious aircraft. In his diary, which parallels Dooley's first journal, he wrote: "At last I feel I am going to be doing something worthwhile in this war."*

He would fly forty-nine combat missions between April and August of 1942 before being assigned as Army Air Forces Materiel Command project officer for half a dozen types of bombers at Wright Field in Ohio. He held positions at Strategic Air Command, was Air Materiel Command's

UNITED STATES ARMY FORCES IN THE FAR EAST
HEADQUARTERS NORTH LUZON FORCE

GENERAL ORDERS)   C.P. VICTOR
NUMBER ......5)   16 Dec.1941

1. The Commanding General notes with pride the
gallant conduct of the troops at Fort Stotsenberg under fire.

11. CITATIONS FOR GALLANTRY IN ACTION:

a. First Lieutenant THOMAS DOOLEY, (O-328542), (Cav),
Aide-de-Camp, having been in Manila with proper authority
prior to the declaration of a state of war was, upon
declaration of a state of war ordered to report at once
to the Commanding General North Luzon Force at Fort
Stotsenburg, Pampanga. He arrived near Clark Field just
as the bombardment of that field commenced at 12:36 P.M.
December 8, 1941. Regardless of his own safety he drove
his private car past the flank of Clark Field during the
bombardment, and reported to the Commanding General,
North Luzon Force as ordered. Under the provisions of
Par. 6, AR 600-45, August 8, 1932, the Silver Star
Decoration is hereby awarded First Lieutenant Thomas
Dooley, (O-328542), (Cav), Aide-de-Camp.

                        HEADQUARTERS
               United States Army Forces in the Far East
                        Manila, P. I.

SPECIAL ORDERS:
NO.   106.   24 December, 1941
                        EXTRACT

20. By direction of the President and pursuant to
authority contained in War Department Radiogram No. 736,
11 December, 1941, the following temporary promotions
of officers in the Army of the United States are announced
effective 19 December, 1941.

NAME, SERIAL NO. & BRANCH   FROM   TO

Thomas Dooley, O-328542, Cav.   1st Lieut.   Captain

            By Command of General MacArthur:

                              R/K. Sutherland,
                              Major General, GSC,
                              Chief of Staff.

The order for Tom Dooley's Silver Star may have been the first issued after the
beginning of hostilities. Dated 16 December 1941, it cites action targeting Clark Field
at 12:36 P.M. on 8 December 1941. The order included his promotion to captain.
Courtesy the Tom Dooley Family.

first Commander of the Ballistic Systems Division, and Deputy Chief
of Staff at Air Force Headquarters before retiring as a four-star general
commanding the Air Force Logistics Command.]

Stopped at Army-Navy Club and called the McAvoys and wished
them a Merry Xmas. Stopped by Stotsenburg on way up and got Tom
[*Gerrity*] a bedding roll and uniform for Venancio Kalaiv—the driver.
Saw Major Montgomery (Asst. G-3) on road and he told me things
were picking up. The Japs (don't know how many) have flanked and cut
off part of our forces. Two of the officers I know. One is Major Martin Moses (Tom [*Gerrity*]'s cousin) and Major Maxie Noble. When got
to camp the 26th had been ordered out to the fray already. Johnny was
in recon up there to see what had actually happened. Came in after I
went to bed and told me about it. He was upset. He had seen and talked
with [*Maj.*] Joe Ganahl. Joe was in scrap. Had been slightly injured. Not
serious. Was still carrying on. Johnny said officers are having "Hell"
there because the Philippine enlisted men are fleeing. That's bad. Trust
the situation can be cleared up. Report before midnight said 15 enemy
transports sighted off San Fernando, La Union. Am on duty from midnight on tonight. Am writing this at 3:00 a.m. on Monday and received
report already that 5 ships off Caba are firing on our men there. Am
going to keep Col. Mohiro awake and try to get a bit of a nap. Am
going with Gen. Wainwright, Col. Nelson and Johnny tomorrow on a
recon of area reported in bad shape.

Monday 12-22-41—Alcala

A terrific day. On duty at G-3 office and the telephone rang
intermittently 'til time to wake Col. Nelson and Johnny. Roused them
at 6:00 a.m. Gen. Wainwright already up and got away about 7:00 a.m.
Gen. Wainwright + Col. Nelson in Packard with Corporals [*Hubert*]
Carroll and Centimo. Johnny and I in G-2 car with Sgt. Franko (a
half-Moro from Co. D, 12th QM) and Manoz (driver), a Manila taxi
driver. Franko was wonderful. He acted as air scout the whole day—
riding most of time with his door open and watching in all directions
for enemy aircraft—which was very active in the Lingayen area all
day. We first went to Urdanetta and Gen. told Gen. Selleck (71st Div)
of his plans. Then to Morong to see Gen. Brougher. [*Gen. James R .N.*]
Weaver (Tank Group Commanding General) was along. He left from

there to contact his Battalion Commanding Officers and we went to San Fabian. Got into an air raid there and I think the Japs were trying to knock out a Battery of 155 millimeters that were in position about 1–1/2 KM in rear of San Fabian. The Gen. and Col. Nelson went on from there to Rosario in a roundabout way and Johnny + I went with Col. Fipps (a Regimental Commanding Officer) to a place called Tabu (Battalion there commanded by Thomas for 26th Cav). They had a tower built there + we went up and looked over the enemy ships in Lingayen Gulf with field glasses. Johnny counted 14 and then 18. I counted 19.

We then went on and met Gen. Wainwright at Rosario. Hung around there. The 26th Cavalry had gone there then to take a position up from Damortis. Gen. Wainwright wanted to know what was going on up there so Johnny + I insisted on going up instead of him. We passed the 26th enroute. Saw Major Trapnell. Saw [*Lt. Gen. Ennis C.*] Whitehead. This location was a Hell of a spot for Cav. but the main reason was that they were the only troops that Gen. Wainwright had that he could move in and also the only troops he could trust. A fracas at or near San Fernando yesterday proved that. A whole Battalion of Filipinos fled—leaving their machine guns and officers. That was when Majors Noble + Moses were caught. But Johnny + I went on to Damortis (passing up we saw spot where the Japs had bombed a platoon of "B Troop" killing 4 men and 12 horses and wounding others) and there we again counted the enemy ships. 11 transports + 8 destroyers. About that time enemy aircraft came over. Johnny + I took cover and luckily no bombs for we later learned that the spot where we took cover was a warehouse with gasoline stored there.

Back to Rosario and Tank Platoon had returned. They had gone up to vicinity of Agoo and had pushed into enemy lines. They scattered the enemy infantry but were immediately met by anti-tank fire and enemy tanks. Six (6) of our tanks went up and five (5) came back. One of the tanks returning had received a direct hit and one man was decapitated. He was buried at the Catholic church in Rosario. I remember the Chaplain getting his home address and it was 220 South 11th Ave., Maywood, Ill., but do not know his name. [*In researching the history of the 192nd Tank Battalion, Mr. James Opoloy (Proviso High School, Maywood, Illinois) interviewed survivors of this encounter. The platoon consisted of four tanks not six. Bob Martin was the driver of one of the three surviving tanks. His assistant tank driver was Henry Deckert (a classmate of the platoon commander, Ben Morin, who signed the paperwork for Deckert to become a tank-crew member). When a shell from a Japanese gun hit Martin's tank at the bow gun port, the resultant concussion decapitated Deckert.*] Johnny + I returned via Monsay with message for 11th Div. Then stopped at Agno Hotel in Carmen and had a beer. On our trip back to Command post, Col. Nunez Pilet and Cpl. Carroll (Gen. Wainwright's American orderly from Paris, Tex.) came over and said "Lt. when you and Capt. Pugh go off again for the 'Old Man' don't stay so long. He was about crazy. That General was afraid you two had been bombed and was about to go after you."

Got to bed about 6:45. Was very, very sleepy. 2–1/2 hrs sleep the night before. Up since midnight. (Oh yes, Johnny + I later discussed our trip and I remarked that the only time I have put on my helmet and the only time I was nervous was when we went up to Damortis and the platoon of five (5) tanks passed us beating it to the rear. He was worried while we were in Damortis.)

Tuesday 12-23-41—Alcala

Got behind with this thing again and can hardly remember what happened. Made inspection trip with Gen. to 21st and 11th Divisions. Rest of day normal.

Wednesday 12-24-41—Alcala

Xmas Eve—you would never know it here except for calendar. Col. Nelson (G-3) went with Gen. Wainwright and me this day. Reports had come in re: fighting in Sison area and we went up to see. Gen. Selleck's Division had dissipated when first shot was fired and left the poor little 26th Cav. with left flank wide open—they immediately put in the 2nd Sq. (hard hit the day before) to protect it. We drove into Birolana while fight still going on. Saw Maj. Thomas Trapnell (O.K.) and Col. Pierce and his staff. They had destroyed two enemy tanks that morn with .50 cal. machine gun and bottles of gasoline. One enemy tank was 1–1/2 blocks (city) away from us and still firing—evidently disabled and could not pull out. I finally got the Gen. to leave. He became very brave because Col. Clinton Pierce gave him a drink of Scotch.

Came back by way of Tayag and saw remnants of the fleeing 71st Div. The most pitiful sight you can imagine. No one knew where they were going. Back to Command post O.K. and Command post was to close and moved to Bamban as scheduled in the General Withdrawal Plan (caused by the untrained + incompetent Philippine Army with not one bit of fight) on Xmas morn. Gen. slept on a Spanish type bed someone had fixed up and I slept in car.

Thursday 12-25-41—Alcala/Bamban

Xmas morn. Gen. Wainwright stayed at Command post until about 9:00 a.m. Went to Carmen—talked with Generals James Weaver (tanks) and Gen. William Brougher (11th Div.). Then to Bamban—shaved, bathed + ate and then back to Carmen. Then to 21st Div. near Mangatarem and then back to Carmen again and then back to Bamban. A busy day with much travel, but not a very Merry Xmas. Oh yes. Johnny asked and was permitted to go to Manila last night to send some Xmas greeting. Tom Gerrity (whom I have mentioned before) wanted to go and asked Johnny Pugh to fly down in an OH-32. They did get to Manila OK and landed at Nichols Field. It was dark. They hit and bounced and rolled thru 2 bomb craters and when they came to a stop they were told that they came in past numerous land mines and stopped 8 feet from a large stack of dynamite. Made it OK though and went on to Manila, danced at Manila Hotel and stayed there that night. Also found out today that MacArthur has taken the field (Corregidor) and Manila declared an open city which everyone knows will not be respected by the Japs.

Friday 12-26-41—Bamban

Went to Stotsenburg this morn and got my woolen uniforms + a few other things from my wardrobe trunk. Found my car had been taken. Adjutant said he saw 2 Air Corps people driving toward Manila in it. Went on to Headquarters Ft. Stotsenburg (in the field) to find the Finance officer. He was not there and everyone there appeared to be scared to death. Even the Commanding Officer. The information I passed on helped calm them down. Went back to Bamban. Carried the Gen. a bottle of Scotch for Xmas gift and he asked me to have a drink. I broke down today for the first time—not to have a drink—but tears came in my eyes from something the Gen. said. I thought that this was Xmas day in the states and Xmas morn at that. Mom, Dad, Cissy + Margaret were probably all there together and had read my Xmas radio (message). I couldn't hold the tears back.

Saturday 12-27-41—Bamban

Went on as duty officer at midnight. Nothing much came in. About 8:00 a.m. the Gen. said he was making a trip to Stotsenburg and the 11th Div. Johnny wanted to go and I wanted to sleep, so I sat around all morn. About 9:30 or 10:00 a.m. Dominick Troglia, whom I lived with at Stotsenburg came walking up. He was reported killed in the Damortis fight. He has escaped across country and came in with 10 enlisted men. Our Command post visited by USAFFE G-3 + G-4 last night. I will not put it in writing, but think that this visit will later have a distinct significance.

Sunday 12-28-41—Bacolor

Moved the Command post this morn. Some sections moved out early. I stayed on 'til 11:00 a.m. and came down with "Gen." Joe Ganahl came in today. Heard his story of his actions on La Union coast and up Naguilian Road to Baguio and then out. I could write a book about what happened this day and history could be made about what I could tell, but I will not put it in writing and just as well, because it is stamped in my brain and never again will I feel inferior to any man. Johnny came in about 8:00. Had been to 21st and 11th Div. They are pitiful outfits. No contact with the enemy, so they sit.

Monday 12-29-41—Bacolor

Our Command Post is in a convent—Saint Mary's Academy—at Bacolor, Pampanga. The structure is 400 yrs. old and smells musty and it's hot, but it's concealment. Walked into the church yesterday morn. The altar is a beautiful thing. Yesterday p.m. some kind of services were being held and you could hear the priest and the choir and it made the day's happenings seem more terrible than they really were. (John Neiger—Gen. George Parker's aide-de-camp came in last night.) Tom Gerrity asked me if I wanted to make a trip with him to the "Rock"— said OK and asked Gen. Wainwright permission. OK again so we left here about 4:00 p.m. + went to Clark Field and got a Filipino bi-plane (BI-01). Took off from Clark Field about 6:15 p.m. Flew at less than 200 feet and wiggled the wings so we would not be fired on by our troops. Nice ride. The natives would wave and I would wave back. There were no guns on the plane except the pistols which we carried. I kept a constant look-out for enemy planes, but saw none. A P-40 passed us going north and I didn't know what to think for a minute. He went directly over us about 50 feet up and was going fast as he could. I imagine about 220 or 250 mph.

Came out over the bay—saw several subs and came over the Rock. Tom Gerrity had never been there before—me either. He spotted the field—we came into the "Rock" across the field—he banked to left and brought it in nicely. Staff Sgt. in charge of field came running out and said, "Lt., you didn't wiggle your wings enough. We almost opened up on you." Hooked a ride in to tunnel. They had had a 2 hr. raid that morn and all were very shaky. Saw Tisdelle and he showed us where to eat and sleep. Quite a day. Lots of fun.

Tuesday 12-30-41—Rock/Bacolor

Had breakfast on "Rock" and went down to docks and caught a small boat out for Mariveles about 8:15 a.m. Got to Manila about 9:00 a.m. On the way over, we had to detour to miss mines that were planted in bay. At Manila we caught a courier and rode up to Medical Corps and found a mess and ate breakfast #2. (Corn-willie hash + coffee). Then on up to Far East Air Force Headquarters. Saw several people there. Jim McCloskey came by. He's a major now. Tom Gerrity had plenty of trouble at this headquarters convincing those people that there were planes still in the woods at Clark Field that would fly. We saw one P-40 and 3 P-35's. [*Capt. Raymond*] Spud Sloan + 1st Lt. Karl Lichter came along; we rode on up with Spud. Stopped at his camp and he gave us 5 cans of Ovaltine[©]. He told a good story. The censor stopped a letter from some private to his Congressman asking to see what he could do about sending us one P-40 as the one we have now has almost worn out.

Got back to Command post about 4:30 p.m. Everything about same. South Luzon Force retreating faster than North Luzon Force. They are having same results as we with Filipinos. Not good. [*Maj.*] Paul [*Mont-*

gomery] Jones (Cavalry) even found some Philippine Army officers and men in officers' quarters at Stotsenburg looting. Why protect a people that do things like that? Johnny and I had a beer and to bed.

Wednesday 12-31-41—Bacolor

New Year's Eve. A Hell of a New Year's Eve this was. Morning pretty quiet. Made a trip with Gen. Wainwright to 21st + 11th Div. 21st at Mabalacat and 11th at Mexico. Saw Joe Ganahl at Mexico. This p.m. an order came thru from USAFFE with promotions. Johnny made Major. I got my Captaincy. Johnny gave me his bars. Johnny Pugh, Tom Gerrity, + I got together for a little New Year's Eve party. Went to bed at 12:02.

Thursday 1-1-42—Bacolor/Hermosa

A lot of bombing raids today. We left from old Command post at St. Mary's Academy, Bacolor and moved to spot south of Hermosa in Bataan. Truck and trailer (Gen. Wainwright's home) was lost and I went out to find it. Went down Highway to tip of Bataan. Finally found it at Lumas. The driver and George (houseboy-orderly) was with him. They had been to "Little Baguio"(on the eastern coast of Bataan)—about 60 km. past where they should have gone. Just past Orion we came on to a spot where bombs had just dropped. The dumb Filipinos—caused a traffic jam. Col. Abraham Garfinkel + [*Brig. Gen.*] Bradford [G.] Chynoweth + I got it straightened out. Bomb had hit next to a taxicab. The driver was only one killed, but he was still at the wheel—one arm hooked out the window—door open—one leg sprawled out—head thrown back—mouth open—a ghastly stare—and to make it worse he had been wearing a dust mask—a horrible picture.

Also there were about 10 Calessi in vicinity when bomb hit. One pony was dead and one had been struck in stomach and guts were hanging out. As I walked up he attempted to get up and struggled forward. He was shot immediately. We missed these raids by minutes on the way down and about 4 different ones on the way back. Casualties were very few, but such a demoralizing effect on everyone. Got the truck and trailer back O.K. and got our stuff out and settled. Supper about 7:30 p.m. and went directly to bed. Slept soundly till 6:30 a.m.

Friday 1-2-42—Hermosa

Nothing much today—a few air raids, but none in our immediate vicinity. Joe Chabot (Asst. G-2 + a major now at 27) cut my hair for me. A good job with clippers, scissors, + razor that I took from barber shop at Club at Stotsenburg I started to cut Joe's and pulled hair with the clippers and Francisco (our ex-cook) took over. He does everything.

Saturday 1-3-42—Hermosa

Quite a day—this one—Air raids close by—worst set fire to Samal —about 5 km south of here. Quite a bit of action on the front— Guagua-Porac line. Made trip early to south with Gen. Wainwright to see Gen. Parker, [*Gen.*] Bluemel, and others. Went over to vicinity of Bagac (on east coast of Bataan). All afternoon read and listened to reports and rumors. Best rumor—that the Russians had bombed Tokyo for 5 hrs. Unconfirmed and un-believed now. Compilation of reports (I on duty 'til midnight) showed we got 7 Jap planes and possibly 8. Anti-aircraft (from the "Rock") got 3. Air Corps on recon—one (Bob Wray) got 2 near Mount Pinatubo—2 Jap Zero fighters—1 shot down in flames—1 hit tree while hedge hopping trying to catch him. Another recon near Cabanatuan got bomber on ground and shot down 2-seat observer in air. Our best day so far. There will be better. Confusing and doleful reports from 21st Div. in late p.m. Johnny + Gen. Wainwright went up.

Gen's. driver and orderly not around—Johnny drove and after dark Gen. insisted on having lights on. Johnny Pugh disliked this as did Command Posts visited. Japs broke thru 21st left and Artillery opened up with enfilade fire on column of Japs—accounting for many. Reserve Battalion sent in and original line recovered by this counterattack. 26th Cav. covering left flank of 21st Division. Cahoon (2nd Lt. in 26th Cav.) went on Recon mission the other night. He and one man left Stotsen- burg Club and worked their way into Angeles. Hid under Nipa shack near highway and watched column of 400 Japs march past. Last squad in column (10) were Jap women. Heard story of escape from cut-off of a Major Monzano (Philippine Army Engineers) from below Calumpit in company of civilian white man. They were hiding in bushes and half-witnessed a Jap officer raping Filipina. He got to Bataan by banca. Have also heard stories of treatment of prisoners—terrible. Japs loot all villages and when they see statues of Christ and different Saints they strike them from wall with bayonets. Such a people can never achieve total victory over a God-loving people.

Sunday 1-4-42—Hermosa

War is Hell—even in a Corps Command post. You wouldn't know that this was Sunday unless I looked at preceding day's notes in this book. The day started off by us hearing lot of artillery firing at "Front" from about 6:30 a.m. to 7:30 a.m. It was the 11th Division. Rest of morning quiet. After lunch (about 1:30 p.m.) we were all exhilarated at seeing about 16 or 18 of our planes (P-40s) in the air. They flew north— presumably to rendezvous—as the Jap bombers (9–8–9) came south along west coast—heading for the "Rock" and Mariveles. [*The numbers appear to reference the number of bombers that flew over.*]

I am just jotting this down about 4:00 p.m. with nothing else to do. Haven't heard what success they had (the P-40s). Tom Gerrity (truly a fine lad) is reading Wm. L. Shirer's *Berlin Diary*. Each time he puts it down I lie in wait and grab it. That book and an early November Collier's is about all the reading material available. Word came in at 3:30 p.m. that the 11th Div. is falling back in the Guagua-Lubao area (north of Manila Bay). Always falling back—but what can we expect— untrained troops—few automatic weapons—and no air support. Not one day 'til this one with its meager attempt have we had air counter-attacks. The Japs float lazily over—pick a target—even on some occasions they take a few practice dives before releasing their "eggs." This I know was done when they got the bridge over the Agno at Carmen.

During a spell when we were up on the hill watching the Nips bomb south of here, the Gen. said, "I suppose they are interning all Ameri-cans in Manila. Think of ol' Tommie Wolff in a concentration camp where he can't have his beer." I remarked, too, that the Britishers will probably be interned. Was thinking of Peggy + Dennis McAvoy. Hope + trust they are alright. Many others I know, too, and pray for. Don't know what has happened to Matilde Zobel (Spanish) + Sylvia Melián. Hope they are faring well. Would like to know about Gerry MacPher-son more than any of them. When I last heard she had been on the *Taiping*—still lying in Manila Bay for 2 weeks. Maybe she slipped out and got to Australia. Too, Gerry's husband—a Col. in British garrison at Hong Kong. I wonder how he fared in the siege and surrender.

I try to keep my hopes up and try not think of the Bataan incident as resulting in a repetition of Hong Kong, but if we don't get help that's what it will result in. That or death to 1,000's of wonderful people. I am not writing this with tears, mind you, but just looking situation over and thinking it out. I am not going to be a prisoner of these inhuman morons if it does result in death. (I know that all this is more terrible to Mom, Dad + Cissy because since Xmas I haven't been able to let them know I am O.K. I thought today of writing letters to home, Margaret, + Gerry in Australia, but know it to be useless. Tom Gerrity may later go to Australia and, if so, he said he would carry letters to be mailed then.)

Monday 1-5-42—Hermosa

Quite a day—left Command post for ride to "front" with Gen. about 10:00 a.m. Saw 71st Div. Command post and crossed Layac Junction bridge and started up Highway #7 to find Command post 11th Div. Stopped several troopers on road and none knew where it was—all the time the "Old Man" sitting up—nervous, griping, etc. + saying "drive on, Centimo." We drove up to Kilometer post 93—saw one lone 3rd Lt. from some Signal outfit with 2 enlisted men straggling back. We asked where 11th Div. Command Post was and he said at Kilometer post 105. It then came about that we were 2 KM in front of our own lines. The Gen. was as nervous as I then, and more so I think. He told Centimo to drive on then but to the rear. On way back after we had turned around we were harassed for about ½ mile by shrapnel fire overhead. Then to 21st Div. at Dinalupihan—Saw Capt. Walt J. Buboltz, supply officer for 26th Cavalry, and Franz Weisblatt (United Press reporter). Then to 11th Div. Command post in Hermosa –Saw Joe Ganahl there. Swell person.

Back to Command post and then "much air activity" took place. Dive bombers razed Hermosa—no casualties. One plane came over our Command post and then banked and started back over and everyone took to "fox holes." Gen. Wainwright scrambled for nearest one and Col. Frank Nelson was already in it. Gen. Wainwright, "Get over, Frank." Johnny Pugh very depressed today. Got to bed at 7:30 p.m. to sleep about 8:30 p.m. Then Johnny Pugh woke me up at 9:30 p.m.

Couldn't get back to sleep until 10:30 p.m. Then Col. Nelson woke me at 10:45 p.m. to go with Gen. to "front." He was to see that all troops were pulled back of Agno River and bridge blown. The General's sentimentality gripes me at times. Like up there at the bridge. He insisted on being the last man back over the bridge. Saw Maj. Trapnell, [Lt. Clifford] Hardwicke [Jr.], + Joe Ganahl there. Bridge blown at 2:00 a.m. Quite an explosion. 1–1/2 tons of dynamite. Gen., Col. [Harry A.] Skerry (Engr.) + I in culvert about 200 yards from bridge. To bed about 3:00 a.m.

Tuesday 1-6-42—Hermosa/West Sector

Gen. relieved from Layac Junction position (northwest of Hermosa) this date per letter from USAFFE and moved to area south of Bagac. Now in command of 1st Corps which covers West Sector. Gen. Parker—East Sector. Encountered no bombers en route. First to Gen. Selleck's Command post. Stopped by Gen. Parker's Command post and saw Lt. Col. O[vid] O. "Zero" Wilson and John Neiger. To new Command post south of Bagac. Nice camp site. Johnny Pugh, Tom Gerrity + I have nice nook fixed up. Tom Gerrity made an unofficial aide-de-camp this date. If we get to Stotsenburg—Johnny a Major or Lt. Col. will be relieved and Tom Gerrity will be air aide. Hope so. Will fly from Cal. to Texas then. Oh yes, about 4:00 p.m. Tom Gerrity and I went down to nearby mountain stream to bathe and shave. Water about 35° it seemed, but surely made you feel wonderful when you get out.

Wednesday 1-7-42—West Sector

Quiet day—no enemy activity. We were put on 2/3 rations today. Breakfast at 9:00 a.m. Supper at 4:00 p.m. A Capt. Lawrence (formerly 1st Sgt. Troop E, 3rd Cav., then Warrant Officer, now Capt.) came by to see the General. When leaving, asked if Gen. would like to have him bring a ham. I nodded yes when Gen. hesitated, so Gen. said, "OK, wish you would." Imagine hesitation at sound of ham. To bed early because I go on duty at 2:00 a.m. tomorrow. Kept awake by Johnny Pugh, Joe Chabot, [Capt. James C.] "Jim" Blanning, Tom Gerrity. having a drink and bulling. Pleasant, though.

Thursday 1-8-42—West Sector

Good day—no Jap air activity at all. Left Command post about 10:30 a.m. to find Finance officer for Gen. Wainwright. Why he wants his money, I can't understand. Carried a Second Lt. of Air Corps—P.E. Ramsey—back to 20th Pursuit Command post. He was shot down. Navy (ours) shot him over Mariveles. Knocked out his engine and he attempted to pancake just off Bagac. Cut his head when plane landed in water. On down to Headquarters Philippine Division (very much confused + with wildest rumors that I have yet heard) and no Finance officer. To another locality where Finance chores were accomplished. Came back by East Rd. and stopped at Limay Gen. Hospital. Saw [*Capt. Theodore*] "Ted" Winship and Juanita Redmond. Red much upset over all this and with a defeatist attitude. I tried to talk her out of that. She asked me to come back some night, bring Tom Gerrity or Johnny, and play bridge. Back by way of Gen. Parker's Command post. Saw no one there (just moving in). Back by Pilac-Bagac road to Command post. Ate and to bed early. [*Dooley mentions 2nd Lt. Juanita Redmond eighteen times between 8 January 1941 and her departure from Corregidor on 29 April 1942. She survived numerous bombings of hospitals and was on one of the last flights out of Corregidor. In 1943 she wrote* I Served on Bataan, *on which the Claudette Colbert movie* So Proudly We Hailed *is based. She achieved the rank of Lieutenant Colonel and helped establish the Army Air Corps Flight Nurses Program. The top award for Air Force nurses is named in her honor. Her name is among those of one hundred military nurses listed on the Angels of Bataan and Corregidor monument dedicated 9 April 1980 on Corregidor.*]

Friday 1-9-42—West Sector

A very quiet day. Nothing doing. Gen. in camp and Col. [*William F.*] Maher to front. Had a good bath in the nearby mountain stream. After we had eaten at 4:30 p.m., Col. Charles A. Willoughby, Gen. MacArthur's intelligence chief, came in. He is USAFFE G-2. Also Col. Pierce + [*Maj. William E.*] "Bill" Chandler [*26th Cavalry S-2 and S-3*] came in. 26th cut off for about 4 days due to Infantry pulling out without notifying them. They had quite an experience in getting back. Tom + I went to our area early. Johnny Pugh and Col. Willoughby came up later to have a drink before going to bed, and we had quite a discussion. Col.

Willoughby (very intelligent—has written several books) took care of most of the talking and he gave the first hint of us actually getting help from the US.

Saturday 1-10-42—West Sector

Gen. MacArthur expected in this area today. Japs starting in again with their bombings about 10:00 a.m. Most of it on East Sector—probably their main effort. Looked thru what papers I have with me this morn. Found picture of Cissy in her $50.00 hat—trimmed snapshot down and now have it in my wallet. General took Johnny to 31st Command post to meet Gen. MacArthur this morn. At breakfast, he said "Tom, we will go at 9:00 a.m. to see the 'Chief.'" I said OK and then Johnny Pugh pipes up to Gen. "Why don't you take me, Gen. I haven't been out of camp in 2 days." So I am left behind. Really wanted to go.

Gen. + Johnny Pugh returned about 12:00 noon and Johnny has notes of their talk. Things look much brighter. Points of Gen. MacArthur's talk with Gen. Wainwright:

- II Corps would stop Jap attack and would counter-attack.
- Jap air superiority was only temporary.
- US and Dutch Air Corps doing work on Davao.
- 20,000 troops in Mindanao.
- Moros being urged into religious war on Japs.
- We will soon re-occupy Manila.
- We have caught imagination of America.

Gen. Wainwright had to celebrate this good word. (An excuse to have a drink.) The monkeys are active in the sector of our bivouac (Johnny Pugh, Tom Gerrity, T.D.). If you leave it for a while and come back quietly, there is a herd all about. This p.m. I was asleep on my bunk and Tom Gerrity came back and as he walked up he saw a big monkey playing with some boot trees near head of my bed. They get mad at times and throw fruit at our beds.

TWO

The Calm in the Midst of the Storm

Sunday 1-11-42—West Sector

Behind again and cannot remember much, but some notes I've made help. A quiet day. Went to 26th Cav. with Gen. Wainwright. I saw Maj. Trapnell first—a swell person. Saw John Wheeler—first time since I stopped on Damortis-Rosario Rd. and shook his hand. That seems like ages ago. John mentioned about Garry Auloff taking his car and then refusing to give him a receipt for same. Will fix that for him. Quiet the rest of the day. Just talk.

Monday 1-12-42—West Sector

Another quiet day. Thank God. Breakfast about 9:30 a.m. Read *Berlin Diary* and slept till about 1:00 p.m. Then took bath in the cold mountain stream. Hard to get started, but a wonderful feeling when you get in. Better still when you get out. Report this p.m. of 300 Japs coming over from Olongapo to first point south. Battalion from 31st Infantry under a Major [*George M.*] Hohl dispatched to meet same.

Tuesday 1-13-42—West Sector

Another quiet day in camp. Gen. Edward King visited today. A grand old gent, would be a pity to see him in the hands of those vandals. Just many bull sessions about camp. Meals are a nice time now. Ten (10) at each meal. Gen., all G's, and Tom Gerrity + self. I have made McKinney + Collin County famous by much talk. Oh, yes, received some newspapers from home. Papers—Oct. 6–Oct. 11. Still good reading. Only mail I've had since before war started. Tom Gerrity and I have started playing Rummy each day or night. Tom leading first time—560 to 550. Good sleeping here in Bataan. Lately I have slept about 11 or 12 hrs. at night and sometimes an hour's nap during day.

Wednesday 1-14-42—West Sector

Col. Frank Nelson went with Gen. Wainwright today so I went with Tom Gerrity to Mariveles and on to Far East Air Force. They are a very jittery bunch. Capt. Ind, G-2, worst of all. Saw Sgt. Whatley—he has lost some weight—he should be up here with us. Stopped at Philippine Air Depot and Tom got 3 flying jackets for Gen., Johnny, + I. Nice. Then stopped at Hospital at Limay to see Juanita Redmond. She still in rather depressed state. Helped her a little on last trip and more on this one. She is a good gal. Told her if we had to take to hills, I was going to take her along. She gave us some much appreciated candy. Back to Command post about 6:00 p.m., ate a good meal. Francisco, our cook at McKinley + Stotsenburg who came with us, is a jewel. Fixes cookies, pies, etc. from nothing. Johnny + I will have to fix him right. Running tonight—I'm still behind. Will catch him, though. Another 12 hrs. sleep tonight. Am gaining weight.

Thursday 1-15-42—West Sector

Went to front with Gen. today. He wanted to inspect beach positions with Gen. Bluemel and front lines with Gen. Segundo. (Place little faith with this fellow). At Moron saw "G" Troop. They are attached to 1st Div. for patrols. Saw Ed Ramsey and Sgt. Ibanez (1st Sgt.). Told them to say hello to Cliff Hardwicke (out on patrol) and to Sgt. [*Julian*] Almonte (supply Sgt + a jewel). Wanted the Gen. to stop in 26th Cav. but he had seen Col. Pierce on the road earlier. E-F Troop under [*Capt.*] John Wheeler is relieving G Troop at Moron tonight. Told John about arranging to get a receipt for his car from Garry Auloff. Saw Auloff yesterday and gave him hell for taking the car when he did. Mine was taken at same time. Mine is with 20th Pursuit. Johnny, Tom Gerrity, and I all took baths in cold stream this p.m. I was on duty this night from 8:00 p.m. to 2:00 a.m. Tom Gerrity sat with me and we played more Rummy.

Reports coming in re: Jap Battalion marching south from Mabayo toward Moron. Col. Maher up and talking with 1st Div. (Philippine Regular Army)—they are a confused lot. Gen. Segundo trying to take John Wheeler's troop and also keep "G" Troop because Japs are near. Wants to put Cav out front so his troops can get away quicker. Johnny slept in G-3 tent on blanket + shelter half until 2:00 a.m. He relieved me then, but I stayed on. Was reading Shirer's *Berlin Diary* and comparing Jap offensives with his account of German drives. A similarity exists of course, but had the Japs been Germans in this campaign so far, we would all be dead or swimming in Manila Bay. About 3:00 a.m. a special courier from Headquarters and Headquarters Detachment brought mimeographed copies of Gen. MacArthur's letter to troops. For immediate delivery to front line troops. Essence of letter: "Help is coming from US." His hedging point though was quite obvious. Time of arrival not known for "they must fight their way through the Japs trying to prevent it." Finally decided to go to bed about 4:00 a.m.

Friday 1-16-42—West Sector

In camp—quiet here and Tom Gerrity and I continued our Rummy. A Jap force of about 300 men came from Olongapo and were coming south and were met at Moron by a Battalion of 1st Div. (Philippine Army) and mostly by Troop E-F of 26th—John Wheeler, commanding. John's troop relieved G Troop at this location only about 30 min. before fight began. Our men did well. Japs were routed with estimated 200–300 dead. Our casualties relatively few. Little contact during night.

On the East Sector, picture it was quite different. The Japs made a thrust at their left flank and the 51st Div. fled. These Filipinos start running when the first shot is fired and what's more they are led by their Filipino officers. No troops have fought under more trying circumstances than these here. I mean American troops. It is generally accepted that all Philippine Army units will not fight, but flee to hills and change to civilian clothes when a fight begins. This due to story that Japs do not harm civilians. Sometimes looks like a pathetic plight.

Saturday 1-17-42—West Sector/Kilometer post 212

Spent this day in camp, too. About 9:30 a.m. the Gen. asked Johnny Pugh to go up front with him. Before they left I asked Gen. if they were going to get close to front where they could do some shooting. He said no, so I went back to Rummy game with Tom Gerrity. As it turned out, he, Johnny, Sgt. Carroll + Sgt. Centimo all got in some shooting. They were at the front lines and saw 5 Japs so they opened fire. The Japs ran into a hay stack and then only 3 ran out when concentrated fire was put on their hiding place. But the ugly part of the day was announcement

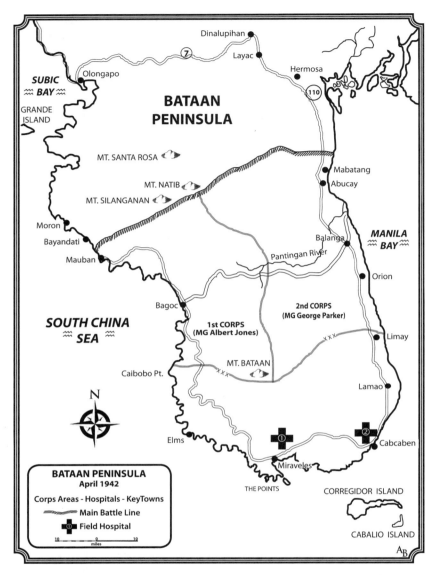

Bataan Peninsula, showing 1st and 2nd Corps areas, initial main battle line, field hospitals, and key towns. Map by Anne Boykin.

of Cliff Hardwicke's (Sherman, Texas) death. He had gone up for some horses that were lost in the fight the day before. He was with Major Bill Thorpe, Capt. Miller, + about 9 others. They saw an officer with some horses who waved to them. They started forward and when within about 25 yards he [*the officer*] laughed and opened fire and also three (3) machine guns opened up. He was a Jap in Filipino uniform. Our patrol got him and 2 of the machine gun crews but they got Cliff Hardwicke. The Japs are a treacherous group of vandals. Before going to bed Johnny had some rum, so as to have some sort of ceremony or thought of Cliff, we drank a toast to him.

Sunday I-18-42—West Sector

Also in camp and my Rummy luck is better. (The story about Gen. + Johnny shooting Japs in haystack happened today instead of yesterday.) Many reports coming in of Japs off Bagac. I think they are bringing supplies into Subic Bay. Gen. is afraid of an attempted landing on our coast. USAFFE pulled dumb trick. Instead of ordering our Reserve Div. (91st—71st) to East Sector to halt the Japs in 51st (fleeing) sector, they ordered 31st Div. (which were in beach positions) here. The reason they gave was because they had not fought yet and 91st had confusion, hardship, inefficiency caused by the move. Reports received from II Corps to effect that Jap patrols had infiltrated thru E-sector lines and attacked groups in rear—21st Division Command post + 66th Pack Train. This was helped along by the flight of the 51st Div.

Monday I-19-42—West Sector

Want to put down some poetry that Tom Gerrity + I wrote. Can put it in here, but were it found anywhere else, we might be tried by court martial.

General Shower
Over the top, men, Shower shouted.
And to your busses, before we're routed.
The enemy's but 10 kilometers away.
So we'll leave the Cavalry to hold them at bay.
The Cavalry are stout fighting men.
So—let the Japs cut them off again.

While others offer a sanguine resistance.
We'll watch the fight from a safe distance.
Pour me some coffee, + here's to us.
Climb on, boys, I've got an omnibus.
The Q.M. has issued us a short ration.
So I've placed myself to watch over the bacon.
So on to Mariveles, I'll lead the way.
Open the road for we want no delay.
We'll eat, and drink, and smoke 'til we're numb.
And when the next fight begins—we'll start swimming, by gum.

General Gower
This is the end of a marvelous career.
General Gower reported + from his eye dropped a tear.
When the grey dawn broke with no Jap in sight.
He turned to his men + said "There's no cause for fright."
Load up the trucks—we move to the rear.
Leave pistols + rifles, but don't leave my gear.
If you see him on Friday when there is no contact.
He has a wonderful division that's ready to fight back.
But then on Sunday if the fight has begun.
He is sad + depressed and says "It's again on the run."
He loads up his kitchens with looted tidbits.
And when they hear Japs, the unit just quits.
So let's fight no more battles with S and G.
Give us some men from over the sea.

Those two poems were based on actions, etc. prior to our movement
to the West Sector. This day spent in camp; reading and a bit of Rummy
with Tom Gerrity. The best thing of the day—hotcakes and ham with
Karo syrup.

Tuesday I-20-42—West Sector
Another day in camp. Many reports especially concerning Japs on
right flank. Here's what happened: "51st Division fled from this point
(position A) and combination of 45th Infantry and 31st US Infantry
retook line, but in meantime about 2000–3000 Japs sifted thru and got

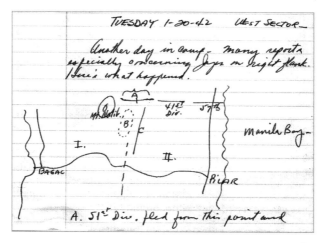

Dooley sketched the action that took place on 20 January 1942. From Tom Dooley's cloth journal.

into position B. Then II Corps placed 31st Div. (which had been taken from us from the beaches) and placed it into position C to protect themselves and left our right flank open."

Wednesday 1-21-42—West Sector

A busy day. Went to our front with Gen. Wainwright + Tom Gerrity. The Gen. was really just going up so Tom + I could slip into 1st Reg. Division Observation Post at Line of Resistance and get some shots at Japs, but when we got to Kilometer post 164, Command post of 1st Div., they notified us that you could not get thru. Snipers had outflanked main line of resistance and had the road covered. Gen. Wainwright had to go forward then. He organized a small platoon + away we went. Heard some snipers about Kilometer post 167+ and we edged down the road. Besides Filipinos, we were of this set-up—Gen. Wainwright, Commander [Tom] Cheek (Navy), Tom Gerrity, Sgt. Carroll (Gen's orderly from Paris, Tex.), Sgt. Centimo (Gen's driver) and two Navy enlisted men. When we got to bad spot, 3 men were wounded and one Filipino officer killed (shot thru head by sniper). Worst case was bullet hit tree about head-height against which I was leaning. Lost no time in getting behind a fallen log. When we went back, Gen. organized another patrol from Philippine Scouts of 92nd Coast Artillery (Battery B.), Major Ball in charge. Back to Command post—good supper—

jittery around Command post until about 9:00 p.m. Then to bed. Gen. sleeping in G-3 night tent to be near phone.

Thursday 1-22-42—West Sector

Waked up at 7:00 a.m. by Sgt. Carroll to go to front with General Wainwright. First to Bagac to contact Gen. [*Luther*] Stevens who has been placed in charge of South Force due to Gen. Segundo being cut off while at Main line of resistance Then to Kilometer post 164 and there got resume of night's proceedings from Col. Albert Dumas (Inf) + Col. Venture (Field artillery). Stayed there short while and then on up to Kilometer post 167+ with Col. John Rodman who was in charge of general advance. (We were with him) (a point in reality). Tom Gerrity, Joe Chabot and Sgt. Drisko joined us. Passed tanks on road. They afraid of log block in road 'til Lt. Spies (26th Cav.) from a right flank patrol came thru in sedan and rolled logs out of way. Tanks started thru and land contact mines blew tracks off. Infantry under Col. Rodman kept going and firing line established by Battery B, 92nd Coast Artillery patrol at Kilometer post 169. We (Gen. Wainwright + I) returned to Kilometer post 164, made arrangements with Gen. Stevens and came back to Command post about 3:30 p.m. Me, with no breakfast, quite hungry. Tom Gerrity and I played a little Rummy (my luck very good). Came down to write this up and about 8:00 p.m. a great outburst of rifle fire was heard up the road north. No doubt it was some Joe with jitters and nervous fingers.

The nights lately have not been conducive to lots of easy sleep, but my habit of dying in bed until morn still hangs on. Still eat (as Johnny says) as if each meal were the last. Carabao steak is very good. 9:00 p.m. word just received that [*1st Lt. Ethan R.*] Bob Cunningham (26th Cav. 1st Lt.) was killed in the jungle right flank patrol action today. A hell of a nice boy. It's things like that that make you feel low and blue and disgusted with the whole blasphemous situation. He + Cliff Hardwicke are worth more than all.

This night looks especially dark. I wonder as do others, if help is really coming from the States. I have begun to doubt it. Normally I live in hope of the best always, but I am rapidly losing that attitude. I believe the War Department looks on us as a brave band and that is all. We do not really count in the big picture of the annihilations of the yellow scourge in the Far East. We must be sacrificed for the fulfillment of the carefully planned movements of the "giant effort." If I do live thru this, when I get back to the States, no matter what the effort costs, I am going to get the true picture to the men in Washington by some means. How can a war be won—even fought—when those who are supposed to be defending their fatherland are forced to the front by Americans. I must sometime give a full account of the exploits of Franz Weisblatt (now in Jap prison camp) who became a friend of mine during our many moves. [*Information on the Battle for Bataan came from a handful of reporters who lived with the troops fighting the invading Japanese. United Press International hired Franz Weisblatt, a freelance reporter, in Manila to cover the Japanese landings on Luzon. Wounded and captured in an ambush on 7 January 1942, he spent three years in Bilibid Prison. When UPI reporter "Doc" Quigg entered the prison in February 1945, a hand grasped his in a dark corridor, and he shouted, "I'm Quigg, United Press." The reply came, "I'm Weisblatt, United Press."*]

Friday 1-23-42—West Sector

A big day for the Japs. Reports from USAFFE that Jap forces landed during night at Aglaloma Bay. They (the Japs) have started in on us with their aircraft again. Till this time the air activities in this sector has been slight with only a few bombings at Bagac, most all day today they have bombed and strafed the "West" sector road. The larger percentage of bombs seemed to be searching for our 155 m.m. guns, which fortunately, they did not hit. This activity appears to me to be covering either a landing operation or a drive in force from the north.

Was happy that the Gen. stayed in Command post today. About 10:00 p.m. Gen. Wainwright received call from USAFFE C. of S. (Gen. Sutherland) with instructions to have Col. Pierce report to advance Command post of USAFFE for orders. He is to be a Brigadier General and take over Gen. Selleck's command with ultimate or primary mission of knocking Japs from Aglaloma Bay. Col. C[onstant] L. Irwin (USAFFE G-3) visited the camp today and one preposterous incident caused me to condemn him. A great deal of enemy air observers and bombers were in action and he asked the question "Do you suppose they (aircraft) have radio contact with their ground troops." When he was told indirectly by me that his own headquarters had listened in on them, he became a bit upset and whipped out pencil and notebook and scribbled.

Saturday I-24-42—West Sector

The Jap bombers started early in our area this morn. All of this bombing I speak of in last few days are by slow flying dive-bombers. They circle + circle and pick out something and then dive with machine guns going wide open. Then as they start out of their dive they lay the egg or eggs depending on size of target. These this morning extremely close to our Command post and the complete staff took to fox holes on numerous occasions.

Much against my judgement the Gen. insisted on going to front (KP 164) to see Gen. Stevens. Frank Hewlett (United Press) went with us. He's a nice guy. We stopped and took to fox holes on numerous occasions and on one occasion it is good that we did. The lone Jap plane circled once, then dived on us with machine guns blazing. Nobody hit. Sgt. Carroll, the Gen's orderly jumped hurriedly into what he thought was a fox hole, but which others had used as a latrine. But those things don't matter when bullets are spitting near you. As we came back, we stopped at 26th Cav. Command post and had some coffee. Talked with Bill Chandler and Trapnell. Trap is one of the finest I've run into yet. He was awarded a Distinguished Service Cross the other day for his actions along with Mickleson (a vet.) at Rosario. Due to Col. Pierce going to Brig. Gen., Col. Vance will be a full Col. and I'm going to see that the Gen. Wainwright gets Trapnell his Lt. Col. leaves. Back to Command post with numerous stops to avoid aircraft. An unpleasant night, but still I slept about nine (9) hours.

Sunday I-25-42—West Sector

Early morn quiet in camp—a pleasant breakfast and then comes in the report that Japs have landed at Aglaloma Bay and at a point on West side of Mariveles Bay. The Marines under Commander [*Francis Joseph*] Bridget of Navy are after the Mariveles group and Gen. Pierce has a hodge-podge group of Constabulary, Air Corps, etc. after the group at Aglaloma. Japs are contained, but not eliminated. Also report came in that Clint Pierce was wounded by sniper fire—later learned not serious. As he described it—an ignominious wound—toe shot off; worst part—ruined good boot. According to plan of USA FFE., troops withdrawn to Reserve Battle position. Went to front with Gen. Wainwright, Johnny, and Tom Gerrity to see about withdrawal of troops from Moron road to rear positions. Much, very much confusion. Buses everywhere. G-4 very inefficient + lazy—no nerve—no brains—because it was ill-arranged with no supervision and no M.P.s Gen. Wainwright very mad and expressed intentions of giving whole staff Hell. Upon return from front went on to new Command post (about 1–1/2 km from old one). Rather confused—new Command post. Went to bed to be able to get sleep as I supposed to go on duty at 2:00 a.m.

Monday I-26-42—West Sector

Tom Gerrity preceded me on duty and didn't wake me till 4:00 a.m. which was OK by me. Sat there in total darkness from 4:30 to 8:00 a.m. Very lonesome for I told the Sgt. on duty to go to sleep. There was a tremendous amount of bombing on roads and coast line in our vicinity this morn. Many reports coming in. I took a report about Noon of 4 of our P-40s that went out and did their recon mission and also downed 3 Jap bombers.

Tuesday I-27-42—West Sector

In camp—no activity on my part—spent most of time playing Rummy with Tom Gerrity. My luck about the same. A great many reports came in today—some true—some windy. Report of enemy landing at Anagasan during night proved true. That is in Gen. Pierce's subsector. Report from West sector of one Battalion that heard desultory fire during night and just walked out of front lines. To bed early.

Wednesday I-28-42—West Sector

Out with Gen. Wainwright, Johnny Pugh, Sgt. Carroll + Sgt. Centimo today. Sgt. Carroll + I rode running board to keep eyes on enemy aircraft. Got extremely dirty. First visited Gen. Pierce's Headquarters at Kilometer post 191. Saw Roy Reynolds while there. Clint Pierce limping around with one toe shot. No bombers on way down. Then to Gen. Jones' Headquarters at our old Command post. Saw Col. Edwin E. Aldridge [*A&M Class of 1916*] (G-3). Then up to

Trail 9. Enemy artillery fire just as we entered trail. No casualties. Saw 26th Cavalry moving to new place on map. Bivouac area. They were initially in midst of some Artillery battery campsites and were moving to get away from counter-battery fire. Saw Maj. Trapnell. Still in wonderful state of mind. He's a peach. Then on to 91st Div. and then to 1st Div. and then to 11th Div. Back to Command post about 4:30 or 5:00 p.m. Commander Bridget of Navy called and asked Gen. Wainwright to request use of *"Pigeon"* or *"Quail"* to go to sea and move in at Longoskawayan Point where we have some Japs cut off. [*Between World War I and World War II the* Pigeon *patrolled the Yangtze River, protecting American citizens and commerce during the revolution in China, and then cruised down to the Philippines with Asiatic Fleet submarines as a submarine salvage vessel. In the same period the* Quail *cleared mines in the North Sea off Scotland, patrolled Cuban waters, the Panama Canal Zone, and Nicaragua, and participated in Caribbean maneuvers. After operating along the East Coast of the United States, it was assigned to Pearl Harbor with some survey work off Alaska. When war broke out, the ship cleared a channel to the South Harbor of Corregidor, rescued submarines and boats from Japanese bombing raids, and hauled tenders filled with supplies for Bataan and Corregidor. The* Pigeon *downed three Japanese bombers and an observation plane attacking Corregidor. When the* Pigeon *and the* Quail *were sunk, their crews joined the marines fighting on Bataan and Corregidor.*] Johnny Pugh left about 10:00 p.m. with Capt. Keeler to join Bridget. Tom Gerrity + I played Rummy in G-3 night tent. My luck better.

Thursday 1-29-42—West Sector

In camp—much enemy air activity. Think they are trying to knock out our big 155 mm guns. Our artillery has done marvelous work throughout this war so far. It is music to hear those 155's leave out. Three P-40's passed over our Command post headed north. People shouted and seemed so happy to see our craft in the air. War is a great leveler. It takes so little to make some people happy, especially now. I gave Peter Perkins a toothbrush today and he was so pleased. He was a hotshot polo player for Los Tamocao and when war started he came in and they commissioned him in Infantry about Dec. 29th. Nice boy. Went to New Mexico Military Institute. Ed Girzi (1st Lt. Field artillery—formerly Asst. Adj. at Stotsenburg and pretty good tennis player) made asst. G-3 today.

One bomb dropped extremely close to our Command post today. Piece of shrapnel landed on G-3 desk. I felt it while it was still hot. Johnny returned from his trip about 7:30 p.m. He had quite an experience. Came in from "*Quail*" about 11:00 a.m. and joined Col. Hal Clark Granberry of 2nd Bn. 57th when they moved in on Longoskawayan Point after a preparation of artillery fire and 3 in. guns from *Quail*. Johnny Pugh said it was marvelous the way those scout soldiers of 57th Infantry moved in. The Japs will not surrender. They fight to the last.

Johnny Pugh saw many just riddled with bullets + shrapnel. He brought the General a sword from officer (dead). Told of one scout Sgt. who had hand cut off by saber—tied handkerchief around it and kept fighting 'til bayoneted thru abdomen—died on litter while being evacuated. Gen. Wainwright gave orders to find out who he was, etc. so he can be given Distinguished Service Cross—posthumously.

Friday I-30-42—West Sector

Also in camp—many reports. One—Gen. Brougher called in asking for use of one Scout Company to clean out some Japs that had filtered through. Word brought in that Gen. Selleck reduced to Colonel. Lt. Todd (military intelligence division) went down to Longoskawayan Point to watch cleaning up of the point. He reports counting dead Japs. About 150 in all. Some committed suicide by jumping from cliff onto rocks. Some (about 30 or 35) attempted to escape in a banca and they were killed by machine gun fire.

Tom + I played Rummy. Tom Gerrity left about 6:00 p.m. to go to Air Corps Headquarters. Another "bucker-up" message received from USAFFE by radio re: naval battle of Makassar Strait and American help being on the way. Wish we had Air Corps to down these Japs that bomb so freely from low altitude. I feel confident that we will be O.K. if help comes soon. Why don't they get here? That's what people all ask. I think it will get here OK. Hope so. I keep thinking about Margaret B. all the time. Hope the attitude that people take during war doesn't affect her. Hope she is around when I get back. That will probably be a good long time off, but soon maybe I can at least call and talk to her or get mail thru, at least. It's going to be great to get back to Texas. One thing about this, I am saving more money now than ever before and making more, too, since my Captaincy came thru.

Saturday 1-31-42—West Sector

Went to 11th Div. Sector this morn with Gen. Wainwright + Col. Nelson. Went to 11th Division Command post and then to 11th Infantry Command post. Gen. Brougher there and he had not yet been to Command post of 45th Bn. which was engaging Japs that had come thru a gap in the Main line of resistance in 1st Div. Sector. Went on up then to Col. Lathrop (45th) on Trail 7 and were within 20 yds. of our front lines. Much rifle + machine gun fire. Gen. Wainwright gave certain instructions + we came back by 1st Division Command post + 26th Cavalry. Saw Maj. Trapnell on trail. Dull evening + to bed early.

Sunday 2-1-42—West Sector

In camp all day. Running with Tom Gerrity during day not knowing what a night was in store for us. About 7:30 p.m. reports started coming in of big boats and 13 barges off W. Coast going south. Whole staff up 'til 3:00 to 6:00 a.m. First attempt under cover of fire from big boat at Aglaloma. Repulsed + barges moved north. We got in touch with Air Corps and 5 P-40's got into the fray. Was good to listen to them strafing with their six 50 cal. guns blazing. Some of the barges got into area between Anyasan + Salaiim Rivers. Number undetermined that got in. It is my opinion that a small percentage of the original group landed. Quite a night.

Monday 2-2-42—West Sector

Left about 10:30 a.m. and took a tanker, Maj. Smyth, to 11th Div. Command post to see about using tanks to annihilate the Japs in corral in that sector. He—a dumb and pompous sort—started telling Gen. B. of previous misuses of tanks especially referring to Gen. Wainwright and I called his hand. Quite a row, but I was in the right and bore him down. Thought my main point was protecting Gen. Wainwright. Tonight was quiet. Navy sent liaison officer to our Command post per Gen. Wainwright's request. I happened to know him previously. He— Lt. [*Cmdr.*] M[*alcolm*] M. Champlin—was + is Admiral Lockwell's aide. [*Champlin was Naval Aide to the Commanding General US Army Forces* in the Philippines, at this time Douglas MacArthur. As a result of his actions during December 1941 and February 1942, he was awarded the Navy Cross and the Silver Star.] A very nice chap. He will stay several days.

Tuesday 2-3-42—West Sector

In camp—quiet. Gen. took Johnny with him and went to 11th Div. sector. I didn't want to go. Took a nap and played Rummy. The G-2 of Gen. Jones' sub-sector staff came in to Command post this morn. A newspaperman—Frank Hewlett—recognized him as Andres Soriano, owner of San Miguel Brewery, Phil. Cold Stores, and various gold mines + property in states making him one of richest men in Manila + previously one of the principal Philippine donors to Franco's Campaign in Spain. [*Frank Hewlett was Manila* United Press *bureau chief when the war started. His dispatches on the fall of Bataan and Corregidor won the National Headliner Award in 1942. Hewlett was the last correspondent out of Manila. His wife, Virginia, remained in Manila as a nurse at Santa Catalina Hospital, but was imprisoned, in spite of having diplomatic immunity. Hewlett found her—thin and unrecognizable—at Santo Tomas Hospital Internment Camp on 4 Feb., 1945.*

Hewlett penned the poem about the "Battling Bastards of Bataan," which he got past the censors in February 1942. The full wording of his poem is:

> *Battling Bastards of Bataan*
> *No Mama, no Papa, no Uncle Sam,*
> *No Aunts, no uncles, no cousins, no nieces,*
> *No pills, no planes, no artillery pieces,*
> *And nobody gives a damn!*

After the war Soriano served as Washington Bureau Chief for the Salt Lake City Tribune *for twenty-three years.*] I asked Johnny Pugh if he knew who he was and Johnny Pugh said only the G-2 of Manor. I proceeded to tell him about Soriano's position and all that and because a Reuter's correspondent named Nat Floyd walked up, Johnny Pugh says that he is not impressed by wealth and that talk and I blew up and off quietly + quickly. This fellow Floyd was originally from Denison, Tex. and at one time worked on the *Sherman Democrat* with

Margaret Jefferson's mother. A surprising spot, this, to find one with mutual friends. [*Nathaniel Crosby Floyd IV, representative for* Reuters *and the* New York Times, *grew up in Denison, Texas, forty miles north of Dooley's hometown, McKinney. After becoming a reporter for the* Sherman Herald-Democrat, *he joined* Associated Press *in Tokyo and later was editor of the* Manila Daily Bulletin. *Clark Lee, writing in the Lawrence, Kansas* Daily Journal *on 9 Feb 1942, said he and Nat Floyd had promised to write each other's obituary. When Floyd asked for bio material, Lee told him just to write, "He died unafraid," but Floyd drawled, "Now you know I couldn't do that. Accuracy is the first rule of newspapering."*]

Wednesday 2-4-42—West Sector

In camp all day—various reports all day—relatively quiet. Took a nap. Tom Gerrity + I played Rummy. Gen. Wainwright in camp to wait and see Gen. Marshall, Deputy Chief of Staff. Johnny Pugh and Joe Chabot went to two points where fights are going on south of here. Had three (3) newspaper men in camp tonight [*including*] Frank Hewlett—United Press and Clark Lee—Associated Press [*Clark Lee served in several AP bureaus before Manila, where he was serving when the Japanese attacked Pearl Harbor and the Philippines.*] Frank Hewlett always brings us something when he comes around. This trip—ham + cheese. Gave me a carton of Camels.

Thursday 2-5-42—West Sector

Quite a day—this one. First, to 1st Division sector with Gen. Wainwright and Col. Maher for a conference with Gen. Jones, Gen. Brougher, + Gen. Segundo re: pocket of Japs behind our front lines in 1st + 11th Division areas. Came back by 91st Division Command post and saw Gen. Stevens. Had some coffee + good cocoanut candy there. After getting back to Command post, Frank Hewlett came down and said that Guiuan Pt. was cleared of Japs and 3rd Battalion of 45th was cleaning up. Frank Hewlett, United Press; Lt. M. M. Champlin—Navy; Sgt. Upton; and I went down and went all the way through to the cliff overlooking the beach. We walked thru area that had been laid flat by our 155 MM fire and it was a ghastly sight. Dead Japs everywhere. We saw what we estimated about 50–60 dead ones in fox holes and lying about. Evidently been dead for several days. The stench was terrific—nauseated me so I spent the rest of the inspection with handkerchief tied over my nose. All the Phil. Scouts + Air Corps troops were rummaging about for souvenirs. I brought back some stuff for G-2 section and saved one sheet—a Jap print for Cissy. Not a very good one, but OK under these extenuating circumstances. The bird that said "War is Hell" must have seen things like I saw today. That makes two points that the Japs have been cleared from. Complete annihilation was forced because the Japs will not surrender. Even when they run out of ammunition they will fight with bayonets until dead. Morale throughout is much higher now and every one feels that we will march out soon. I personally feel that way. On duty tonight till 2:00 a.m.

Friday 2-6-42—I Corps Command post

I have been listing location as W. Sector and that has been wrong designation. We are the I Philippine Corps and have been since withdrawal to Reserve Battle Position which we now occupy. Went to front today with Gen. Wainwright and Frank Hewlett (United Press). Very interesting. My cold worse and a long rough ride with my head closed up made a very uncomfortable trip. Gen. Wainwright had a conference at 1st Division Command post with Gen. Jones, Brougher, and Segundo re: action on north front—it must be cleaned out. Saw Peter Perkins + Jack Walker ('35 T. A&M) this morn. Back to Command post and supper was fun. [*James R.*] Bob Lindsay (Artillery Officer) sounded off at supper table. He just gave Col. [*Frank Dow*] Merrill hell re: pessimistic attitude of people in general. He had had a stiff drink and all these thoughts had been griping him for some time and he loosened up and gave out. Really a nice fellow. Wonderful sense of humor and extremely hard worker.

Saturday 2-7-42—I Corps

This day spent in camp. Felt terrible all day with cold. Played Rummy with Tom Gerrity and slept. Bad night with reports of enemy attempts to land. Our P-40s up and strafing barges. Our artillery at work. There are about eight 155 M.M.'s in this vicinity. They make terrific amount of noise and lay concentrations all night. Normally they don't wake me, but with this cold I have spent restless nights lately.

There is one battery about 1500–2000 yds. away. That practically dumps you out of bed when they fire a salvo.

Sunday 2-8-42—I Corps

To front with Gen. Wainwright this a.m. First to 1st Division Command post. Gen. Segundo not there, but Gen. Wainwright notified Col. Dumas that Segundo was being relieved and Dumas placed in command of that Division. Gen Wainwright didn't get the replacement he wanted due to paper technicalities of rank, a drawback to our army. Even at that, there are others whom I think could have been chosen to better replace Segundo. Went on then to 11th Division + thence to 11th Infantry. At 11th Division Command post Gen. Wainwright tore up dust because his orders to move a 155 Howitzer Battery to certain spot had not been done quickly enough. Col. [*James C.*] Hughes— 11th Division Artillery Officer—at fault. Hughes does not impress me. Saw Gen. Brougher at 11th Infantry Command post. Then to Battalion Command post 45th Infantry. Col. [*Leslie T.*] Lathrop (commanding) appears to be capable. As we left here we stopped at 45th Clearing Station and talked to a Medico. His observations were that most Philippine Army casualties were injuries to hands, arms, or feet, while Philippine Scouts were usually hit in eyes or chest. Tends to indicate some instances of self-inflicted wounds. Boats reported attempting to land this night. Our artillery working on them.

Monday 2-9-42—I Corps

Went south with Gen. Wainwright this a.m. Went first to 57th Infantry Command post They are in charge of cleaning up Jap landings in area of Anyasan and Salaiim Rivers. Saw Col. [*Edmund J.*] Lilly, [*Maj. Harold Keith*] Johnny Johnson, + Dr. Francis (bunkmate in Washington). Spud Sloan (Air corps) has a detachment of Air Corps men on beach and he was there with Jap they had captured after he swam in. They were trussing his hands with telephone wire when we came up. Gen. Wainwright had him released and gave him a cigarette. He said, "Thank you." Am sure he could speak English fluently, but later turned out to be quite insolent. Tonight was pleasant in Command post. Nice chatter with Bill Ward, M. M. Champlin (Navy) + Engineers (Col. Skerry + Steve Malevich). Tom Gerrity + I played Rummy + then to bed about 11:30 p.m. Slept like the dead. Speaking of death—I thought my time had come day before yesterday when Gen. Wainwright + I were returning from front. About ½ km from our Command post we received enemy artillery (105 or 155) fire. Two shells hit road about 20 to 30 yds. directly in front of our car. Too close for comfort.

Tuesday 2-10-42—I Corps

Spent in camp. The Gen. took Col. Nelson + Champlin to 11th Division sector, but I asked to stay in due to my cold. Feel as if I can hardly breathe. Though I knew it would do my cold no good, I took a bath this a.m. before breakfast for I felt filthy. Went down + got some medicine from the Medicos + then to bed for a while. Had two Jap prisoners in camp today—one this a.m. seemed stupid—both picked up from swimming in sea. The one they brought in about 5:30 p.m. was a nice looking specimen and seemed quite willing to talk, but could speak no English. We had a Chinese cook talk with him by writing and he was quite grateful that he had come into hands of Americans + said he would be glad when the war was over. He was a sergeant in some medical unit. Had been in sea for 20 hrs. and had been shot thru the chin.

Had supper with E-F Troop who are on guard here. [*First Lt. William H.*] Bill Ward asked me up. Received letter from F. F. Thomas (on duty with 13th Philippine Army Infantry) asking me to see about his promotion. He had sent it in a Jap envelope that they had taken from dead Japs killed by one of their patrols. Had a good session in the G-3 tent tonight. Tom Gerrity and I played Rummy and then talked with Johnny Pugh, M. M. Champlin, Joe Chabot, [*2nd Lt. Joe T.*] McIntosh (an Engr.). To bed about 12:00 p.m. and thought would sleep like a log, but was awakened at 2:00 a.m. by artillery fire. Johnny Pugh was awake and we talked about it and what woke us was artillery fire from Jap naval vessel off to the west. You could hear the whine + then the explosion. Not so near our Command post.

Wednesday 2-11-42—I Corps

Spent in camp—asked the Gen. if I couldn't stay in because of my cold—seemed worse than ever before. Progression reported from both north pocket and Anyasan-Salaiim sectors. I heard report that Spud Sloan (Air Corps) wounded near Salaiim sector. Played Rummy this night—4 handed—Steve Malevich, Tom Gerrity, Bill Ward + self. (Gen. Wainwright in camp—Col. Maher out.)

Thursday 2-12-42—I Corps

Gen. Wainwright went to North front today—Johnny Pugh + Lt. Rosebear went with him. Tom Gerrity and I went south today. Went first to Air Corps Headquarters. They griped me—especially a Col. [*Kirtley J.*] Gregg and Capt. Lundy. High + mighty attitude—Lundy reports that we will have Air Corps support soon. Spoke of all the stuff we now have in Australia, but still you ride in open cars so you can watch for "Charlie" and duck out at a moment's notice. Went on to PNAD to get Gen. Wainwright some flight coveralls. Then saw [*Col. Henry Edward*] Pete Warden. He seems to work pretty hard—a little too confident in his rash talk of what to do. Went then to Hospital No. 2 to see John Wheeler. On the way in saw Col. Baccus and Karl Lichter who was looking for Spud Sloan. They were inseparable. Worked, lived, + played together. Had heard he had died. Saw "Hutch" Hatchett at #2. Went then to Hospital #1. Went in and had supper with Juanita Redmond. There verified Spud Sloan death. Terrible to hear. He was shot 6:30 a.m. yesterday and died 6:30 p.m., but was conscious to the end. Juanita Redmond looked much better, but still feels that Japs will grab her if she steps out of the house. That is a dirty trip and my cold seems no better. Am almost convinced it is serious trouble. Played little Rummy.

Friday 2-13-42—I Corps

Went to front today with Gen. Wainwright and Lt. M. M. Champlin (Navy). Went to 11th Division Command post + then to area of North Pocket which was finished yesterday in the p.m. 45th Philippine Scouts were sweeping area. Gen. Brougher was there and we all went up Trail 7 where some of the fighting had taken place. Champlin seems a pretty good judge of people. Col. C. L. Irwin (USAFFE G-3) in camp tonight + Gen. Wainwright with twinkle in eye told Artillery Officer Bob Lindsay to have 155's working most of night. First salvo at 9:00 p.m. was quite a blast. The situation looks rosy here for the time being. All landings (Jap) have been cleaned from our West Coast and total Jap dead should come close to 1200. There are over 300 dead in the pocket.

If we can only get help here we could clean Luzon. Hope this happens. Everyone is getting fed up with this Bataan life. If the rainy season finds us here it is going to be bad.

Johnny Pugh + Tom Gerrity accusing me of selfishness because I did not share a carton of cigarettes with them which FrankHewlett gave me. I smoke much more than they and the Camels were gone before they had finished their prior supply. The Gen. is in good shape + good humor these days. Trust that we have changes for better by receiving aid here soon. Am sure the Gen. will receive another star if we get more men here and start on an offensive. Should he get this, I might get home from this war a Major. Spoke to him yesterday re: Regular Commission.

Saturday 2-14-42—I Corps

In camp today. Gen. Wainwright stayed in as something he ate made him ill. Was glad he did as I did not feel like going out. The doctor believes I have serious trouble. Played some Rummy with Tom Gerrity and Bill Ward. Gen. Marquette visited the Command post re: replacement for 8 Ball. Went to bed almost 9:30 p.m. and couldn't sleep. Head so closed up I could hardly breathe. Got up and dressed + came back to Command post and talked to Frank Hewlett + Ed Gunzi about Japan. Frank H. not encouraging re: navy losses at Pearl Harbor.

Sunday 2-15-42—I Corps

This is the day I had told Juanita Redmond that we would be back in Manila. Had it marked in my date book. Missed that one. Went to front this a.m. with Gen. Wainwright + Commander [*James Seerley*] Clark of the Navy. General's regular Command Car driver, Notah, was ill and they gave us some driver who was no good. When we got to 11th Division Command post, I had him get out and wait there and I drove rest of the day. Terrific roads. Went to Col. Lathrop's Command post and then to Col. [*Glen R.*] Townsend's 11th Infantry Command post. Gen. Brougher at the latter. Got back to Command post about 4:00 p.m. Took bucket bath + clean clothes. Some I still had that were pressed + people looked at me as if I were a mannequin. A lot of artillery fire since about 6:30 p.m. Enemy bombers dropped eggs on our front lines and then their artillery opened up + then ours opened up + the rumblings + blasts keep you jumping for a while. Remainder of night fairly quiet. Talked with Steve Malevich, Col. Lindsay, + Frank Hewlett for a while + then turned in.

Monday 2-16-42—I Corps

In camp today. Johnny Pugh + Tom Gerrity left early to go south. Tom to see Air Corps + Johnny Pugh to see Major Stu[art] Wood at Hospital #1 at the tip of Bataan. Spent most of day reading Damon Runyon + [*Capt. William T.*] Sexton's *Soldiers in the Sun*. Fighting still in 11th Div. sector—reported (enemy) almost cleaned out. Next on duty at 8:00 p.m. for Tom Gerrity. Tom + Johnny returned about 11:00 p.m. and told of day's happenings. To bed about 12:00.

Tuesday 2-17-42—I Corps

To front this a.m. with Gen. Wainwright + Frank Hewlett. Went direct to 11th Infantry Command post + Gen. Brougher was there + immediately announced that the main line of resistance was closed now + that it was his birthday. We went then to front and saw where the last Japs had been killed. Saw about 20 of them just "freshly dead" as the Gen. said it. Gen. Wainwright then personally directed the laying of barbed wire. Saw Parnell (on same boat) and it was his outfit where break had occurred. He has been right with his men for some time on the front. Saw Gen. Jones Command post on way up this a.m. Jones recovering from fever. Command post in good spirits when we returned. Notice received that USAFFE going to take some of our troops for their island defense. Have my opinion of that group.

British are not highly thought of in these parts due to their surrender at Singapore. Wonder how that will affect us. And another thing—I wonder when we will get aid here. There are many things to consider, I know, but it seems to me that there has been ample time for aid to come. At least some sort of Air Corps activity. Nothing but Jap planes all day long. Rations are not so good these days either. Never again will Mother have to insist that I eat more when at home. Notice in Navy news about conscription in states. Wonder how Winston will be affected.

Wednesday 2-18-42—I Corps

Spent in camp—my day a short nap and otherwise reading and "discussing world news" with anyone. Our discussions of world news always end up or are interspersed with how it will affect our situation here. Usually, in the past, I have not wanted to go out every day that the Gen. goes, but my cold + sinus is some better and feel that going somewhere is better than sitting around camp and thinking—also we are issued no sugar since Sunday and everyone seems to have a "sweet tooth." Gen. Wainwright gets nervous and impatient when we stay in and he said tonight "Tom, let's go visiting tomorrow." I thought at the first of the war and sometimes later that maybe I should ask to be relieved and go to the 26th Cav. but Johnny Pugh is G-2 and really not acting as an aide and I sometimes think I may be doing the Gen. some good where I am. I rarely have anything to do, but I never try to discourage the Gen. by habitually reminding him of the great odds we are against, as some do.

Lt. M. M. Champlin (of Navy) after having been gone for several days returned this a.m. He is a very likeable fellow and always good for a discussion of the naval view on our receiving help. Col. Frank Nelson surprised everyone the other day by really playing a clarinet which he had asked some "tankers" to retrieve from Stotsenburg. Gen. Pierce visited the Command post today at Gen. Wainwright's request re: movement of troops in S.S.S. It is hard to understand the decisions of USAFFE. They are in much worse mental condition over all this than the front line units. Yesterday was first day since Jan. 16 that our Corps had not been actively fighting and first day since Jan. 23rd that the Jap had not been somewhere in our lines in force. By captured documents, maps, etc. it is rightfully believed that the I Corps has not only repelled a vigorous main coordinated attack of the Jap, but have inflicted heavy losses. We killed about 2500 Japs + do not know losses from artillery nor losses to fighting units by injuries. To bed early tonight because I go on duty at 2:00 a.m. Will write some letters, too, for chance they will get out.

Thursday 2-19-42—I Corps

(Note: About 4 days behind in writing this up.) In camp this date. Went on duty at 2:00 and had intentions of writing letters, but read

Sexton's *Soldiers in Sun* and finished it. Took a "bucket bath" this morn and then played Rummy with Tom Gerrity and spent some time reading "Prisoner of War Reports." Quiet day.

Friday 2-20-42—I Corps

Left early this morn with Tom Gerrity and Capt. [*Houston*] Farris (from 26th Cavalry—took Jim Blannings place—and whom I have very little regards for) to go to rear and try + get some additional food supplies for the Gen.'s mess. Went first to Headquarters Philippine Division—Gen. [*Allan C.*] McBride was out and could get no satisfaction from Col. [*Pembroke A.*] Brawner G-4. He suggested though that I see Col. [*Alva E.*] McConnell (Quartermaster) who proved to be the key man in the food supply of Bataan. He was very nice and most liberal with the items he had that we asked for. Even got ham + syrup and a few fresh vegetables, including onions. This all took quite some time. Back by Air Force Headquarters to pick up Gerrity + had supper at Sgt. Martin's Air Corps Mess. Would have stopped by the Hospital to see Juanita had the Farris person not been along. He's a gross individual. During day saw Jim McCloskey, Medical Corps, and Bill Jones, Field artillery. Back to Command post about 9:30 p.m.

Saturday 2-21-42—(KP. 210.7) I Corps

To front this a.m. after a good breakfast—pancakes with butter (oleo). Gen. Wainwright, Johnny Pugh + I went first to 91st Div. Command post—Gen. Jones, Gen. Stevens, + Gen. Brougher all there. Gen. impressed on them the need for more work during the quiet period and warning not to relax. This quiet period came about after Jap penetration pushed from 11th Division Sector. Now our patrols that work out to front have no contact with Japs. There are several opinions as to what they are up to, but of course no one really knows. Most probably they know that our force is contained here and they have realized that we cannot be driven out with the force they have here. So they pull back and sit while we sit. Their distribution of forces will not enable them (with their main operation in Java) to put added strength here. Therefore they wait until southern problem cleaned up and additional forces brought in from there or China to polish this place off. Gen. then wanted to go on to new road across to II Corps and we followed it across the Pantingan River. 14th Engineers working this road. Saw [*Maj. Frederick G.*] Freddie Saint with much beard. Back to Command post, took bath and then at about 7:30 p.m. headed south with Champlin (Navy) and Tom Gerrity. Tom Gerrity being ordered this date back to Air Corps presumably preparatory to going south to rejoin his Light Bomb Group. Tom has been with us since Dec. 20, 1941, and is a swell lad. We have been playing Rummy all along. Left Champlin + me at Mariveles at Quarantine Station to spend night with Commander Harrison. He's a nice guy. Had shower in real bathroom before going to bed.

Sunday 2-22-42—I Corps

Had good breakfast with Commander [*Harry John*] Harrison this a.m. and then Lt. Champlin and I took boat to "The Rock." Went to Navy Tunnel and to Admiral Rockwell's office. Looked about the place. Saw Hank Henry + [*Lt.*] Warwick [*P.*] Scott. Went then to Army Tunnel + to Quartermaster to get Champlin some clothes. Then to Hospital to see some Navy Medico. Saw line forming for lunch and ate again. USAFFE in tunnel, only people in entire set-up that eat 3 meals a day. Talked with Tisdelle a while and then went back to Navy side. Talked with Hank Henry for about 2 hours + he gave me some mints, razor blades, + cigars for General Wainwright. Ate third meal with Navy. Very good. Left "The Rock" about 6 for Mariveles. Thru mine fields over + back. Comdr. Harrison had arranged for a car for us and went to Hospital #1. Had date with Juanita Redmond and enjoyed talking with her very much. Lt. Champlin went up to Headquarters Philippine Division and saw Col. Wong, Chinese Army and then we got back to Mariveles to meet our courier with whom we rode back to our Command post. A good day—lot of fun but accomplish little. Just a day off. Oh, yes, saw Tom Suddath at Navy before leaving Rock.

Monday 2-23-42—I Corps

In camp this date—did not wake up til 9:30. Had breakfast. Gen. Wainwright, Johnny Pugh + Lt. Champlin went to P.C. on our right front on inspection. Spent most of day reading and napping. Had excellent supper. To bed early.

Tuesday 2-24-42—I Corps

Out with Gen. Wainwright, Col. Lindsay (Bobo), + Lt. Champlin to inspect artillery positions. Went first to 91st Field artillery Col. Hunter technically in command, but [*Maj.*] Alva [*Revista*] Fitch (A Btry, 23rd Field artillery) is the real ramrod—considered the "best gunner on Bataan." Went then to "Eight Ball" on Saysain Point. Gen. Wainwright not pleased at all with that outfit. Then to 24th Field artillery. Saw "Chuck" Samson, + Capt. [*Don G.*] Whitman. "Mike The Monk." Back to Command post with no excitement. Took soapy bath + had good supper in new Mess Hall. Have rigged up some tent flies over bamboo poles and have strung mosquito bars around sides. This has helped a great deal. Formerly we had to shoo flies with one hand and eat with the other. Beautiful moonlight night tonight and Gen., Col. Maher, + G-3's busy preparing plan for artillery fire + follow up by patrols.

Wednesday 2-25-42—I Corps

Row with Johnny Pugh early this morn re: water for brushing teeth. Heard story yesterday that might show Whitehead alive. Whitehead is alive. Have just received confirmation. He reported in to General Bradford Chynoweth at Iloilo. Very happy and phoned to 26th Cavalry. Got Paul Jones and he had heard rumor and this confirmed it. They all very happy. Stayed in camp all day. Read Edgar A. Poe. Francisco made me some candy. Everyone listens to Voice of Freedom at 7:30 p.m. now since [*H. P.*] Houser got his radio working—did so by hooking to telephone. Beautiful night. Saw orders today re: Tom Gerrity. He was transferred to 20th Pursuit and is now with Gen. George's Headquarters.

Thursday 2-26-42—I Corps

Also in camp. Gen. Wainwright had conference of Sub-Sector Commanding Generals re: rations size + distribution and sanitation. There is considerable griping re: food greatly among Americans. Sanitation important because many cases of sickness being reported. Our new mess hall is a great help in this respect—also my putting signs in latrine area is helping. Tonight—a beautiful moon also. Had long talk with Lt. Champlin re: general situation and subversive activities. Joe Chabot talked with me today.

Dooley arranged for Wainwright's staff to pose for this Signal Corps photo taken 27 Feb. 1942 in the I Corps area during Japanese artillery fire and air raids. When Wainwright autographed it, he added, "To Tom Dooley from the Battling Bastards of Bataan." Left to right: Capt. Thomas Dooley, Aide-de-Camp; Maj. John Pugh, Aide-de-Camp; Maj. Gen. Jonathan Wainwright; Lt. M. M. Champlin, Navy File; and Sgt. Hubert Carroll, Driver. Photo courtesy the Tom Dooley Family.

Friday 2-27-42—I Corps

To 2nd Battalion 72nd Infantry today with Gen., Johnny Pugh and Lt. Champlin to inspect front lines. Were close in to Bagac. Our artillery firing overhead all day. Jap artillery opened up as we were coming back and we stopped off in 3rd Battalion Command post for reports. Lot of walking and it's beginning to get hot. Took good soapy bath upon return to Command post. Also on return to Command post Signal Corps photographer was here to take pictures of Gen. and he had Lt. Champlin, Johnny Pugh and Sgt. Carroll + me in with him.

The poor Filipino Troops on front are without smoking tobacco or cigarettes. Battalion Commanding Officer had one package and he was giving one cigarette to each squad of 6 or 8 men. Pitiful. I gave them all I had, as did Gen. Wainwright. They gave us in return a bunch of cashew nuts. Fruit of this tree also good. Listened to Voice of Freedom tonight. Read Navy news. All cheered by general reports of Allied actions in Java area. But it all seems so terrible. Nothing is worth the loss of American life that is inevitable should all this continue. Orders tonight issued posthumous awards to Bob Cunningham and Cliff Hardwicke.

Saturday 2-28-42—I Corps

The meals are the pleasant time around here now. Fun with Monty [*H. E. Montgomery*] + Houser. He always telling food stories with recipes. Went with Gen. Wainwright + Monty this a.m. to inspect beach defenses of 1st + 3rd Battalions of 71st Infantry. Saw Major Hickes + Capt. _____ drive thru 45th bivouac area. Monty + I fired our Garands at rocks to see just how they shoot. Are excellent. Back to Command post early and had coffee with Gen. Wainwright had conference at 2:00 p.m. this date with Gen. Jones + Gen. Brougher to settle some disturbance and put records straight re: Terol Pocket victory. Farris (from 26th—took Jim Blanning place) being so nice to Johnny Pugh + me so as to get promotion to Major. Has even asked Johnny outright to ask Gen. to promote him. He's a gross individual in my opinion.

Pleasant supper with much bickering between Monty + Houser. Heard Voice of Freedom. Johnny Pugh + Lt. Champlin left with courier about 7:25 p.m. to go to Mariveles + then to the "Rock." Johnny Pugh going, I think, because I did it last week. This morn early, Col. Maher got on him about being late at G-Section area. This put Pugh out. I have not mentioned it before, but when there Johnny Pugh was cited the first time it was for his work at Damortis just before Jap attacked. Gen. said after citation was out, "Oh, you were with Johnny, weren't you?" "But you already had Silver Star." Now Johnny Pugh has been given oak leaf cluster for accompanying Navy off Longoskawayan Pt. and to buck himself up, I overhead Champlin telling him that he had volunteered to go because people thought the road closed because of snipers. [The *certificate accompanying Champlin's Silver Star says, "On 20 February 1942 Lieutenant Commander Champlin voluntarily went forward to the front lines in order to ascertain if Naval gun-fire could be of assistance, and in so doing, advanced well beyond a line of enemy snipers in order to fully reconnoiter for possible artillery targets."*] Listened to radio + talked with Col. Nelson and then to bed early for I go on duty at 2:00 a.m. in place of Johnny Pugh.

THREE

The Battling Bastards of Bataan

Sunday 3-1-42—I Corps

On duty at 2:00 a.m. Relieved Joe Chabot. Read + wrote. After breakfast went to front with Gen. to inspect front lines of 1st Infantry. Good work being done there. Went first to 1st Division Headquarters. Col. Berry out. Talked with Chief of Staff Col. Fields. On way out on Trail 17 to Trail 9 stopped by 26th Cavalry. Saw Paul James + Henry Fleeger. Maj. Trapnell out with Col. Vance on recon. On way back from front we ran into rain in 11th Division Command post sector. On returning to Command Post had coffee with Gen. Wainwright in his trailer. He gave me a bar of much-needed soap and some ammunition. We are going to try to get a Bantam for narrow trails and saving of gas. If so, I will drive and Gen. will sit in front and Carroll + Bearden in rear. Major Allen sick so I am going on duty again tonight from 8:00 p.m. to 2:00 a.m. Voice of Freedom news not so good tonight. Have heard via KGEI that Japs have established beachheads on Java. Someone said this went past censors to States:

> We're the Battling Bastards of Bataan.
> No mama, no papa, no Uncle Sam.

No Air Corps and no aid prompts that—easily understandable.

Monday 3-2-42—I Corps

In camp—got Bantam from motor pool and tried it around camp today. My idea to use it for Gen's trips and save gasoline. Had lunch—cocoa, bread, + peanut butter, with [*Capt. Joseph R.*] Joe Barker + [*Col. Edwin P.*] Ed Ramsey in Cavalry Guard Camp Command post—"G" Troop on guard since Sun. Took 1st Sgt. Ibanez some cigarettes. Johnny brought the Gen. a bottle of Scotch from Corregidor the other day and today the Gen. started on it early. He is a completely different person when he does that and I don't like being around him. His mind goes blank and he gets the "brave attitude" and all-in-all it's not right. He had Col. Lilly, 57th Infantry with him and his "glorious attitude" brought to fire by whiskey prompted him to give his rifle to them as a gift from him for their fight on the beaches. "Johnny" Johnson—S-3 of 57th—came with Col. Lilly. Enemy artillery fell in vicinity of our Command post today. Also on Bopo Point. About 7:45 p.m. reports came in re: Air Corps actions at Subic Bay this date. P-40s worked on that section all day—bombing + strafing. Sank 5 ships, set fire to another—set fire on Grande Island and fire on Subic shore. Strafed personnel also on docks.

Tuesday 3-3-42—I Corps

Out this date in "Peep"—Gen. Wainwright, Sgts. Carroll + Bearden, + self to Gen. Pierce's Command post, then to Quinauan Point. 34th P.G. (A.L.) in this section. On returning to Command post, was in Gen's trailer having coffee with Gen. and Johnny Pugh and Johnny habitually pessimistic in his conversations with the General. Gen. plans to visit rear area for the first time tomorrow.

Wednesday 3-4-42—I Corps

In "Peep" with Gen. Wainwright + 2 Sgts. to rear. First—to Gen. Pierce's Command post, then to advanced USAFFE where Gen. Wainwright talked with Gen. Frank re: gasoline. Went then to see Cavalry horses. Then to Quartermaster office where Gen. thanked Col. McConnell for food I picked up there before. Stopped in at Hospital #1. Col. [James W.] Duckworth already gone to South to establish new hospital. Gen. saw + spoke to Mike Nash. I saw Juanita Redmond for minute. Stopped again at Gen. Pierce's Command post on return. Lt. Champlin returned today. Artillery fire and bombing near our Command post while we were away. According to reports, the Japs are using the 155's that were disabled and left on Maubon Point. Hope they run out of ammunition soon.

Thursday 3-5-42—I Corps

Spent in camp. Francisco gave me a haircut today. I gave him some cigarettes—also gave Pvt. [Isabelo S.] Torio, 26th Cavalry radio operator, some cigarettes. Gen. Wainwright + I had some coffee and cookies—interrupted by Jap artillery fire and air raids. Read for about an hour. Johnny Pugh went out on normal staff inspection of positions. Photographer from Signal Corps here to take pictures. Wanted picture of Gen. Wainwright + staff. I arranged the picture. Johnny Pugh was disappointed upon return that he was not in picture.

Friday 3-6-42—I Corps

In camp. I was left in due to Johnny Pugh's planning. Gen., Johnny Pugh, Lt. Champlin went to front and took with them a Signal Corps photographer. Car so crowded I just didn't go. Read and talked with everyone about. Went up later in p.m. and talked with Joe Barker + Ed Ramsey with G Troop 26th Cavalry (my old troop). Gave Sgt. Ibanez (1st Infantry) some cigarettes to distribute to troop. No enemy action this date.

Saturday 3-7-42—I Corps

Gen. planned to stay in the Command post today so I took a command car (drove myself) and went back to Quartermaster Dump to see Col. McConnell and get a few items for the Gen.'s mess. Took Lt. Champlin and Col. Skerry (Engineers) to Mariveles where they took a boat to Corregidor. Went on and got OK from Quartermaster to draw foods—(even got a ham on the list and also jelly). Went up then to Hospital #1 and saw Ted Winship and Juanita Redmond. Had cup of the best coffee + a doughnut about noon. Went over then to Air Corps Headquarters and picked up Sgt. Whatley (from Normangee, Texas) who was formerly the General's driver and now Staff Sgt. in Air Corps. Went over to Bataan Field to see Tom Gerrity who was formerly with us here (my Rummy playing friend). He still in good spirits. Had been up once in plane since he left here. Stopped by Quartermaster Dump with OK slip and got the foods and then to Mariveles to meet boat to pick up Col. Skerry. He had changed plans and didn't ride back with me so I had a long drive with dim lights back to Command post. Quite tired and to bed early.

Sunday Mar. 8, 42—I Corps

Lt. Champlin came in early this morn with Navy news sheet that mentioned convoy in Pacific with much aid. Cheerful start with that. Went to front with Gen. Wainwright in "Peep" to 12th Infantry sector and inspected front line. Quite a bit of walking. Back by 11th Division Command post. Gen. Brougher is getting ready for rainy season with bamboo huts and all. Almost has a barrio there now. After supper tonight, Joe Chabot, H.P. Houser, + H.E. Montgomery and I have a long discussion about the many better things we would like to have to eat. One thing I insisted on was lots of cold sweet milk and added some liver + onions. [*Collecting recipes was a favorite pastime. It gave the soldiers something to think about besides their terrible living conditions, and it created moments of humor in their otherwise drab surroundings. Recipes ranged from the simple to the complex:*

Corned beef mixed with tabasco, A-1©, horseradish. *Toast in oven, then for top slice of cheese melted in bread, add chipped onion, rye or whole wheat bread.*

Col. Sage's sandwich. *Garlic buttered bread, cheese melted in top slit, Canadian bacon fried, circle of onion fried, place latter two together + then fry egg over top. French bread.*

Baked Stuffed Fowl, Polish Style. *Use old bread, 2 diced onions, 3 cloves garlic diced, 2 green apples diced, 1 teaspoon cloves ground, ½ teaspoon nutmeg, 1 teaspoon paprika, 1/4 lb. fat bacon diced to 1" cubes, 1 teaspoon sage ground. Salt + pepper to taste. Fowl dressed—take juice of lemon and rub inside. Bread—soak in water, then render out water. Onions, garlic, etc.—braise in skillet, then mix into bread and stuff into fowl. Bake, starting with a little beef stock.*]

Monday 3-9-42—I Corps

Joe Chabot upon waking up this a.m. complained he didn't sleep well because of indigestion. Monty + I accused him of eating too much of what we talked about last night. Went with Gen. Wainwright, Johnny Pugh, Lt. Champlin this day. Took the "Peep" (Bantam car) and went by way of new road across mountain to II Corps (East Side of Bataan). As we came into clearing on top of mountains a Jap plane dived at us with machine gun blazing. Lt. Champlin first saw plane and I saw him bank to dive at us. Johnny was driving and we told him to stop quick. He did, luckily, as we all jumped out and scampered into the bush, the machine gun bullets landed alongside of car and between car and us. He circled back twice after diving and we stayed in bush and attempted to get in some depression as we were afraid he would drop a bomb. He didn't. I was scared stiff. Went on and came out on East Road at Limay. Then on down to II Corps Headquarters. Saw Gen. Parker, Zero Wilson (Lt. Col.—also from Normangee, Texas), John Neiger, [*Maj. Hueston R.*] Bish Wynkoop and others. Wilson, Wynkoop, Neiger, + [*Gen. Royal*] Reynolds [*Jr.*] (57th Infantry) lived next door to us at Fort McKinley. Came back by way of lower road thru Mariveles. We were very dirty + dusty upon arrival at Command post. Looked like men from Mars or Hell or something. To bed early. [*The close call on March 9 was described in Bill Sloan's* Undefeated:*"The next morning, during a tour of the front, Wainwright narrowly escaped death when a strafing Japanese Zero put seventy-two bullet holes in the staff car in which he and two aides, Captain John R. Pugh and Lieutenant Tom Dooley, were riding. They were forced to bail out and take cover in some bushes, but fortunately, after the Zero left, the car was still sufficiently drivable to get them to the Mariveles dock, where they were met by a cabin cruiser with Lieutenant James Baldwin at the controls."*]

Tuesday 3-10-42—I Corps

Early this morn a secret letter came in for the General and I took it over to his trailer. He was ordered by Gen. MacArthur to come to Corregidor for conference. Few minutes later he received telephone call and so Gen. Wainwright, Johnny Pugh, Lt. Champlin + I left early + went to Mariveles and got boat from there. Gen. Wainwright was immediately whisked off to conference with Gen. MacArthur + Gen. Sutherland (Chief of Staff). I was standing in the Malinta Tunnel and talking with Capt. John V. King (Master Sgt. at Texas A&M when I was in school). Gen. MacArthur passed by. I saluted and went on talking with Capt. King. In minute here was MacArthur peering into my face. I thought there might be some error so I said, "Sir, I am Captain Dooley" and before I could say I was Gen. Wainwright's aide, he said, "Yes, I know. I was talking to your Chief outside and just wanted to shake hands with you." Made me feel very good that he should remember

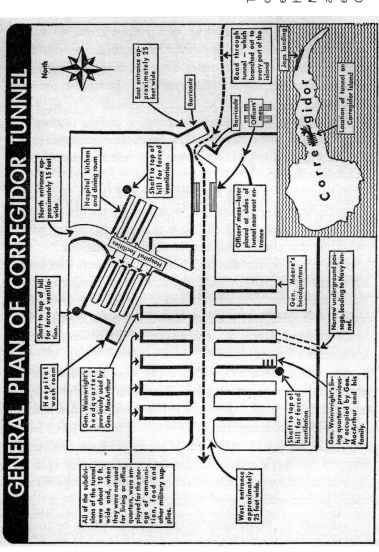

The Malinta Tunnel complex on Corregidor Island had eleven main laterals, including headquarters for Generals MacArthur and Moore, and a separate hospital wing with eight laterals. From Wainwright, *General Wainwright's Story.*

66

me—had met him once before at Fort McKinley. [*John V. King*
accompanied former A&M Commandant Col. George F. Moore when
Moore was reassigned to Corregidor in 1941. King survived the siege of
Corregidor and years in POW camps only to die on the Hell Ship Enoura
Maru *in 1945.*]

Many changes brought to light today. Gen. Wainwright told us
of the reorganization on the boat back to Mariveles. Under the new
plan—MacArthur is to head the General Headquarters, Wainwright
the Luzon force (which makes him an Army Commander now instead
of a Corps Commander). Brig. Gen. Bradford G. Chynoweth will have
the Visayan Forces and [*Brig. Gen. William F.*] Sharpe, the Mindanao
Force. Gen. Wainwright is to move his Command post and take
over new job on Thurs. with new staff. Only Johnny Pugh and I are
going with him. We are taking with us the two Tech Sgts. (Carroll +
Bearden), Sgt. Centimo (driver) and Francisco and Jacob (Francisco
was our cook at McKinley + Stotsenburg). Saw Gen. Weaver (Tank
Commander) on road. Had late supper, the four of us, and Gen. gave
us a long cigar that Gen. MacArthur had given to him. (Pres. [*Manuel*
L.] Quezon had given them to him.) Gen. told his staff about the
change tonight. All hate to see him leave. Johnny + I are to go to new
Command post tomorrow to make arrangements.

Wednesday 3-11-42—I Corps

Had Cholera shot this date. Forgot to mention that yesterday when
we got back to Command post that 2 ambulances were leaving with
wounded men. Japs had shelled gun position on hill above us and
killed 2 men + wounded seven. Johnny, Sgt. Carroll, + I went to new
Command post this a.m. and talked with Gen. [*Arnold J.*] Funk (new
Chief of Staff) re: Gen. Wainwright change. Got everything settled and
stopped in Hospital #1 on way back and talked to Juanita Redmond
about 15 minutes. Also stopped at Section Base in Mariveles and had
some ice water and talked with Mr. Gonzlea (Navy). Sent our regards
to Comdr. Harrison. Back to Command post + took bath. Very dirty
road—dirty trip. Saw no Jap planes. Enemy artillery fire this night—
we fired counter-battery. Am going to try to get a telegram home soon.
Think there is a way. Houser (G-1) and I slipped into mess tonight and
finished the extra piece of apple pie that was left over.

Thursday 3-12-42—Kilometer post 168/Luzon Force

Moved to new Command post today just after breakfast. Told everyone goodbye—was held up about 45 minutes by air raids. All the I Corps Headquarters officers were gathered at Command post to tell Gen. Wainwright goodbye. They really hated to see him go. I took the "Peep" with Francisco + Jacob and led the truck with the Gen.'s trailer down. After having several Jap bombers over this a.m. The entourage looked like a freight train. Gen., Johnny Pugh, Lt. Champlin, + the 3 Sergeants went down in Packard. New Command post is in nice spot at Kilometer post 168 (Little Baguio) and with some much needed reorganization + planning, will be nice. Gen. issued orders for Capt. Bill Lawrence to come here as Headquarters Commandant. I started work on small mess for General's personal staff. To bed early.

Friday 3-13-42—Luzon Force

Yesterday—I forgot to mention—I told Lt. Champlin goodbye + gave him some radiograms to send for me—one to family + one to Margaret. I worked today on new mess by going to Quartermaster and talking to Col. McConnell. He gave me some extra food and then suggested I requisition thru him some utensils. Gen. held staff conference after supper and I sat up until about 10:00 watching some people play bridge.

Saturday 3-14-42—Luzon Force

Had terrible breakfast—oatmeal and rice and "drbie" coffee. Went with Gen. first to Hospital #1 where he visited Chaplain Duffy—I Corps Chaplain. I talked with Ted Winship and Juanita Redmond. Told Juanita to get a letter written and I would get it out for her. Tom Suddath reported as Naval Liaison officer this a.m. to replace Lt. Champlin. Champlin is going south. While at hospital went thru "Prisoner of War" ward. 33 Japs. Had cup of coffee and delicious fig "tart." Went then to Headquarters Philippine Division where Gen. discussed food situation with Gen. McBride, Service of Supply. I saw report and heard discussion and it is very discouraging. Six out of eight of the last supply boats that have tried to get thru to us have been sunk or captured. Rice supply, by cutting to minimum to allow 5 oz. per day for Americans + 9 oz. for Filipinos, will last 30 days. All other supplies—a lot less—some items only 5 days. The 26th Cavalry horses are being slaughtered at rate of about 30 each week for food. I have not yet been forced to eat any. Back to Command post and after supper (we eat at 5:00) went with Tom Suddath to Mariveles where we took small boat out to a larger one. We were going to load torpedoes on submarine that was due in, but job postponed. That's how I was going to get letters and radios off and how Champlin was going south. Had some coffee with bread, real butter, + blackberry jam while on "Ranger." Brought Johnny 2 sandwiches. NOTE: Frankly things look darker now for this force than ever before. I still have hopes that it will all come out alright but something must take place in next 30 days. Will not put story in writing until some announcement is made about Manila but I do know about it all.

Sunday 3-15-42—Luzon Force

In and around Command post all day. Gen. Edward King + his aide Tisdelle came over last night and are now settled here. Went down to Hospital #1 and talked with Gen. Pierce, Chaplain Duffy, and Juanita Redmond. Pierce—not knowing his trouble—think it is heart trouble. Told Juanita to write telegram and would get it off tonight. The new mess hall and kitchen is coming along. Nipa roof and servale sides. Got a case of bacon from C+E Dump. Went with Tom Suddath to Mariveles—Left about 6:00 p.m. Stopped and picked up radiogram for Juanita. Took boat at Section base in Mariveles out to Ranger last night. Had coffee with biscuits, butter, + jam. About 9:30 p.m. Champlin and the other "passengers" from Corregidor came aboard. Talked with him 'til Permit came alongside about midnight. [USS Permit SS-178, a Porpoiseclass submarine, penetrated the blockade to the "Rock" and rendezvoused off Corregidor on the night of 15–16 March, landing ammunition and taking on board forty officers and enlisted men, including thirty-six cryptanalysts from the intelligence station CAST.]

Went aboard "Permit" and found that [Lt. Cmdr. Wreford G.] "Moon" Chapple was skipper. Looked all around sub and talked with officers—[Lt. Cmdr. Henry S.] Hank Monroe, [Lt. Cmdr.] Jack [M.] Seymour, Fred Tasch. Had coffee on board with real cream. A naval Lt. (jg), Vincent Edward Schumacher, who had one of the motor torpedo boats, was aboard with his crew.

Monday 3-16-42—Luzon Force

Went last night with Tom Suddath (Navy) to Mariveles. Caught boat out to *"Ranger"* to await submarine. Champlin + other navy officers came out. Sub came alongside and I went aboard and stayed for about 2 hrs. Talked with all officers—Mason Chappell, Hank Monroe, Jack Seymour, Fred Tasch—missed Fluch. Tom went along—got mail + radiograms off. Got in about 6:00 a.m. and to bed—got up at 9:00—missed breakfast. Worked on Gen. Wainwright's mess all day and to bed early to get sleep before going on duty at 2:00 a.m.

Tuesday 3-17-42—Luzon Force

Went to II Corps today with Gen. Wainwright. Stopped at II Corps Command post and picked up Gen. Parker + John Neiger. Saw "Zero" Wilson—sick in bed—better. Went to Sectors A + B—saw lot of Air Corps people. Called Jack Kelly—"Liz" Bush's husband—still OK. At "A" saw Murphy. ["X *Jack Kelly"—noted in top margin of page.*]

Wednesday 3-18-42—Luzon Force

Stayed in camp today. Gen. Wainwright + Johnny Pugh went to "Rock" on business this date. Got Johnny to fix up my allotment—it is now $242.00 per month to Collin County National Bank effective April 1, 1942 running "indefinitely." Got mess started at evening meal—had soup—tenderloin steaks—sweet potatoes—peas—peaches. [*Lt. Alfred L.*] Al McMicking [*executed with his wife, Helen, in Manila January 1945*], [*Capt. Thomas H.*] Tom Delamore and I went to Hospital #1 tonight. Talked with Gens Pierce + Stevens. Three of us talked food with Miss McDonald. Al McMicking admitted reason he felt so low was he had $25.00 of candy on return trip of the *"Legaspi"* [*a US Army ship, on charter from Philippines, shelled and scuttled off Luzon 1 March 1942*], and it was not reported arriving off Mindoro.

Thursday 3-19-42—Luzon Force

When got back last night—Johnny Pugh on duty—told me I would not have to get up early as planned. I was going to meet Col. Manuel Roxas—former Secretary of Treasury—and show him around. Glad that's off. Went to Hospital #1 with Gen. Wainwright—he to get haircut. I talked with Fraley (Navy) re: electric refrigerator. Went on to

Mariveles to see about Frigidaire, but Commander Bryant not there. Bill Lawrence with me and we went on to Motor Pool #4 to get spoons, chairs + toilet paper. Got them from Major [*James W.*] Cavender—former manager Manila Hotel. Johnny Pugh, Al McMicking, Tom Delamore, + I played bridge tonight.

Friday 3-20-42—Luzon Force

Went with Gen. Wainwright to I Corps Command post this a.m. Saw Gen. Albert [*M.*] Jones, Cols. William Maher, Frank Nelson, Lindsay, Joe Chabot, Houser. Stopped at 26th Cav. on return—saw Maj. Trapnell, John Wheeler, Col. John Vance, Red Jones, Jim Blanning, Bill Chandler. Gave Trapnell + John two cartons Camels. While at 26th Gen. Wainwright got telephone call from Gen. Arnold Funk—Chief of Staff—informing him that KGEI had announced his being made Lt. Gen. He was happy as was I. He told me he would probably make Johnny Pugh a Lt. Col. + me a Major. When got back I fixed up a celebration dinner. Put "Saigon" tablecloth on table—had candles—and good meal. Bill Lawrence got me some native gin and Johnny Pugh + I mixed cocktails and we drank toast to the General. He very happy about it all. Invited Juanita Redmond, but she couldn't accept. Johnny Pugh, Tom Delamore, Tisdelle, + I played bridge. On duty till 2:00 a.m.

Saturday 3-21-42

This morning before breakfast the Gen. had call from Gen. [*Lewis C.*] Beebe from Corregidor to the effect that War Department orders were received placing him in command of all Philippines and he was to have Headquarters at "Rock" with same set-up that MacArthur had. Gen. Wainwright left about 9:30 a.m.—I went with him to Cabcaben and then back to Command post to get gear. Johnny Pugh + I with 3 Sgts. got to Corregidor about 1:00 p.m. Went up to Hospital #1 and gave Juanita Redmond 4 cartons cigarettes + some matches. Major Burton R. "Bob" Brown, Gen. Moore's ADC, met our boat and got us settled. Gen. Wainwright temporarily in quarters with Gen. Beebe + Johnny Pugh + I in Gen. Moore's quarters. Even had lunch. Dinner tonight with Champagne and ice cream. Gen. Wainwright had received congratulatory notes during day from President Roosevelt + Gen.

MacArthur. Much publicity going out via radio. Frank Hewlett—United Press, Mr. [*Dean*] Schedler—Associated Press etc. Beautiful night.

Sunday 3-22-42

We start starving today at noon—Jap propaganda dropped on 3-20-42. Have copy of letter pasted on this page. Sunday morn—radio when first turned on playing Presbyterian songs. Wonderful breakfast. To tunnel with Gen. about 9:00 a.m. Went over to Navy tunnel—saw Hank Henry + Warwick Scott + Willis. Smoked outside + talked with several people. Col. Haines, Maj. [*Joseph E. H.*] Stevenot. Wonderful dinner tonight. Manuel Roxas to dinner. He is leaving tonight by plane to rejoin Quezon.

Gen. Moore received radio today from T.O. Walton [*President, A&M College of Texas*] **to effect that new building there will be named for him** [*bold type added*].

Monday 3-23-42

Went on inspection of "Rock" Defenses this a.m. with Gen. Wainwright + Moore and Bob Brown (Gen. Moore's aide). Visited Antiaircraft Battery, 155 Battery, + Marine Beach defenses and 12-inch gun battery. Col. [*Jesse T.*] Traywick + [*Lt. Frank F.*] Carpenter [*Jr.*] reported in tonight.

Tuesday 3-24-42

Started out on another inspection with Gens. Wainwright + Moore + Bob Brown this morning, but we were interrupted while at Battery Monja by bombs. We were all in 155 casemate when first stick came down. About 15 yds on one side + about 25 yds. on the other. Went then to nearby tunnel. Finally went back to Malinta Tunnel. Continuous air raids during day and also into the night. Slept in tunnel.

Wednesday 3-25-42

Bearden left last night on regular 7:00 o'clock boat for Bataan. Back to Pack Train. Johnny Pugh and I were at Quarters this a.m. when Air Raid alarm sounded. We went to Battery Kysor. Went to Main Tunnel about 11:30 a.m. Went back to Quarters this p.m. + moved my clothes

Your Excellency,

    We have the honour to address you in accordance With the humanitarian principles of "Bushido", the code of the Japanese warrior.

    It will be recalled that, some time ago, a note advising honourable surrender was sent to the Commander-in-Chief of your fighting forces. To this, no reply has, as yet, been received.

    Since our arrival in the Philippines with the Imperial Japanese Expeditionary Forces, already three months have elapsed, during which, despite the defeat of your allies, Britain and the Netherlands East Indies and in the face of innumerable difficulties, the American' and Filipino forces under your command have fought with much gallantry.

    We are, however, now in a position to state that with men and supplies which surpass, both numerically and qualitatively, those under your leadership, we are entirely free, either to attack and put to rout your forces or to wait for the inevitable starvation of your troops within the narrow confines of the Bataan Peninsula.

    Your Excellency must be well aware of the future prospects of the Filipino-American forces under your command. To waste the valuable lives of these men in an utterly meaningless and hopeless struggle would be directly opposed to the principles of humanity and, futhermore, such a course would sully the honour of a fighting man.

Your Exellency, you have already fought to the best of your ability. What dishonour is there in avoiding needless bloodshed? What disgrace is there in following the defenders of Hongkong, Singapore and the Netherlands East Indies in the acceptance of honourable defeat? Your Exellency, your duty has been performed. Accept our sincere advice and save the lives of those officers and men under your command. The International Law will be strictly adhered to by the Imperial Japanese Forces and your Excellency and those under your command will be treated accordingly. The joe and happiness of those whose lives will be saved and the delight and relief of their dear ones and families would be beyond the expression of words. We call upon you to reconsider this proposition with due thought.

    If a reply to this advisory note is not received from Your Excellency through a special messenger by noon of March 22nd, 1942, we shall consider ourselves at liberty to take any action whatsoever.

COMMANDER-IN-CHIEFS of
the IMPERIAL JAPANESE ARMY and NAVY.

March 19th, 1942.

To His Excellency Major-General Jonathan Wainwright, Commander-in-Chief of the United States Forces in the Philippines.

ANY ONE WHO GETS THIS LETTER IS REQUESTED TO SEND IT TO THE COMMANDER - IN - CHIEF OF THE UNITED STATES FORCES IN THE PHILIPPINES.

Above: Japanese propaganda letter to Wainwright calling for surrender 19 March 1942. Copy folded inside Dooley's journal.

+ things to tunnel. Air raids again at night. The damn Japs won't leave us alone.

Thursday 3-26-42

The cook—Filimon—was killed last night. Think he died of shock. Was not struck by bomb fragment, but ran into wall in the dark + probably died of shock. The air raid alarm started at 10:00 a.m. this date and very few + very short intermissions. Gen. Wainwright last night received radiogram from Gen. George Marshall to the effect that Wainwright has power of Independent Army Commander. About 7:00 p.m. Gen. Wainwright said to go see Gen. [*Carl H.*] Seals and wait for him. The order was out on promotions and I got promoted to a Major. Johnny made Lt. Col. Pilet + [*Lt. Col. Nicoll F.*] Galbraith + Lt. Col. Stuart Wood made full Colonels. Also Lee Vance + Sledge. Trap made Lt. Colonel. But the joy of receiving promotion was deadened by the report that Jim McCloskey was killed today in Bataan by bombs. He was a swell guy. Had talk with Maj. Horace Greely (Air Corps). Bob Brown told that he was going to be promoted. [*Following the start of hostilities, Dooley went from first lieutenant to major in ninety-three days.*]

Friday 3-27-42

Today rather uneventful in one sense. Continuous air raids all day and into the night. Outside many times to smoke—during raid alarms + "all clears."

Saturday 3-28-42

Left "Rock" at 7:30 a.m. for Bataan. Gen. Wainwright, Col. Irwin, Sgt. Carroll + self. Gen. Funk met us at Cabcaben dock + we went first to Bataan Field. Talked with Capt. [*William Edwin*] Ed Dyess + Tom Gerrity. Then to Luzon Force Headquarters. Gen. Wainwright talked with Gen. Edward King. Thence to 5th Interceptor Command Head-quarters to look into settlement of command status since Gen. George's exodus. Then back to Luzon Force Headquarters. Gen. Wainwright had conference with all Gen. officers of Bataan except General Parker, who was sick. While here I got upset for first time of war. Was nervous

+ jittery to point of nausea. Came back to "Rock" and upon reaching tunnel another raid started. Bob Brown, Johnny Pugh, Ted Wallace, and several nurses and I had gathering in sound proof radio room.

Sunday 3-29-42—Corregidor

The first raid this a.m. was at 9:45. [*Capt. Raymond*] Finley, Quartermaster Corps and I were outside and we heard the planes coming and started walking inside. About 20 feet in, the bombs started hitting near mouth of tunnel. We dodged behind a sandbag baffle. No one hurt. About 3:30 p.m. went with Bob Brown to Battery Crockett for dinner. Herman Hauk, Battery Crockett, very nice. Plenty to eat and Herman showed us around. Watch alert drill. Two 12-inch disappearing guns. Watch through glass while Battery Hearne fired on Jap minelayer—out of range. While at Battery Crockett, Bob received phone call that the order was out on his promotion. Another gathering in radio room. Air raid—to powder room.

Monday 3-30-42

Another day of raids—the 7th. First this a.m.—8:45. Gen. Wainwright had conference today with Capt. Kenneth [*M.*] Hoeffel—Navy—re: blockade. Continuous raids all day. About 5:00 p.m. two (2) Jap bombers came over and the anti-aircraft got both. Everyone happy about that. Report came in today that Hospital #1 was bombed today. One killed and several wounded. No nurses, patients, or officers hurt. Night raids again. I go on duty at 10:30 p.m.

Tuesday 3-31-42

First raid this a.m. at 9:00. Relatively quiet. Raid alarms intermittently during whole day. Played bridge this p.m. with 2 nurses + a navy medico. Stopped by broadcasting studio at 10:00 p.m. and Lt. [*Wallace E. "Ted"*] Ince (formerly studio mgr. KZRH—Manila) was making test broadcast in preparation for Army Day broadcast. He asked me to read some poetry for "Voice Carry Test" as he did not want Japs to have opportunity to recognize his voice. Raids during night as usual.

Wednesday 4-1-42—Bataan

(Gen. Wainwright—$10,000 Govt Insurance—effective this date). To Bataan this morn with Gen. Moore and Bob Brown. Left North Dock at 7:00 a.m. and landed at Mariveles. Car which I had called Tisdelle for was not there so walked up to Pack Trail Rear Echelon to see about horses. Some oats left and plenty of green grass for grazing. Walked on up road to Naval Antiaircraft Battery + called Bill Lawrence for car. Went on then to 20th Pursuit Headquarters on Mariveles Cutoff for package which Capt. Moore flew up from Ciba. Stopped at Hospital #1. Saw where bombs were dropped in the area. Asked Jap prisoners what they thought of it.—"It was a mistake, sir." Talked with Col. Duckworth. Capt. [*Jack E.*] LeMire [*Adjutant of Hospital #1*] "licking boots" all over the place. Talked with Juanita Redmond. During their bombing, she fainted under the ward desk. Asked if she wanted transfer to "Rock." She said yes, so told her it could be fixed.

Went on to Luzon Force Headquarters—Gen. Edward King not there. Met Gen. Moore + Bob there and we went on to Cabcaben and caught the boat. Back on Rock—with air raid on—in time to have lunch. I am always hungry these days—as is everyone. Have utmost faith in our receiving food + help soon.

Thursday 4-2-42

First raid this morn started 9:05 a.m. Started work in G-1 Section under Colonel Pilet. Today spent observing papers + study of regulations. In two raids this morn the Nips dropped 2 heavy sticks. Tunnel rocked. Direct hit on quarters where Gen., Johnny Pugh + I were living prior to start of continuous raids. Gen. sent notice to Surgeon to transfer Juanita Redmond to "Rock." She will be better off here. No raid alarms after 1:00 p.m. 'til after midnight. Spent time with Dick Smith and later with Dean Schedler + Wallace "Ted" Ince in K2VF (Voice of Freedom radio station).

Friday 4-3-42

Up at 5:30 a.m. Couldn't sleep from thinking about Gen. tying up his broadcast last night. Cleaned up, shaved and walked up to look at quarters. Looked like large pile of enlarged toothpicks. Orders issued this date re: Juanita Redmond's transfer to "Rock." Called her re: same and told her to keep quiet as possible and to let me know when she was coming over and I would meet boat. Talked while tonight with Dean Schedler, Associated Press correspondent. He felt very low about the whole affair here. Had coffee in Ted Ince broadcast studio. Reports coming in re: pretty strong attack going on in 41st Division Sector. Japs attacking in force.

Saturday 4-4-42

Arranged last night for Sgt. Carroll to get early morn coffee from Ah Poo (Chinese "Mess Sgt."). Since coming in tunnel, the Gen. hasn't had it. I must seem lax about that. Reports during night show continued action in 41st Division Sector and also an attempted landing operation at Kitang [*Quitang*] Point on East Coast. (Reported that 42nd Infantry had disintegrated.) Japs advanced past 41st Division sector Main line of resistance. May not be as bad as it seems but the physical condition of the troops will not permit much hard fighting. This p.m. Bob Brown + I mixed some chocolate milk—condensed milk, cocomalt, + water. Noticed Col. George [S.] Clark out working today. He commanded 57th Infantry (a good outfit) at first of war and then he broke and was relieved. Gen. Wainwright, after taking command of US Forces In Philippines (USFIP), sent for him and tried to put iron in his soul, to no avail. Then he begged Gen. not to send him back to Bataan, but to get him South on first available transportation. Gen. agreed and have heard him say nothing more re: affair.

Sunday 4-5-42

Easter morn—no eggs to hunt, though. Went with Gen. Wainwright and Sgt Carroll to Bataan. Left "Rock" at 7:30 a.m. Went first to Headquarters Luzon Force. Gen. Edward King and staff at breakfast. Morale seemed very low. In my eyes "DEFEAT" was written all over them. This was also true at II Corps Headquarters, where we next went. Gen. Parker's attitude in general seemed "lax" and "unoptimistic." Saw Col. Harrison [C.] Browne [*Chief of Staff, Philippine Division*]. He had been acting as Chief of Staff II Corps in absence of Col. Charles [L.] Steel, who has been sick. Got back to Corregidor about 12:30 a.m. in time for bowl of soup. Gen. received radio from [*Brig.*] Gen. [*James A.*] Ulio [*Asst. Adjutant General, War Department*] this p.m. with message from

Mrs. Wainwright. He quite elated re: same. Also Gen. Ulio had called Johnny's wife who is in Washington and told her that Johnny Pugh with Gen. and well. Wish he would include Mother in a radio and Gen. Ulio could wire collect to McKinney. But I will probably get radiogram off from Cebu soon.

Monday 4-6-42

Most of day spent back + forth with no specific duties. Checked reports from II Corps. Situation there confused. 45th Infantry, 31st Infantry (American) + 57th Infantry moving up to stop Japs. They were able to push in unopposed thru 41st Division sector when that Division disintegrated. I think this was due to poor physical condition caused by lack of sufficient + proper foods, living conditions (no relief from front lines), continuous unopposed aerial bombardment, and continuous artillery fire which was observed by unopposed Jap observation planes. Morale has gone down noticeably in past 2 weeks due mostly to the much talked of "help" that has never arrived. Never has anyone thought that Americans would be in a position in which the United States would be termed "impotent."

The Japs have a large "V" driven into the II Corps front which takes in Mt. Samat which is not so good. Ten nurses from the Tunnel Hospital are being transferred this p.m. to Hospital #2 in Bataan and this proved to be the opportunity that we had been looking for. The Gen. today ordered that the few civilians (women) that have done nothing but sit on fat fannies and read books + ate much food are to be put to work in the hospital. I take some credit in agitating this move. There were three noticeable cases—a Miss Benly, (Manila debutante who does not let you sit for 1 min. without mentioning same), a Mrs. Ryder (Navy wife), and an Air Corps officer's wife (sent home by Army Transport last spring who shipped back by Norwegian freighter.) Thus far, they have been burdens + food eaters (precious food). They will probably continue as burdens due to their attitudes toward work. Arranged (per her request) for Juanita Redmond's transfer to be revoked. All in all the outlook here is not bright. But "hope springs eternal in the human breast" and this is especially true in my case. I still believe that something will pull us out of here, as miraculous as it may now seem.

Two news correspondents, Frank Hewlett—United Press + Dean Schedler— Associated Press, were talking to me last night to see if they could talk with Gen. about getting out of here and down to Mindanao. They claim there is nothing more to write about here and the big news will shift to Mindanao. I bluntly told them why not admit that they just wanted to get out and they would not come back once they did get south. Also heard tonight that Dōmei news said that American aid to Philippine Islands was due April 15th and added, "but it will be too late."

[*"The day before the Fall of Bataan April 8, 1942, a group of American and Filipino pilots (among them future Philippine President Carlos Romulo) escaped from Bataan by flying out a Grumman Amphibious Plane that they had repaired.*

"Lt. Tom Gerrity who had served as a bomber pilot, fighter pilot, ground liaison to Gen. Wainwright and infantryman on Bataan organized the repair and flight of the aviators. They would evade Japanese naval and air units and make it to Dole Field on Mindanao where they would meet Gen. Rosie O'Donnell (not to be confused with the contemporary icon) and fly to Australia. Gerrity would fly B25 Missions against the Japanese in the Bismark Sea; sink 28 ships; and become a leading force in American Air Power."—from 1965 dedication of the Leo High School War Memorial in Chicago in honor of General Thomas P. Gerrity for the Veterans program held in 2009.]

Tuesday 4-7-42

The only good news today was the order re: civilians reporting to Hospital at 8:00 a.m. for work. The II Corps has been badly shaken. Filipino troops shed arms + uniforms and flee. [*Brig.*] Gen. Mateo Capinpin (Philippine Army 21st Division) missing. All American troops and Philippine Scouts are committed to try and stop the Nips. The Japs, for the 3rd time, struck Hospital #1 which is already marked with large Red Crosses. Several of the buildings were hit and one large bomb hit the main ward. 43 were killed and about 60 severely wounded. Two nurses, [*Lt. Rosemary*] Hogan [*sent to set up a 1,000-bed hospital on Bataan*] and [*Lt. Rita G.*] Palmer, injured. They were brought to Corregidor last night. Not serious. The Japs are sinking lower each day. Imagine a deliberate bombing of a clearly marked hospital. They had the troops on run and deliberately bombed the hospital to make more confusion and leave us with no hospital to care for casualties. Talk this evening with Johnny and Stuart Wood, (G-2). The situation looks blacker all the while. Why can't the almighty US do something to relieve this group here. Four months have passed. Gen. Wainwright is worried over the whole situation. Too worried. He must think clearly not of himself, but of the people on Bataan.

Wednesday 4-8-42

Bataan fell! [*Dooley added this entry in the top margin after recording the event.*]

A new day which I hope proves to be no worse than yesterday. The II Corps pulled back during the night to a line approximately thru Lumao. All Filipino troops have disintegrated except about one regiment. The I Corps will have to pull back to conform. They (the Nips) continue their bombing of the new areas. These must be some salvation for the Americans on Bataan. Why do the American people at home parade and rejoice in the glory of "all out" war when these poor devils here daily watch the seas and skies for the aid of the US which now appears too late. I have held hope all along for something to happen to get this mess straightened out and, mind you, I still have hope, but the situation is desperate. The reports all day are bad. I took report at 7:00 p.m. which means the end of Bataan. Col. [*James V.*] Collier called from G-3 Luzon Force and said that Philippine Army troops on right flank of II Corps line had fled and the Japs pouring thru. Proved to be double envelopment as Nips were also coming around II Corps left flank. Col. Irwin (G-3) and Col. Galbraith (G-4) went to Bataan this p.m. with plans for evacuation of certain units to "Rock." During night Ordnance + Engineers busy destroying ammunition + other such few supplies as need be.

Gen. Wainwright in conference most of day with Chief of Staff Gen. Lewis Beebe (who is quite sound). Gen. Wainwright quite upset. Two days ago Gen. Funk came to "Rock" for Gen. Edward King to say he was going to capitulate. Gen. Wainwright gave two direct orders— one—do not surrender—two—attack with I Corps toward East. Later the second order was modified. Last night when things looked so bad and plans for evacuation of certain units were made and order was given to Gen. Jones (I Corps) to make a frontal attack with his Corps and attack Olongapo. Went to bed about 1:00 p.m. Frank Hewlett, United Press, wanted me to wait up and see the Bataan episode, but I didn't want to watch it. I feel sick when I think of it and feel that I should be there with them, but I started this war with the General (and before it) and will stay around 'til ordered differently.

[In her 1943 book, I Served On Bataan, *Army nurse 2nd Lt. Juanita Redmond wrote,*

"If aid could not reach us while Bataan still held, we all knew (though the words were seldom spoken) that no relief could be hoped for now. But there was true comfort and a quickening of pride and faith in the words that went from General Wainwright's Headquarters to the people at home:

"Bataan has fallen. The Philippine American troops on this war-ravaged and bloodstained peninsula have laid down their arms—with heads bloody but unbowed they have yielded to superior force and numbers of the enemy. The world will long remember the epic struggle that Filipino and American soldiers put up in the jungle fortresses and along the rugged coast of Bataan. They have stood up uncomplaining under the constant and grueling fire of the enemy for more than three months. Besieged on land and blockaded by sea, cut off from all help in the Philippine Islands and America, these intrepid fighters have borne all that human endurance could bear.

"For what sustained them through all their months of incessant battle was a force that was more than merely physical. It was the force of an unconquerable faith, something in the heart and soul that physical hardships and adversity could not destroy. It was the thought of their native land and all that it holds most dear, the thought of freedom, dignity and pride, in these, most priceless of all, our human prerogatives. The adversary, in the pride of his power and triumph, will credit our troops with nothing less than the courage and fortitude that his own troops have shown in battle. Our men have fought a brave and bitterly contested struggle, all the world will testify to the almost superhuman endurance with which they stood up until the last in the face of overwhelming odds.

"But the decision had to come. Men fighting under a banner of unshakable faith are made of something more than flesh, but they are not

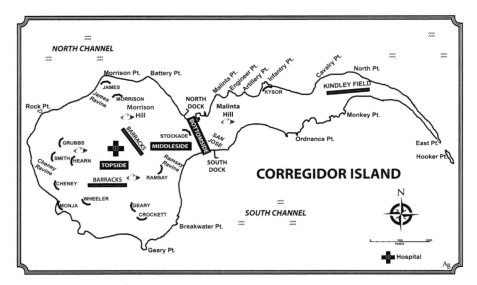

Map of Corregidor Island showing key points, gun emplacements, and area nick-names. Map by Anne Boykin.

Finance Section, Lateral 12, Malinta Tunnel. A typical installation in the laterals. Photo courtesy Texas A&M University Archives.

made of impervious steel. The flesh must yield at last, endurance melts away and the end of battle must come.

"Bataan has fallen, but the spirit that made it stand—a beacon to all the liberty-loving peoples of the world—cannot fall."]

Thursday 4-9-42

History certainly being made this date. After I got up I went to get a bite of breakfast and all thru the tunnel were new faces—those who came out of Bataan during the night. All that could be said was that it was a mess. Went then to Gen. Wainwright's quarters and he + Johnny Pugh were just up + Col. Traywick was on phone talking to Gen. Funk and the report was that Gen. Edward King had sent his representative to front with the white flag. This, of course, was just complying with Wainwright's orders, but I can certainly understand when I know the real person that Gen. King has always been. He did it to forestall more deaths and suffering. He could see the cause was hopeless. The men left on Bataan and the Gen. are the ones I feel so deeply for. It certainly looks from our side of the picture as if we were sold down the river. Had not reports conveying the wrong idea been continually sent to War Dept. + Press we would not be in this predicament today.

With a minimum of aid Bataan could have been held. Continuous, unopposed enemy aerial activity is the key to the downfall of Bataan. What now will happen to the "Rock?" Already this morn the Japs have started to bomb again. Air raid alarm on all morn. When the Nips move their heavy artillery up within range from Bataan this place will be a living hell, besides the shortage of food and water probably after our supply has been demolished. Can the American people stand by without a determined effort to relieve this place? Checked up and all nurses brought over. Redmond OK and in good spirits. Those poor girls have gone thru a nerve-wracking few days. Telephone lines to Gen. King's Command post still working 'til 6:00 p.m. Every staff officer that received calls there asked that radiogram be sent home if possible to say "Keep chins up—see you in Frisco."

Confusion in tunnel among those arriving from Bataan. There had been a plan, but it blew up due to confusion among troops. The sad part is that the good troops that we had planned to pull over here were cut off and what arrived here but Philippine Army Quartermaster officers, etc. Several of us got together tonight—Redmond, Bob Brown, Ted Ince.

Friday 4-10-42

Radio from President Roosevelt arrived late last night. It was three-page affair and stated he understood and told of confidence + faith he felt for Gen. Wainwright. Yesterday p.m. we started receiving shell fire from Bataan. Could not fire back because our troops were still in the area. The Gen. early this morn told Gen. Moore that he could + would fire on definitely located enemy batteries. No area firing though. At 8:37 a.m. this date the Luzon Force radio signed off with this message. "Ordered off air by Japanese commander—see you in States." No reports in all day re: Gen. King. Saw few 26th Cavalry troopers but could get no information re: officers. I pray that Trapnell + John still have their lives.

Continuous air raids all day long and also shell fire from Bataan + Cavite Provinces. Sent radiogram out tonight to Dad and told him to inform Boyd that I'm still with Wainwright and well. Get-together tonight in V. of F. studio—Bob Brown, Redmond, Charles Smoke, Ted Ince, Beethoven, Winnie Madden, Johnny Pugh. Stayed up late talking with Stuart Wood. Story re: Air Corps officers stealing plane.

Saturday 4-11-42

Another day up on the Japs. No reports re: Gen. King nor outcome of terms of Bataan surrender. Heard some stories from late arrivals from Bataan but second-hand stories, etc. You can not believe those. Corregidor under continuous air raid all day. They dropped a lot of bombs but the casualty report for the day was only two. One serious wound—one slightly injured. Gen. Wainwright prepared letter today to be published to all troops on Corregidor that we will hold here and not surrender.

You can't keep from thinking about all those wonderful people on Bataan and what will be their treatment by the Nips if they lived thru those terrific days prior to the truce. Stayed up till about midnight talking with Stu Wood. We mixed some Class C coffee + ate a biscuit.

Sunday 4-12-42

Another day up on the Japs. Morale of this spot is going up. All think we can hold out here and trust that the united effort will eventually wipe the Japs from this area. No reports (except Domei news) re: Gen. Edward P. King and others on Bataan. Some few still coming over, but their stories may well be affected by the excitement they have gone thru in the last few days. Am going to attempt to get this out with copies of certain orders so that if it gets home the folks will know what has gone on here. I still feel that we will come out of this OK. My confidence grows every day. The news just now of some of our planes bombing in Luzon has made everyone quite happy. My health is still OK. There are very few people here who do not think we will come thru victorious. It will be wonderful when we have finally achieved victory and I can get back to Texas.

I am going to include 3 orders—Silver Star Citation—Promotion to Captain—promotion to Major. I have recently made an allotment of $290.00 per month effective May 1st. Will also include brief notation of pay status to date. Besides insurance policy with Central States Life I have one (1) $10,000 government policy which was obtained in January by radio from Ft. Mills.

If this comes thru, tell Margaret Boyd all is well and let her read same if she would like. Hope all of you are well and please don't worry for all is for the best and we will certainly come out of this fracas better men than we went in.

I certainly don't add financial data in the form of any will, but just to let you know how things stand. Please arrange for all drug stores at home to keep well stocked with the ingredients for malted milk, because I will order many when I get home. My love to you all and say again—try not to worry as everything will be alright in the end. Say hello about for me to all except Don Bagwill—I don't want to appear in Y.H.T. Again all my love and sorry this war started before Xmas because was looking forward to receiving those pictures. Have one small picture of Margaret and one small one of Cissy. But will see you soon and hope you can meet the boat in Frisco. I love you all and please don't worry –

[On April 18, 1942, just three weeks before the surrender of Corregidor, Lt. Col. James Doolittle led eighty army airmen on a daring bombing raid

General Wainwright's surrender was refused by Japanese Lt. Gen. Masaharu Homma (second from right). At left side of photo are Lt. Col. John Pugh, Lt. Gen. Jonathan Wainwright, Brig. Gen. Lewis C. Beebe, and Maj. Thomas Dooley. From Beebe, *Prisoner of the Rising Sun*.

over Japan. Sixteen modified bombers launched from the USS Hornet *on the 750-mile mission to Tokyo. Piloting the fourteenth plane was Doolittle's second-in-command, Maj. John A. Hilger (Texas A&M Class of 1932). Lt. Robert M. Gray '41 was the third to take off. Other Texas Aggies participating in the mission included Lt. William M. Fitzhugh '36, Lt. James M. Parker Jr. '41, and Lt. Glen C. Roloson '40. Because this occurred several weeks before the fall of Corregidor—where there's a gap in Dooley's journals—it isn't clear what soldiers in the Philippines knew about the raid.*

At this point, on April 12, Dooley signed off on his first journal and packed it, along with General Order #5 (granting his Silver Star and promotion to captain), the order promoting him to major, and other personal notes and papers, to be sent home on the next plane leaving the Rock. He started a new diary and for two weeks repeatedly noted air raids and shell fire, but the entries from this diary appear only in Ken Foree's Dallas Morning News *series, which was published in October 1945, after the war had ended. The following is excerpted from that series:*

"Spent the night of 27th and day of 28th at Battery Smith (all batteries on Corregidor had names) topside—a twelve-inch, barbette mount, seacoast gun. . . . Intermittent barrages all during the night.'

American and Filipino troops surrender at the mouth of Malinta Tunnel May 1942. Photo courtesy Texas A&M University Archives.

"*April 29 was Emperor Hirohito's birthday. . . . The Americans knew it by two means. First, Domei broadcast it. Then the Japs celebrated it. 'A terrific artillery bombardment from 12:30 to 5 p.m.,' wrote Dooley.*

"'*That night, 'As scheduled, two Navy PBYs came in, landing on water between Fort Hughes and Fort Drum' (Corregidor's satellite forts).*

"*And then followed a strange parting. From the hosts of the condemned, G-1 (Personnel) had carefully picked a little handful to be flown out to civilization—and life. A few were officers with valuable data and reports. The rest were nurses.*

"'*I went down to the dock and said good-by to Juanita Redmond and Stuart Wood, then sat on the path to watch the planes take off. Beautiful sight to see flames from the exhaust streaking across the water in the dark of night. They are to land at Lake Lanao on Mindanao, spend daylight hours under cover and proceed to Australia the following night.'*

"Concerning events on May 3 he wrote, 'Submarine in tonight. Taking out a few staff officers with reports to Washington and nurses. Sent last letter home by Colonel Irwin.'

"It was the last link with the outer world. Three and one-half years later he met Brig. Gen. C. L. Irwin in New York and thanked him again for taking out that letter just three days before the Corregidor curtain came down.

"May 5. 'According to weather forecasts and time schedules on hour of moonrise, those who have studied it believe Japs will land tonight.'

"They did, sneaking over in the darkness and operating on the beaches at moonrise.

"'A busy night. Reports pouring in to G-4 (operations). About midnight first report of Jap landing near Cavalry Point. Thirty minutes sleep.'

"'Out on the beaches there was hell going on. The twelve-inch guns could not be brought to bear. The others had been knocked into junk. There was only rifle fire and machine guns left.' But, according to the recent testimony of one [Lt. Gen. Masaharu] Homma, they did right well. Half of sixty barges were sunk, he said. But the rest formed a beachhead for hordes to follow.

"'Morning of May 6. 'Situation hopeless. Conferences of Generals Wainwright, Moore and Beebe, Col. [Samuel L.] Howard (4th Marines). Decision to capitulate. Dark hour.'

"It was the end of Corregidor. The beginning of prison."]

FOUR

Capture and Imprisonment

[*Shortly after the US surrender, Dooley began a new journal in a wallet-sized brown leatherette 1942 calendar notebook labeled "Engagements." Helpful information printed in the book included a calendar for 1942 on which Dooley marked April 8 (labeled "Bataan") and May 6 (labeled "Corregidor"). He circled June 4, Aug. 12, Sept. 29, Dec. 3, Dec. 18 and Dec. 25. Then on a 1943 calendar he circled the birthdays of his parents, his girlfriend, his sister, and other unidentified individuals with initials GT, MJ, and OB.*

The notebook included numerous reference charts that helped him stay aware of everything from populations of principal cities, public holidays, eclipses predicted for 1942, standard time zones, the rising and setting times for the sun and the moon, and even a scoring guide for contract bridge (which received frequent use).

On 9 May 1942, three days following his confinement in the Manila University Club, Dooley began this journal with the entry "Old diary thru April 12, 42." Then he skipped back a few days to record the surrender of Corregidor on May 5 and 6.

The Kenneth Foree series in the Dallas Morning News *described General Wainwright's unsuccessful attempt to surrender to General Homma, commander of the Japanese forces in the Philippines. "After dodging an artillery barrage, Wainwright's contingent was taken over to Bataan to meet Homma at a Filipino house near the Cabcaben airstrip. After the Japanese general finally arrived, Wainwright attempted to begin negotiations, but Homma abruptly walked out without receiving the surrender and sent the Americans back to Corregidor. Wainwright would sign surrender papers with a Japanese colonel. Immediately after the signing, enemy batteries on Bataan began pounding Corregidor's exposed middle side and top side barracks and the Jap commander donned his field equipment and left to lead 'the attack on middle side, against men who had been disarmed since noon!*

Following the surrender, Dooley's journal entries become brief and often repetitive, owing in large part to the privations of captivity and the austere and brutal conditions the prisoners were forced to endure. However, his slim missives do illustrate the boring aspects of imprisonment and provide nuggets of information about how small things become meaningful, such as his interrogators' inability to extract even minimal strategic information from him. The books he mentions barely hint at the massive amount of reading material the prisoners managed to obtain. Dooley's third, fourth, and sixth journals list upward of two hundred volumes. To dismiss the entries covering the last eight months of 1942 would compromise any chance of understanding the experiences of Dooley and his fellow captives.]

Saturday May 9, 1942
Bob Brown's Birthday. 2nd Lt. Eumara [*first Japanese officer they met*]—very kind to us all.

May 5–6, 1942
Corregidor surrenders.

May 7, 1942
To Lumar + Manila. Broadcast—Univ. Club.

5–7 to 11, 1942
Gen W., Col. Nunez C. Pilet, Johnny Pugh + self under guard.

May 11, 1942
Traywick returns Beebe, Lawrence, Carroll with baggage.

May 12, 1942
Doctor (Japanese) with Maj. Bill Lawrence. Bridge + reading. Bill Lawrence worse—Dr. says pneumonia.

May 14, 1942
Bill Lawrence died at 11:05 p.m. this date.

Maj. Bill Lawrence, right, with Maj. Tom Dooley, was the first Wainwright aide to die in captivity, on 14 May 1942, owing to a lack of treatment for pneumonia. Lawrence joined Wainwright's staff as Hq. Commandant in mid-March 1942. Photo from captured enemy film.

May 15, 1942

Gen. Wainwright, Gen. Lewis Beebe, Col. Pilet, Col. Jesse T. Traywick Jr., self, Johnny Pugh, Sgt. Hubert Carroll buried Lawrence with Father Gd. (Ermita C[*atholic*] School) officiating. Buried at Fort McKinley Cemetery.

May 16, 1942

Bridge + reading. Washing clothes. Exercise on roof this p.m. Ice cream—gift of *Lt. [(j.g.) Toshio]* Kusamoto.

May 17, 1942

[*Brig.*] Gen. [*Guillermo B.*] Francisco + Lt. [*Robert C.*] Silhavy [*missing in action less than two weeks later*] joined us. They are going south.

Japanese mission. Bridge. [*Card games were played constantly to while away the time.*] Read—*The Wayward Man.*

May 18, 1942

Routine. All hands ravenous—dress at clatter of dishes. Johnny Pugh—Gen Beebe—no rice.

May 19, 1942

Hot—Bridge. Read. Exercise on roof after breakfast—hour on roof after dinner.

May 20, 1942

First rain today. Noticeable on Luneta [*a park in Manila*]. Bridge— read. University Club Library accessible.

May 21, 1942

Read *R.A.F.*—started *Master-at-Arms* by Sabatini. Bridge—coffee. Bridge 'til 12:00 p.m.

May 22, 1942

Rain this p.m. Col. Nunez C. Pilet (G-1 USFIP), Col. Jesse T. Traywick, Carroll + self bridge. Purchased mangoes + papaya. Good meals today.

May 23, 1942

Gen Francisco, Johnny Pugh, Silhavy to South today. Bridge—rain.

May 24, 1942

Read—Bridge—rain. Candy—cocoa. Corregidor people marching past. Water—off—bought newspaper.

May 25, 1942

Still water off—on roof. Moved this PM to 1st floor—very dirty— much work to clean up—stove in bath. Bridge—read newspaper.

May 26, 1942

Routine—Carroll fixed ice tea, cocoa, coffee. Bought candy, sugar, salt today. Read—bridge.

May 27, 1942

Good breakfast—sunned on roof. read—bridge. Coffee—cocoa.

May 28, 1942

New guard. Breakfast—roof- read. Taught new guard English Comp—OK. Purchased paper—candy—sugar—cocoa.

May 29, 1942

Routine—Gen. Wainwright questioned by Japanese military police this a.m. Pilet—Traywick—myself questioned this p.m. After 3 hrs., Jap remark to me: "I cannot see how you are the general's aide and know so little."

May 30, 1942

Good breakfast—roof. Read—bridge.

May 31, 1942

Routine. Johnny Pugh returned 2:30 p.m. Bridge—read. Dumb party.

June 1, 1942

Roof—good sunning. Read—"*The Doctor*" by MRR [*Mary Roberts Rinehart*].
Bridge—new cards taramfer.

June 2, 1942

Routine—roof—read—bridge. Lt. Eumara with artist visited this p.m. bringing ice cream. He very nice + very thoughtful.

June 3, 1942

Routine—roof—sun—read "*Sabotage*"—bridge—coffee—washed clothes. Japanese military review this a.m. on Luneta.

June 4, 1942

Routine—sun on roof. Hospital ship in this a.m. Read "*Sabotage*" + "*Silver Bride*" by Dell—bridge—ice cream—Carroll baked creamy raisin pudding.

June 5, 1942

a.m.—routine—sun on roof—read. p.m.—bridge—Lt. Eumara visited with ice cream—photos of group on floor #5. Good supper.

June 6, 1942

Routine—sun on roof. Read *"Frozen Inlet Post"*—Haycox's *"Trail Smoke."* Food—not so good today.

June 7, 1942

Routine—no sun this a.m. Read *"National Geographic"* and *"I Was a Nazi Flyer"* by G. Luke. Papaya + mangoes. Bridge.

June 8, 1942

Routine—sun on roof. Read—bridge. Johnny Pugh ng.

June 9, 1942

Sun on roof—Then Lt. Eumara announced we are all now prisoners of war and move to Tarlac this a.m. Arrived Tarlac Camp 1:30 p.m. Many old friends and word of Trapnell + John.

June 10, 1942

Roll call 7:00 a.m. + 7:00 p.m. Routine—Calisthenics. Food—no good. Read—bridge- P.X. Walk with Gen. George F. Moore [*A&M Class of 1908*]. Rummy with Bob Brown.

June 11, 1942

Routine—"Pork." Japanese officers questioning re: artillery. Read—bridge. Bed—hard.

June 12, 1942

Routine. Coconut candy. Read—rummy, bridge. Made good bunk replacing wooden slats with piece canvas from Gen. Wainwright bedroll (32 years old).

June 13, 1942

Routine. Read—finished Mary Roberts Rinehart book *"K."* Played rummy + sunned with B. Brown. Wrote essays required by Japanese.

June 14, 1942

Songs with breakfast. Bridge—N. C. Pilet– Jesse Traywick—Bob Brown—self.

June 15, 1942

Routine. worked in garden. Bridge. good supper, but not enough.

June 16, 1942

Routine. worked in garden. new regulations. good supper, but not enough.

June 17, 1942

Routine. work in garden pleasant. good P.X. automatic issue.

June 18, 1942

Routine. Gen. Wainwright quite sick during night. Ptomaine? Work in garden. Food still ng. Hair cut very short.

June 19, 1942

Gen. Wainwright better this a.m. Work in garden. Sun in p.m. Roll call 8:00 p.m. Bridge.

June 20, 1942

Routine. Worked in garden. Sleep, bridge.

June 21, 1942

Songs at breakfast. Col. Ho, Jap Col., visited bringing mangoes + milk. Read—good supper.

June 22, 1942

Routine—worked in garden—bridge—walked in sun with thought— bridge. Candy on auto issue. Rain.

June 23, 1942

Worked in garden. Walked in sun—read Kipling "*Naulahka*" n.g.— No P.X. Bridge. Good sleeping—rain.

June 24, 1942

Walked with Gen. Moore. P.X. this a.m.—no candy. Read (C.S.) Forester's *Capt. from Connecticut*. Rain this PM. Carabao + calf brought in.

June 25, 1942

Washed clothes + sunned—Bridge. Col. Ito, Jap in command of concentration camp, visited—brought candy—now newspaper. Rain—p.m.—good sleep.

June 26, 1942

Routine. Japanese sentry time moved so that we are up about 5:00 a.m.

June 27, 1942

Routine—no P.X. Walked—sunned—bridge—good sleep. Col. Galbraith returned from Baguio—news + rumors.

June 28, 1942

Songs at breakfast. Routine.

June 29, 1942

Routine—P.X.—no candy—bridge—walked—washed clothes.

June 30, 1942

Routine—talk of exchange of prisoners. Just hope, I think.

July 1, 1942

Up early—sunned—bridge. Routine.

Send set of bamboo furniture to Juanita Redmond for birthday. [*This entry is circled and labeled "Impossible."*]

July 2, 1942

Cats + drunk sentry during nite. Routine. Japanese G-4 visited—inspect. Bridge—no news.

July 3, 1942

Routine. Sun—bridge—read.

July 4, 1942

Big day. Reveille one hour later. Bananas + milk—patriotic songs—breakfast. Chicken + dumplings—lunch.

July 5, 1942

Songs at breakfast—milk, sugar, lg. doughnuts + coffee. Nice lunch. Bridge.

July 6, 1942

Routine a.m. up at 6:30 (5:00). Swept, cleaned up, breakfast, washed clothes, sunned. Dull. Talk of Jap troops moving out. Aired woolens.

July 7, 1942

Routine. More talk of troop movements. Food—no good.

July 8, 1942

Routine. Bridge—sunning. Watched chess play.

July 9, 1942

Routine—sun—bridge—news. Started K. Roberts "*Oliver Wiswell.*" Some people condemn others for faults they themselves commit in turn.

July 10, 1942

Routine—rain all day—read—bridge—charge of quarters from night roll on—Nothing eventful.

July 11, 1942

14 Cols. arrived—Stu Wood—little news—mess received heifer this date. read—slept. C.Q.

July 12, 1942

Songs at breakfast. Coffee + doughnuts noon. Group very talkative. Stu Wood sick.

July 13, 1942

Routine—read *Oliver Wiswell*—washed clothes.

July 14, 1942

Routine. Stu Wood still sick. Rice only at meals.

July 15, 1942

Rations yesterday—14 sacks rice—½ sack sugar. Beef + dumplings—supper. Vienna sausage with Gen. after 8:00 p.m. roll call.

July 16, 1942

Routine. Stu Wood up + about. Rain.

July 17, 1942

Rain all a.m. Bridge—Col. Barry, Edwin F., Ordnance, Marshall, Tex. died 10:45 p.m. strep throat.

July 18, 1942

Raining still—Formation for Col. Edwin Barry's funeral. Col. Ito present. Later Col. Ito requires essays of certain officers. Bridge.

July 19, 1942

Coffee + doughnuts—songs for breakfast. Tong-Kong for supper.

July 20, 1942

Results of Tong-Kong overnight—can-can. Bridge—rotation of partners each rubber.

July 21, 1942

Routine—bridge—mom—afternoon + night. Roll call change to 8:00 p.m. Gabi for supper with rice.

July 22, 1942

Sun this a.m. (first in a week) aired woolens + linens.

July 23, 1942

Routine. Bridge—volleyball, horse shoes.

July 24, 1942

Routine.

July 25, 1942

Routine. Bridge, volleyball, horse shoes.

July 26, 1942

Breakfast—do-nuts + coffee. Songs. Good day. Gen. Stevens moved to O'Donnell Hospital.

July 27, 1942

Johnny's birthday. Stu Wood gave dinner—corned beef, tomatoes, pork + beans, cherries.

July 28, 1942

Read + slept—a.m. p.m. slept—volleyball—J.T. Traywick displays poor sportsmanship. I get mad—pop off.

July 29, 1942

Japanese General expected. All day spent in uniform playing bridge, washing. 4:00 p.m.—no general. Japanese Col. called on Generals W. + King.

July 30, 1942

Rain all day—bridge—slept. Gen. made pay account voucher. Nick + Johnny Pugh lost bridge 1st rd.

July 31, 1942

Paid tribute to Gen. Wainwright's 40th year in Army. Sang "Happy Birthday" to Gen. Moore. Rain all day. Japanese Gen. expected—no appearance. Bridge + talk with Stu Wood.

Aug. 1, 1942

a.m. Rain + waiting for Japanese Gen. p.m.—Read—New Jap Lt. in charge of camp. Cpl. Nish relieved. Rumor of reading material, athletic equip + radio. (Proved purely rumor.)

Aug. 2, 1942

Hot cakes + coffee—rice in coffee. Col. Ito came to say goodbye. Also said we would be moving from Tarlac. Rumor later make move to Japan.

Aug. 3, 1942

Formation at 8:00 for Jap Gen. [*Iichiro*] Morimoto [*named Commandant of Philippine POW camps two days earlier*]—little time spent. Washed clothes + sunned woolens + aired linens. Bridge + talk.

Aug. 4, 1942

Breakfast lugao + weak milk Lunch—Rice + grease. Supper— +. Bridge + songfest.

Aug. 5, 1942

Routine. Bridge + sleep.

Aug. 6, 1942

Food—still not good—Japanese newspaper mail in today. Notified of move to Taiwan or Japan in about one week.

Aug. 7, 1942

Routine. Bridge—rain.

Aug. 8, 1942

Rain all day—Bridge, all day. Canned beef—lunch. Pineapple after supper.

Aug. 9, 1942

Hard rain all night—Coffee for breakfast. Physical exam by Japanese Medical Corps. Bridge + packing.

Aug. 10, 1942

Rain all day—packing. Announced that we leave Tarlac early Tuesday. Good lunch + supper.

Aug. 11, 1942

Reveille—3:30 a.m. Left Tarlac Camp 6:40 a.m. walked to RR + left about 8:00 a.m. Arrived Manila (Tondo Station) 1:30 p.m. by truck to Pier 7 to *Nagara Maru*. Food OK. Crowded bins in hot hold. Generals Wainwright + King given stateroom.

[As Gen. Wainwright was being driven to Pier 7 in Manila a GI truck driver told him the Marines had landed at Guadalcanal four days earlier. Within two weeks, after the Marines had secured the airfield and beaten off a fanatical Japanese attempt to recapture it, the first planes landed.]

Aug. 12, 1942

Aboard *Nagara Maru*. Pulled away from pier about 10:00 a.m. Laid outside breakwater until about 2:30 p.m. Required to stay in hold until 8:00 p.m. Very hot + stuffy. Margaret Boyd's birthday—hope Cissy sent her something as asked in my last letter.

FIVE

Shipped to Camp Karenko, Formosa

Aug. 13, 1942

At sea—very calm—food—good. tried to sleep for while this p.m. but too hot. Called on Gen. Wainwright this a.m. He + Gen. King OK.

Aug. 14, 1942

Arrived Takao Harbor [*Taiwan*] about 9:30 a.m. Stayed on board ship all day. Very hot and miserable. Stu Wood—Brown—I drinking cocoa + talking with Japanese. Too hot to sleep in hold. Physical inspection.

Aug. 15, 1942

Still aboard ship—about 3:00 p.m. disinfected + transferred to 1000 ton vessel *Suzuya Maru*. Half in aft hold—our half in forward hold. Allowed on deck for 40 min. Laid in Takao Harbor all night.

Aug. 16, 1942

Pulled out of Takao about 8:00 a.m. Smooth sea—making about 10 knots all day—allowed on deck—1 hr. this a.m.—30 min. this p.m. + 30 min. after supper. Bunk cool, but hard.

Aug. 17, 1942

Pulled into Karenko Harbor about 8:00 a.m. Stayed in hold— came on shore 12:00 a.m. Marched in column of 4's—hot—asphalt hiway about 3 miles to camp. Stood in hot sun undressed for inspection—Finally—sponge bath. Slept on mats. Shorts + blankets issued.

Aug. 18, 1942

Bowed to pole for movie camera. Washed clothes—received some baggage—food—soup + rice. Rise 6:00 a.m. Morn roll call—6:30 a.m. Bow to pole—Eve roll call—8:00 p.m.

Aug. 19, 1942

Rearrange squads. Made to be squad chief, 6th squad. Assigned to room with Col. Samuel Howard + Col. Donald Curtis—USMC. Squad chiefs conference—same type food—beds with straw mat. Uncomfortable.

Aug. 20, 1942

Washed clothes—received all baggage except shoes—everyone's feet + legs sore from wearing wooden shingles. Squad chiefs conference a.m. + p.m.—Shakespeare's *Much Ado about Nothing.* Food—no good—Arm bands issued.

Aug. 21, 1942

Weather + scenery very nice. Shoes returned for cleaning. Name badges issued + sewed on. Col. Howard + self food carriers. Shoes turned in to certain room overnight.

Aug. 22, 1942

Weather still nice—mountains. quite nearby—high + especially pretty in early morn. Formation for Gen. of Jap General Staff this p.m. He—nice countenance.

Aug 23, 1942

Vigilant officer—1:00 a.m.—2 a.m. Routine thru day—washed clothes. Nap from 1:00 p.m.—3:00 p.m. Slight cold—made coffee for breakfast. Sewed underwear + socks and made cork for water bottle + soap dish from corned beef can.

Aug. 24, 1942

Routine—walked in sun. Played Rummy with Col. Edwin O'Connor + Navy Capt. Lyle [J.] Roberts. Lift from breakfast coffee. Went on

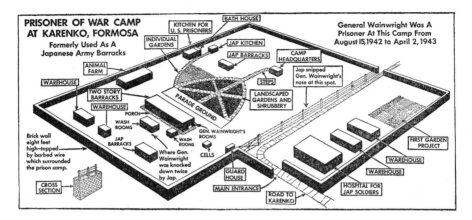

The Prisoner of War Camp at Karenko, Taiwan, housed more than four thousand POWs between 17 August 1942 and 6 June 1943, beginning with the officers under General Wainwright's command at Bataan and Corregidor. In his third journal (with a red stripe on its cover), Dooley included a roster of 157 American officers held at Karenko. From Wainwright, *General Wainwright's Story*.

as Officer of the Day (O.D.) at noon. Opened sardines. Squad moved downstairs this p.m.

Aug. 25, 1942

New squad not as pleasant as old. Played Rummy + walked. Talked with Gen. Wainwright. Bath today by order.

Aug. 26, 1942

Coffee (the last) for breakfast this a.m. Washed clothes and played Rummy. Talked with Gen. Wainwright, Johnny Pugh, Stuart Wood, Bob Brown. Nap this p.m. and nice breeze this eve. Received order of tea.

Aug. 27, 1942

Routine—6:00 a.m. up—6:30 roll call—breakfast—7:00 a.m.— lunch—12:00—supper—6:00 p.m.- Eve roll call—8:00 p.m.- Lights out 9:00. Received some tea. 1–1/3 bananas for lunch.

Aug. 28, 1942

Routine. Played Rummy—had tea at 4:00 p.m.

Tom Dooley kept monthly records of his weight gains and losses while a prisoner of war.

Tom Dooley's Weight Record at Karenko:

Aug. 30, 1942	66.5K	=	146.3#
Sept. 13, 1942	63.5K	=	139.7#
Oct. 20, 1942	57.5K	=	126.5#
Dec. 12, 1942	57.1K	=	125.6#
Jan. 25, 1943	58.5K	=	128.7#
Mar. 24, 1943	54.0K	=	118.8#
May 20, 1943	58.6K	=	128.9#

Tom Dooley's Weight Record at Shirakawa:

July 30, 1943	61.4K	=	135.08#
Sept. 18, 1943	62.6K	=	137.72#
Oct. 15, 1943	65.0K	=	143.00#
Nov. 22, 1943	66.0K	=	145.2#
Dec. __, 1943	64.3K	=	141.06#
Jan. 28, 1944	62.8K	=	138.16#
Feb. 23, 1944	63.3K	=	139.26#
Mar. 25, 1944	63.7K	=	140.14#
Apr. 22, 1944	64.7K	=	142.34#
May __, 1944	62.0K	=	136.4#
June 22, 1944	61.9K	=	136.18#
July 21, 1944	61.7K	=	135.74#
Aug. 21, 1944	60.1K	=	132.22#
Sept. 25, 1944	59.1K	=	130.02#
Oct. 20, 1944	59.2K	=	130.24#
Nov. 17, 1944	60.2K	=	132.44#
Dec. 14, 1944	58.8K	=	129.36#
Jan. 17, 1945	57.7K	=	126.44#
Feb. 15, 1945	57.2K	=	125.84#
Mar. 11, 1945	57.1K	=	125.6#
April 11, 1945	56.9K	=	125.18#
May 5, 1945	57.0K		
May 23, 1945	57.1K		
June __, 1945	58.4K		
July __, 1945	57.5K		

Aug. 29, 1942

Scrubbed floors + cleaned windows 8:00—11:00 for inspection. Capt. George J. McMillin, Governor of Guam, arrived 10:45 p.m. Assigned to our squad.

Aug. 30, 1942

Talk with Capt. McMillin thru breakfast—Col. [*Charles G.*] Sage + self conducted Protestant services. Rummy + tea with Col. Edwin O'Connor, Capt. Lyle Roberts + Col. Edgar [*H. "Jack"*] Keltner. Last few days remind me of early fall at home. Weight—66.5 K

Aug. 31, 1942

Routine morn. Rummy + tea this p.m. Pay received at 4:00 p.m. Mine listed in back of 2nd journal. Cool night.

Sept. 1, 1942

Routine. Bath this p.m. Rummy + talk. Had dysentery shot. On Vigilant duty 12:00—1:00. Many thoughts of home and what is happening.

Sept. 2, 1942

Routine—Rummy + nap. Walk with Col. Sage—washed clothes. Talk with Gen. Wainwright. More thoughts of home + when I'll be there.

Sept. 3, 1942

Walk with Col. Sage + rummy this AM. Nap + fire drill this p.m. Tea at 4:00 p.m. Talk with Gen. Not enough food.

Sept. 4, 1942

Walk with Col. Sage this AM. Nap + bridge this PM. News of Britishers to arrive on 8th. Rice + soup—day in + day out—2 bananas thru P.X.

Sept. 5, 1942

AM spent cleaning barracks—scrubbed floors alongside Gov. of Guam. Bath + bridge. Sugar issued—85 cubes. Stomach cramps— Low—physically + mentally.

Sept. 6, 1942

Sang with choir—Protestant services. Read *Fortune* magazine. Feel better this date—2 bananas issued today. Discussion of war.

Sept. 7, 1942

Washed clothes—walked + talked with Col. Gordon Sage. Letter being written this date asking permission to increase ration by our purchases. We are now on about 1/3 rations. Talked with Gen. Wainwright—after supper sat outside alone and thought of home. Formosa really a beautiful spot but we are not appreciative under the circumstances—2nd Dysentery shot.

Sept. 8, 1942

Played bridge this a.m.—Stu Wood—Nick G.—Bob Brown. Nap + bath this PM—Talk of world situation at supper—Rations still very light. Talked with Gen. Wainwright. Outlook not so bright here, but what a glorious day when we do get home. Pray that Mom, Dad, Cissy + Margaret are safe.

Sept. 9, 1942

62 officers—30 enlisted men, British, Dutch, Australian arrived 10 p.m. last night—a.m. spent in discussion with them. [Lt.] Gen. Sir [*incorrect; was not awarded a knighthood*] [*Arthur E.*] Percival + [*Maj.*] Gen. [*Merton*] Beckwith-Smith called on Gen. Wainwright. General outlook brighter—chances of exchange look less after discussion.

Sept. 10, 1942

Walk with Col. Gordon Sage—Talk with Col. [*Kent*] Hughes—Australian—met Gov. of Sumatra [*Tjarda van Starkenborgh Stachouwer, Governor-General of Dutch East Indies*]. Nap—rummy—Talk with Capt. George McMillin after supper. Greeting formation British-American at Reveille this AM. Food still scarce.

Sept. 11, 1942

Appointment this a.m.—Gov of Sumatra to call on Gen. Wainwright.—His story—sad, but interesting. Major catastrophe—Enlisted Man fell + spilled the squad bucket of soup.

Sept. 12, 1942

Vigilant Guard 1:00–2:00 a.m. Scrubbed squad room this a.m. Nap, Rummy, bath this p.m. Rain—steady—last 2 days. Discussions with various groups including British + Australian.

Sept. 13, 1942

Still raining—church services inside. Sang with choir. Nap—case of diphtheria—British enlisted men. Some people caught + boiled snails this date. I am hungry all the time.

Sept. 14, 1942

Washed clothes—no rain this AM. Arranged for Gen. Wainwright to call on Dutch officials. Face masks issued—no visits—Japanese version of hygiene—diphtheria control. Masks a nuisance.

Sept. 15, 1942

Weights taken—63.5 K. loss of 6.6# since 30th of Aug. Average loss in squad 3.15# per man. Food very short today. Typhoid shot this p.m.

Sept. 16, 1942

Bridge this AM. Breakfast slightly larger, but noonday meal very light. [*Sir Geoffry Northcote*], Gov. of Hong-Kong arrived last p.m. but put in detention room for not signing non-escape pact. Released this a.m. Brought little news. Rumors at bedtime.

Sept. 17, 1942

Washed clothes—Rumors of exchange in December. Walked, sat + talked with Col. Sage outside. More rumors of exchange—optimism— bridge—walk with Col. Gordon Sage after supper.

Sept. 18, 1942

Walked this AM with Col. Gordon Sage—sat outside + talked with Gen. George Moore. Nap + bridge this p.m.—Received Vitamin B pills. 4 ounces rice per man per day. 1–1/2 bowls vegetable soup.

Sept. 19, 1942

Cleaned squad room—bridge—walked + sat outside + thought of home + how it will be when I return. Remainder of day—routine.

Sept. 20, 1942

150 for church services—choir practice at 9:30—Services at 10:00 a.m. Bridge + nap this p.m.—Bananas received—Buoyed by the sudden thought of how pleasant everything will be when we are free again. Gave my cards to Gen. Wainwright.

Sept. 21, 1942

Washed clothes—sunned linens + wools. Walked with Col. Gordon Sage—Sat in sun—walked with Stu Wood—Gen. Wainwright seems more optimistic now than before. Ate snails + broth at supper.

Sept. 22, 1942

Walked with Col. Gordon Sage—haircut very short—rumor of more + better food. Talk with British Gen. Beckwith-Smith—Rice still very short—Col. Charles S. Lawrence beaten by 2 Jap cooks this date—2 British slapped by sentry.

Sept. 23, 1942

Cool this AM. Col. Lawrence repeat this a.m. Bob Brown—Dr. Roberts kicked—Col. Nelson popped. Sat outside in sun—talked with Gen. Wainwright + Johnny Pugh. Outlook not bright with this tirade. Tirade quelled, I think. Nap + walk alone this PM. Talk of food at bedtime—can feel pangs of hunger.

Sept. 24, 1942

Cool at Reveille—walk with Col. Gordon Sage—sat alone in sun and thought of what pleasures I would have when I get home. Took Gen. Wainwright + Gen. King to call on Dutch. Slight earthquake at 1:00 p.m. News—1 battleship + 2 submarines sunk in Aleutians. Jap repatriated + report of ill treatment in States.

Sept. 25, 1942

Long talk last p.m. with Navy Capt. George McMillin (Governor of Guam)—very nice. Spot of tea at 10—Sat outside in sun. Much harassment from Japs. Food very short today—small portions of rice + soup practically all water—very few vegetables. Gens. Wainwright + Parker in conference with Jap Officer of Day.

Sept. 26, 1942

Cleaned squad room—breakfast smallest meal so far—harassing by sentries continues. Yesterday conference unsuccessful. Bath + nap this p.m. Hate climbs steadily. Duck soup at supper—smoked ducks bought by us. Out of cigarettes.

Sept. 27, 1942

Choir practice + church this a.m. Nap + rummy this p.m. New prisoners expected this date. Col. Samuel Howard gave me a cigarette after lunch. Quite stimulating.

Sept. 28, 1942

4 Generals, 20 Colonels + 16 Enlisted Men from Mindanao + Luzon arrived last night. News of [*Lt. Col. William S.*] Bill Van Nostrand— OK. Good news of war in Southwest Pacific. Food back to routine today—walk with Gen. Wainwright. He down in spirit—very hungry this p.m.

Sept. 29, 1942

Cissy's birthday. Wish I could see her. Rain all day. Rations still very light. Everyone always hungry. Many thoughts of home—would like to have taken Cissy to dinner on this day especially.

Sept. 30, 1942

Rain all day—very dreary—bridge. Cigarettes received this p.m. 10 packs per man. Velatis (Wash. D.C.) caramels thought brought forth by Col. Edwin O'Connor upon returning. Will get some when there next.

Oct. 1, 1942

Still raining—bridge with British Team. Morale very high today. Japanese gave notice of air raid drills to come. Thoughts of home + future + food. Navy Capt. George McMillin Japanese pipe tobacco —Momoyama.

Oct. 2, 1942

Clearer this a.m. Little sunshine. Bridge with British. Good news. Breakfast—smallest to date. Tobacco—3rd, 13th, 28th.

Oct. 3, 1942

Nothing eventful—snail soup at supper. Bath—Got + read *"Walking The Whirlwind"* by Brigid Knight. Food—still light. Air raid drill.

Oct. 4, 1942

Choir practice + services this a.m. Read all p.m. Food light—eternally hungry. Good news today re: President Roosevelt's statement in paper. Air raid drill this p.m. [*Roosevelt's Sept. address on the Pacific War recounted US victories at Coral Sea and Midway and said the navy would hit the enemy "and hit him again wherever and whenever we can find him." From http://www.britishpathe.com/video/roosevelt-speech-on-pacific-war/query/Roosevelt+on+Pacific+War*]

Oct. 5, 1942

Finished—*Walking the Whirlwind*—very good. Air raid practice. Bridge—tea. Sun bath—bridge. Talk of food with Col. Sage who has cut off mustache + beard—hardly recognizable.

Oct. 6, 1942

Cigars, bananas, bath—big day—Made bet with Gen. Wainwright re: Philippine Islands. Bridge with British. Food extremely light this day.

Oct. 7, 1942

Good news. Tokyo bombed rumors. More rice at noon + supper. Trust it continues. Gen. Wainwright in better spirits. Morale in squad better. Thoughts of home + thick malted milks.

Oct. 8, 1942

Breakfast better—SOIREE—8:30–10. Soiree practice this p.m. Food better—Hope it continues. H.F.J. seethes inside—grows daily. Cleaned squad room.—everyone worked for tomorrow's inspection.

Oct. 9, 1942

Breakfast—very small—officers swept ground outside. Inspection by Jap Commanding General of Taiwan. Gift—pig. Thoughts of Jim, Ben, John + I getting together. Thoughts of repatriation. How good that would be.

Oct. 10, 1942

Had pig soup noon + night—very good. Long talk with Gen. Wainwright this a.m. Read Jap newspapers + *Evangeline* this p.m. Fat in rice very good. Discussions. Talk with Col. Gordon Sage of home at Xmas + New Year's.

Oct. 11, 1942

Breakfast—menial—choir practice + church. Walk alone in area. Talk of Graham Crackers + malted milk with pecans. What I would like—mother's hot biscuits + hash with buttermilk + hot mince pie with cheese. Later armed forces radio—popcorn + chocolate.

Oct. 12, 1942

Pretty day—sun—morn routine. Sat alone outside in sun + thought of home. Gen. Wainwright allowed to put in letter to states today. We will be allowed to write soon—they say. Talk of food with Gen. Wainwright + Col. Sage.

Oct. 13, 1942

a.m.—routine—talk of war + possibilities of exchange. Rumors of ducks + more food. Duck soup at supper—Jap Lt. "50 more prisoners coming here." Thoughts of home + good foods. Talk with Capt. McMillin + Col. Sage. Am eternally hungry.

Oct. 14, 1942

a.m. routine—walk with Col. Sage + sat alone in sun. Nap—Played Liverpool Rummy with Gen. King, Col. Sage, Vic C.—Smoked cigar with Gen. Wainwright after supper. Talked of food + what we would do when reached states. Sleep about 11 hrs. day now. Possibly lack of food.

Oct. 15, 1942

a.m. routine—walk with Col. Sage. Food today—least we have had so far. Starvation rations. Cigar with Gen. Wainwright. Jap Lt. harassed 5th squad tonight. No issue today of sugar, salt, tea.

Oct. 16, 1942

Rations still very small—food is all we can think or dream about. Sun bath this a.m. Hope a real offensive is beginning in South. Still have hope of repatriation.

Oct. 17, 1942

a.m.—cleaned squad room—Service for Feast of Harvest [*Jewish Festival of Pentecost*]—15 minute formation. Nap—bath—bridge with Gen. Percival + B—S. Food still light—Pangs of hunger. Discussions of food + good places to eat in states.

Oct. 18, 1942

a.m.—cool—put on woolens for choir practice + church services. Food still very little—received Jap paper this p.m. Played Liverpool Rummy. Gen. Wainwright gave me pack of Chesterfield this a.m.

Oct. 19, 1942

a.m.—walked + sat alone outside. Nap + solitaire—Good talk this p.m. with Col. Sage + Col. Kent Hughes, Australian. Talk of food. Learned new sandwich today—Canadian bacon, onion + cheese.

Oct. 20, 1942

Wt.—57.5 K—126.5#. a.m.—walk alone outside. Weights taken—have lost 19.8# since arrival. Tea + bananas issued. Why don't they feed us more? Peanuts—2/10 #, sugar ½ #, tea 1/4 # issued for 1 month—salad—rice, sugar, bananas, peanuts.

Oct. 21, 1942

Haircut—walk—copied names of British—Aussie—Dutch contingent. Jap papers—naval battle. [*Possibly Battle of Leyte Gulf.*] Hungry—Jap Medical Corps says loss of weight expected—that's it. Food—uppermost in every mind.

Oct. 22, 1942

Routine—out of cigarettes—food still very light. Rumors of more food. Am afraid they will not pass rumor stage.

Oct. 23, 1942

a.m. routine—7 bananas issued this p.m.—quite unexpected—chip them up fine and eat over rice. Discussion of food after supper with Col. Sage + Col. Kent Hughes.

Oct. 24, 1942

a.m.—cold—walk in wind outside. Colder this p.m.—bath—like ice. Took Gen. Wainwright pair of woolen breeches. Col. Edwin O'Connor + Col. Donald Curtis civilian coats. Late p.m.—very cold—farm work announced.

Oct. 25, 1942

a.m.—choir practice + services outside—some warmer this a.m. Talk with Gen. Wainwright, Johnny Pugh, Stuart Wood + Gen. King this p.m. re: repatriation rumor. Thoughts of home in this cold weather.

Oct. 26, 1942

a.m.—no work on farm yet. Food still very light—still out of cigarettes. Everyone started work today at 1:00 p.m.—Then supper— still no increase in food as promised.

Oct. 27, 1942

a.m.—Slight increase in food—worked in Prisoner of War garden this a.m.—Rain—No work this p.m. Fish in soup at noon—Bean at supper. News. cigarettes + salt issued this p.m. Have slight cold.

Oct. 28, 1942

Some Japanese holiday—no work in prisoner-of-war garden. Cold worse today. Read—Discussions of all sorts today—Repatriation— Noticeable change in our treatment. Good soup last night—beans and carabao beef.

Oct. 29, 1942

Work in Prisoner of War Garden today—not hard—beautiful day—sun—cold better. 1st + 2nd squads issued rice cookies. Nicer treatment—gramophone recital last night—Beethoven's *Fifth Symphony* + *How Still The Night* [probably "Still of the Night"]—Very Good.

Oct. 30, 1942

Paid this a.m.—no work in prisoner-of-war garden. Capt. McMillin trunk arrived yesterday. News of letters received. Rumor of leaving here by 15th. Food not so good today. Morale high tonight.

Oct. 31, 1942

No work in garden—cleaned squad room this a.m. No work this p.m. Nap + bath. Had been promised ducks this day, but none came in. Bean soup at supper—good. Talks re: repatriation + war in general. Received canteen (Jap as ordered). Many thoughts of home.

Nov. 1, 1942

Choir practice + church service outside this a.m. Nap this p.m. Discussions. Nothing eventful. Music this p.m.—[*Gershwin's*] "Rhapsody in Blue" + Strauss selections—excellent.

Nov. 2, 1942

Japanese propaganda party in camp—no work. Gen. Wainwright photographed here + downtown. 1st trip outside of compound. Church service simulated + photographed. Light rice.

Nov. 3, 1942

Gerry Treacy birthday—Happy Birthday—General. Jap holiday— no work—formation at 8:30. Bananas given by mess, 3 each. What is reason for better treatment here? Double amount soup this p.m. with pork. Gen. Wainwright questioned today by Prop. officer.

Nov. 4, 1942

Spent a.m. walking + sitting outside—thinking of home—read Jap newspapers. Work this p.m. "Boots" left this a.m. early. Hope no return + good supper—extra vegetables from Col. R + S + R. Col. Edwin O'Connor cooked—cookies issued—concert this p.m. Jap Officer of Day called after roll call—very friendly.

Nov. 5, 1942

No work this date—had cup coffee this AM. PM spent writing memos in new notebooks. Talked with Gen. Wainwright after supper. Beautiful days lately. wonderful weather.

Nov. 6, 1942

A beautiful day—Talk with Gen. Wainwright + Col. K-Hughes. No work—Enlisted men worked on stock farm buildings. Musicale this p.m. Some quite optimistic this date.

Nov. 7, 1942

Earthquake—6:25 a.m. Pretty good shake. Pictures of everyone in camp taken this date—after squad rooms cleaned. Bridge—food—not heavy. Musical program this p.m. Closed my eyes and was at home for 1 hour.

Nov. 8, 1942

Choir practice + church this p.m. Bridge—Nap—Musicale this p.m. Brahm's *1st piano concerto*.

Nov. 9, 1942

Routine—Bridge—discussions. Domei reporters in camp. Some selected to broadcast messages to states.

Nov. 10, 1942

Marines birthday. Squad gardens started. I am Sq. 6 representative. News of French actions. Everyone allowed to write a message to be broadcast. Boots back. Treatment continues better?

Nov. 11, 1942

Major General Merton Beckwith-Smith, Commanding General. 18th English Division, died at 7:30 a.m. this date of strep throat plus malnutrition. Formation + church service at 3:30 p.m. Food ration shorter this date.

Nov. 12, 1942

Back on starvation ration—Rain—bridge—news of Americans landing in Morocco + Algeria. Much discussion re: above.

Nov. 13, 1942

Routine—pretty good supper. Work in squad garden.

Nov. 14, 1942

Cleaned squad room—worked in garden. Bath in p.m. Bridge—Bananas issued—both like balsa wood.

Nov. 15, 1942

Did not attend church this a.m. Talked with Gen. Wainwright. Had tea with saccharine. Thoughts of home—draft of letter to Dad + Mother. Rations very light.

Nov. 16, 1942

Gen. Wainwright + Gen. Lewis Beebe + I had discussion of my staying in Army. Gen. Wainwright said if he was accepted favorably in states upon return, he would promise my commission.

Nov. 17, 1942

No barley with rice. Rain—Bridge—Issue of tea, salt, + sugar, + bananas. Shark meat in soup at supper.

Nov. 18, 1942

Food server this date—food not good. Worked in garden—put it in shape to plant—several slackers in squad. News of last Solomons naval battle. [*Maj.*] Gen. Frank Keith Simmons [*commander of Singapore Fortress when it fell*]—British—slapped by Commandant this a.m. Bridge.

Nov. 19, 1942

Rain + cold. Finished reading John Erskines' "*Give Me Liberty*"—work this p.m. Gathered papaya + snails. Had cigar with Gen. Wainwright.—Musicale.

Nov. 20, 1942

a.m.—cleaned snails—washed clothes. p.m.—work in garden. Good supper. Music tonite. Get records of tunes from Carmen. *"Prelude."*

Nov. 21, 1942

Cleaned squad rooms—bridge—nap—newspapers. Good supper soup—Hot bath—musicale—much interest in camp re: American action in North Africa.

Nov. 22, 1942

Good breakfast—larger than usual. Bridge. Gen. Wainwright had coffee date with Dutch. Planted radish + carrots in garden. Music.

Nov. 23, 1942

Jap holiday—watered garden. Jap enlisted men very drunk. Best chow today so far—Talk with Gen. Wainwright. Bridge—discussions of African front.

Nov. 24, 1942

Work this a.m. Nap + bridge this p.m. Soup very poor this date. Have placed Margaret's picture in spot where I can often see it + it gives many bright moments during day.

Nov. 25, 1942

Work this a.m.—breakfast—very poor—cleaned snails + gabi—no sun today. Sgt. Carroll sent bowl of snails this eve. very good—music. Promise of good chow for tomorrow.

Nov. 26, 1942

Thanksgiving—church service this a.m. Rabbit stew this noon. Watered garden—bridge. Duck + bean soup this p.m. Music.

Nov. 27, 1942

Work both a.m. + p.m. Chow better than usual. Routine—Rumors galore tonight.

Nov. 28, 1942

Cleaned squad rooms. Bridge. Inspection by Capt. this p.m.

Nov. 29, 1942

Missed church—bridge—washed clothes. Read—sunshine—beautiful day—garden growing nicely.

Nov. 30, 1942

Sunshine—beautiful day. Worked this p.m. gathered snails. Bridge. Rumors. Food—not so good today. Visitor in camp. B.P. sakied up

Dec. 1, 1942

No news as expected—food very poor today. Japanese-made clothes brought in today—very cheap stuff. Those who tried it on make a good comedy act for vodville [*vaudeville*]. Music this p.m.

Dec. 2, 1942

Routine—work outside—worked in squad garden—cleaned snails. Food less than before—soup practically water. Music this p.m. Brahms *1st piano concerto.*

Dec. 3, 1942

Margaret J.'s birthday—wish I could send her a radio. Work in squad garden this a.m. Work on chicken + pig build. p.m. Food still terrible. Diphtheria shot—Tues.—Dec. 1.

Dec. 4, 1942

Very cold this date—no work. Bridge—all clothes utilized. Jap clothes not warm—my woolens envy of all in camp. Food little better—small ant meat at noon—Squad drew peanuts + potato cake.

Dec. 5, 1942

Still very cold—just sat + walked around trying to keep warm. Food—worse. Lt. Gen. [*Sir*] Lewis M. Heath—British + Brig. Gen. Duncan S. Maxwell—Australia—arrived 10:15 p.m. this date.

Tom Dooley kept a close record of his inoculations.

TYPHOID SERIES	APRIL, 1928
	MAY, 1931
	MAY, 1934
	SEPT. 15–25, 1942 AT T.P.C. #4, KARENKO, TAIWAN
SMALL POX	FEB., 1926 – REACTION – GOOD SCAR
	MAY, 1931 – NO REACTION
	MAY, 1934 – NO REACTION
	JULY, 1940 – NO REACTION
(CARABAO VACCINE)	MAY, 1941 – NO REACTION
	(FT. STOTSENBURG, PAMPANGA, P. I.)
CHOLERA	MAY 1942 – IN BATAAN
TETANUS ANTI-TOXIN	AUG., 1941 (3 SHOTS - FT. STOTSENBURG)
BLOOD TYPE –"O"	SEPT., 1941 – TAKEN AT FT. McKINLEY, P. I.
DYSENTERY	SEPT. 1-8, 1942 – T.P.C. #4, KARENKO, TAIWAN
DIPHTHERIA	DEC. 1, 11, 19, 1942 – T.P.C. #4, KARENKO, TAIWAN
SMALL POX	APRIL 5, 1943 – T.P.C. #4, KARENKO, TAIWAN
DYSENTERY	SEPT. 15, 1942
	SEPT. 25, 1942
	APRIL 7, 1943 (1 SHOT-ACTIVATION)
TYPHOID	APRIL 15, 1943 (1 SHOT-ACTIVATION)
TYPHOID	JUNE 9, 1944 (1st SHOT)
	JUNE 15, 1944 (2nd SHOT)
DYSENTERY	JULY 7, 1944 (INOCULATION)
TYPHOID	OCT. 13, 1944 (1 SHOT-ACTIVATION)

Dec. 6, 1942

Still cold—slept in clothes last nite. News this morn via new arrivals. Very good. Very cold all day. Bridge.

Dec. 7, 1942

Still cold—work today—food still not good. I am still always hungry, but it is not so pronounced as during the real "starvation period."

Dec. 8, 1942

Warmer this date—formation at 10:30 a.m.—reading of the Imperial Rescript—Tone quite different. Bridge—worked this p.m. Potato cake this noon.

Dec. 9, 1942

Bob Bullock [*hometown friend*]'s birthday—Routine this date— work—bridge—washed clothes this a.m. Sunshine today. No news lately. Col. Samuel Howard + I won 41 rubbers at bridge this date.

Dec. 10, 1942

Work this p.m. Took warm bath this a.m. Cold starting this evening. Bridge—food still very light.

Dec. 11, 1942

2nd Diphtheria shot this a.m. No work. Bad weather—rain—played bridge—food still bad.

Dec. 12, 1942

Weights taken this a.m. 125.6# 57.1 K. Loss of .4 K from last wt.— sewed on flight cap—played bridge. Cold much worse—feel terrible. Music this p.m.

Dec. 13, 1942

Black-out air raid practice 5:00–7:30 a.m. Choir + church. [*The word "church" is scratched out.*] Cold + damp. Rumor—Tokyo bombed this a.m.—food still bad—never enough to eat. Played bridge.

Dec. 14, 1942

Clear this a.m.—worked on chicken coop fence. Cold worse this date—feel terrible—bath + bridge this p.m. 2 oranges issued today. Good music this p.m. Some news.

Dec. 15, 1942

Clear—cold better. Worked outside wall in garden—bridge. Food very poor. Gen. Wainwright sick—cold, chills + fever.

Dec. 16, 1942

Routine—no work this date—inspection by Jap Medical General—bridge. Some sweet potatoes in rice this p.m. Music this nite.

Dec. 17, 1942

Bad day—washed clothes—sugar issued. Col. Edwin O'Connor beaten by Jap sentry. Music this p.m. More harassment by sentry. Col. Leonard [R.] Crews + Maj. Dean Sherry beaten. Made soup dipper.

Dec. 18, 1942

Not a happy spot to spend one's birthday. Col. Gordon Sage's birthday gift + greeting—dull day—work. Thoughts of home + how I'd like the box of fudge that Mother would send. Wonder if Margaret remembers. Hope that 30th birthday not spent here.

Dec. 19, 1942

Dull—cold + rain—cleaned squad room—made roster of American officers—read newspapers—made bootees + jacket from blanket. Dull day—Practice for songfest.

Dec. 20, 1942

Cold + rain—choir practice = church. Practiced Xmas carols. Practiced octette for songfest. Talk with Gen. Wainwright. Read "*Don Desperado.*"

Dec. 21, 1942

Cold + wet—no work for 6 Sq. Bridge—practiced octette. Food—no good. No news from Jap officers for week. Music this p.m.

Dec. 22, 1942

Pretty day—sunshine—Inspection 1:00 p.m. by Jap Quartermaster general. Breakfast + dinner—no good. Supper better—some gabi today—bridge—Gen. Wainwright sent Xmas greetings to English + Dutch. Choir + octette practice. Thoughts of home at this time make me ache.

Dec. 23, 1942

Routine—clear—bridge—practice choir + octette—talk of what Xmas will be like. No news.

Dec. 24, 1942

Clear day—washed clothes—practiced octette singing for Sun. night. Brig. Gen. Luther [R.] Stevens, Cols. John Horan, Eugene H. Mitchell, Hiram W. Tarkington arrived this p.m. from Philippine Islands. News. Carols sung thru barracks by choir. Decorated table Xmas tree.

Dec. 25, 1942

J. Coldwell [*hometown friend*]'s birthday. Hope he is safe + happy. Really a happy day—amazing spirit shown—Church service + carol singing. Pork soup—noon—duck—supper. 2 bananas, 1 orange, peanuts, potato cake, piece of bread. Thoughts of home—hope they are happy + enjoy Xmas. Really good thoughts this date. Rice trick.

Dec. 26, 1942

Another good day—Food better than usual—surprise—bridge— song + fun fest this p.m.—7:00–9:00 p.m. Gift (sake) to entertainers from Japanese Captain. Marine Col. Donald Curtis sick.

Dec. 27, 1942

Cold + damp—food surprisingly above par today—church—Sake in Gen. Clinton Pierce's room. Bridge—supper—extra rice kept + given to Col. Curtis. Talk of another funfest for New Years.

Dec. 28, 1942

Dull—cold + damp—bridge—a.m. Work p.m. Col. Curtis feeling better—watered garden—chow better than usual at supper—music this p.m. Beethoven's 7th, the Unfinished Symphony. No news for 2 weeks of world situation.

Dec. 29, 1942

Routine—clear pretty day—washed clothes + played bridge. Music this p.m. Food—fair today—Promise of pork for New Years.

Dec. 30, 1942

Clear day—cleaned squad room for inspection. Octette practiced for songfest—bridge—B.P., says "good news" for prisoners postponed to end of Jan. Newspapers—no news.

Dec. 31, 1942

Cleaned squad room—inspection at 1:00 p.m. Nothing unusual. Played bridge. Octette. practice. Music this p.m. Thoughts of home + Margaret + what we would be doing were I at home. Exchange talk rising again. Outlook for 1943 much brighter.

SIX

A New Year—A New Journal

Jan. I, 1943–Jan. I0, 1943—Karenko Prison Camp

The small diary that Gen. Wainwright gave to me in Nov. 1941 has been filled and so far I have not kept a daily note of happenings, but it is just as well. Prison life is a dull routine.

But the holiday season (that which is normally considered the holiday season) was not so bad here as was generally expected. I am sure it was in every man's mind that Xmas day would dawn with a black cloud over the whole affair, but it did not. Prior to Xmas itself, I worked rather diligently on choir practice. Lt. Gen. Arthur Percival (British) was in charge of the Xmas Day church services and a group had selected carols which were familiar to all—American, British, + Dutch. Then he (Gen. Percival) proposed a carol singing on Xmas Eve which was OK'd by the Japanese officers and so between supper and roll call on the 24th of Dec. the choir went about the barracks and sang carols. While moving from one location to another we sang "Silent Night! Holy Night!" and "Hark! The Herald Angels Sing." This helped the occasion quite a bit. Then Xmas Day dawned bright and beautiful. The sun was out and it was really a beautiful day. I had fixed a few gifts and, meager as they were, I think they helped the occasion.

On the 24th I fixed up some decorations of a sort. Col. Samuel L. Howard, USMC, brought in a periwinkle plant in a can and had it on the table. I put some tinfoil and colored paper cut into stars, etc. Then on Xmas Day, Dr. Lyle J. Roberts, USN, brought out a clean sheet and we had a table cloth at our table. Capt. George McMillin USN (Gov. of Guam), myself, Col. Donald Curtis USMC, Col. Samuel Howard USMC, and Dr. Lyle Roberts (Capt. USN) make up our table roster.

The Gen. had a good day and the spirit of the whole group was unexpectedly high. Then too, the ration helped that day. The breakfast was as meager as usual but we drew an orange and two bananas and a cupful of peanuts before noon. Then, too, we got a bit of bread (about 1/5 of a pound)—the first that we had had since our arrival here on the 17th of Aug. It was poor quality and sour, but at that it was bread and I cramped lump sugar into mine and made a sort of cookie. The noon rice had been cooked with diced pork and pork fat was in the soup. We then were issued one of the potato cookies in the p.m. and had duck soup for supper. One incident that cannot go unnoticed, I must mention. In the afternoon a notice was sent around that there would be no rice issue for supper because bread was already issued. Of course, having received the bread in the morn, almost the whole camp had already eaten it and the supper outlook was quite dull. Due to inquiries made into the situation by the Officer of the Day, the rice was issued and no calamity occurred.

All during this period I have continually thought of home and how I would like to be there. Of all times of the year, this season is the most enjoyable for me. How I would like to have had eggnog and fruit cake in mother's kitchen on Xmas morn. I have thought of what gifts I would have bought and what Margaret was doing and an incessant line of thoughts bordering on same.

Rumors persist and in this period one has been reborn. All of us had about given up any hope of repatriation but it burst forth again thru remarks of the two Japanese lieutenants and now we hold hope again of being exchanged or of being transferred and interned in a neutral country. I hold hope for at least the latter. In that case, we could get enough food and a correct diet. Just today I have noted the number of people whose legs and feet are swelling from lack of nutrient. Chile has been resolved by most as the likely spot for internment. Something is in the air and maybe (I hope) this is right. Also Gen. Luther Stevens, Col. John R. Horan, Cols. Eugene Mitchell + Hiram Tarkington arrived here the 23rd and from odd talk it is gathered that several Dutch officers will arrive about the 15th.

The Lt. Gens.—Wainwright, Percival + Lt. Gen. Lewis M. Heath + three Governors—Adrian I. Spitz (Dutch Sumatra), Sir Mark [A.] Young (Hong Kong) + Sir Shenton Thomas [W.] Thomas (Singapore) have all been excused from work along with those over 60 yrs. old. This, too, has added to the thought that something is in the air.

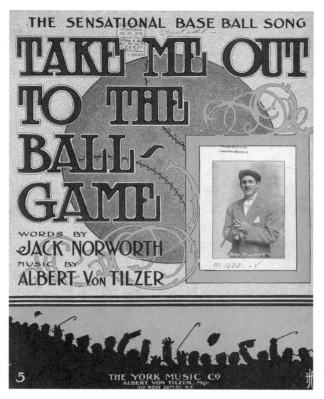

In 1941 players such as Ted Williams, Joe DiMaggio, and Bob Feller were leading the major leagues. Singing such songs as "Take Me out to the Ball Game" gave POWs a break from the mind-numbing routine of captivity.

Also we had a formation (Banzai) on the 1st.

On the 26th + the 1st we were allowed to have a songfest. British + Americans formed two sides of the program. On the 26th I was a member of an octette comprised of: Melody—Col. Edmond J. Lilly + Brig. Gen. Charles C. Drake; Tenor—Col. Edwin O'Connor + Capt. William H. Wilterdink [*USN*]; basses—Col. Charles G. Sage + Capt. Robert G. Davis; and baritone—Col. Theodore [*M.*] Cornell and myself. We were good or so our nice friends told us. On the 1st, the same octette sang and I led the groups in some old songs—"Take Me Out To The Ball Game," "Smiles," + "Sweet Rosie O'Grady." They were a nice break in the dull routine.

"Dull Routine" is certainly what it is. I will try to keep entries for every day, but if things keep on as they are—only a few things will appear.

Sunday night and I have finished this. Last night I felt very low + tonight is not much better. We did have some sunshine and a hot bath which helped, but I am hungry. Have eaten too much of my 1# of sugar as rationing goes, but I won't have it to worry about when it is gone. We have had no newspapers for about two weeks and it is hard to go without food and news both.

Had an inspection this morn. Worked yesterday morn and cleaned barracks yesterday p.m. They seem to be bent on us working in the garden more and more.

My love goes with my thoughts for Mother, Dad, the Mintons + Margaret. May they stay healthy, happy + keep faith that we'll be together soon.

Monday January 11, 1943

Today has been our coldest thus far. Yesterday we had sunshine and then early this morn the wind came up and at a.m. roll call the weather was quite brisk with a misting rain. It gradually got colder and more rain about 9:00 prevented us from working in the garden plot. Everyone sat around in all of the clothes they could put on. Then the rain stopped and so we were ordered out to work at 1:00. The American group weeded the first plot we ever worked—inside the brick wall— and we only stayed out about 1-1/2 hours. My feet got and stayed cold and it is now 7:30 p.m. and they are still freezing. Here is what I have on besides my underwear—my 28 oz. cavalry breeches, two pairs wool socks + a pair of booties made from an olive drab blanket and my feet are further wrapped in a Jap issue blanket. I have on an undershirt made from a wool blanket, a woolen Olive Drab shirt, a heavy khaki shirt, my blue topcoat, an Air Corps flight type cap which I made from a woolen blanket, and a pair of pigskin gloves. My feet did get a little warm for a few minutes because I made a foot warmer from my canteen filled with hot water. This brought to mind—and I asked Capt. George J. McMillin if he had done it—the hot bricks that Mother used to put in the oven after supper, then wrap in newspapers and put into the foot of the bed. How good that would be now and how I would love to be with Mother and Dad in that back room at home, sitting by the fire, reading and listening to the radio, and eating candy or popcorn balls or having some hot egg custard with fruitcake.

And how often at night have I thought of calling for Margaret and going out to dinner. How much fun it would be now—as it was then—to go to the Mexican spot and have a Mexican dinner. I talked with Col. Gordon Sage for quite a while last night re: Margaret. I wonder if she thinks of me or if she has fallen in love and married someone since this damnable war started. I would not blame her the least bit were she to do what I have just mentioned. I realize I have been gone almost two years, but my estimation of this world situation does not look forward to seeing me stay away another two. We received some newspapers today with little news, but one item mentioned the Japanese Foreign Minister sending greetings to internees in America and elsewhere. If we could only send and receive letters from home! Maybe this month will bring news of our going to Chile or some other neutral country. I pray for it—I do so hope that you all are not worrying about me.

Tuesday January 12, 1943

Another cold day. We worked both this a.m. and this p.m. up on the hill. The sun came out for a while and it was quite pleasant, but with late afternoon the cold is coming back. Breakfast + noon were meager fares both, but supper as Taiwan Prisoner Camp meals go, was better—we had some flour in the soup. With this cold weather I have eaten all my sugar—finishing the last after supper tonight. One of the Jap lieutenants put out some news of a battle going on down south and that the Japanese unit could not be supplied because the US Navy has control of the seas in that area. Just so I will not forget—we have a Col. of Infantry in our squad who is certainly the modern version of Dominie Sampson.—([a learned but socially inept tutor] in Sir Walter Scott's Guy Mannering.) Impossible. Also tonight the Jap authorities have asked for a list from each squad listing names and addresses of friends, relatives or acquaintances of prisoners in Japan. I must list none. This is a monotonous existence. What joy it will bring when we leave this place for home.

Wednesday Jan. 13, 1943

Nothing unusual today. I didn't wear my cap this morn but the Jap Lt. on duty was displeased + harangued at length about the officers wearing homemade head gear—flight helmets especially. For winter months the routine is this—First call—6:30 a.m. Roll call—7:00— Breakfast 7:30—usually to work at 9:00 or 9:30 a.m. Return to work 11:00 to 11:30 a.m. Lunch at 12:00—work 1:00 or 1:30 p.m.—Return 4:00–4:30 p.m. Supper 5:30. Eve roll call in rooms at 8:00 p.m. and lights out at 9:00 p.m. Today I was a food carrier. In our squad we have this system: Two food carriers and two food servers. The carriers assist. We each in the squad put out 2 bowls—all on one table. We each now get 7 to 8 ozs. rice per day and 3 bowls of soup. Breakfast + noon is very thin—mostly water boiled with few vegetables—very few vegetables the last few days. Very few.

Thursday Jan. 14, 1943

Routine day. I was food server today. Worked in squad garden after regulation work and was so dirty that I had to take a bath. Had to take cold one outside, but the weather has warmed up considerably today. Sunshine all day. Talked with the Gen. this p.m. The 3 governors of Malaya, Sumatra, + Hong Kong and the 3 Lt. Generals—Wainwright, Percival + Heath along with men over 60 years are not required to work in garden but they are required to stand watch during the day over our herd of goats. Nice work for men of their position in the world.

On the days that we work both a.m. + p.m. we get 10 Kilos additional rice—that amounts to 22 lbs. for about 320 men or about 3 spoonfuls each. That is about 44¢ gold and we pay for it. Doesn't seem right. Incident furthering question of exchange yesterday. First, it is pointing to what will happen. After nearly two years in the Far East my idea of Heaven is the United States. What a day it will be when you are not hungry all the way thru.

Friday Jan. 15, 1943

Routine day. Sunshine was nice—worked both a.m. + p.m. This p.m. I worked one 30 minute period without shirt and next period under wraps. This place is like Texas in that the weather changes so quickly. Read James Hilton's *"The Passionate Year."* Col. Joshua A. Stansell came to the squad from hospital. He has been in hospital since middle of June. A swell gent and a welcome addition. A bad time at morning roll call this a.m. Hoots and laughter is a result of an announcement re: voluntary work. Newspapers tonight—no news.

Saturday Jan. 16, 1943

Worked this a.m.—Cold wind blowing. We have finished clearing the American portion of the garden plot. Now the men with shovels are spading and those with hoes are helping on the Dutch portion. Cleaned barracks this p.m. + played bridge. Had flour in soup tonight. A welcome addition. Rumor has it that we will get flour in the soup twice each week—*misan* (soy bean curd) twice a week and cooking oil once per week. Also tonight's rumor has it that the Japs are slaughtering beef on Taiwan for the Army and we may get some odd bits such as stomach, liver, kidney, hooves, etc. Hope so. A group like this—really hungry—will eat almost anything. Talked with Gen. Wainwright tonight. He is good spirits. He herds the goats for one hour per day now. Tonight is quite cold. Quite odd to see people remove only their hats to retire. I don't do that. My head gets cold.

Sunday Jan. 17, 1943

Been here 5 months today. Today is memorable in that we had tripe for supper (in the soup). B.P. went down and made the arrangements at the slaughter house where they are killing beef for the Japanese army. He got for us the heart, liver, and stomach of the beef. We had tripe at supper and promise of heart, liver, + kidney for breakfast. "Edible awful" is the term some applied to our meal. Other than that the day was uneventful with inspection and church in a.m. and bridge in p.m. A cold day.

Monday Jan. 18, 1943

A beautiful day. Worked both a.m. + p.m. Sunshine + warm. Food good today. Heart, liver + kidney in breakfast soup. Tonight had discussion re: exchange (repatriation). Brought about by exchange of talk with Jap Lieutenant re: news that will be of utmost interest to the prisoners but cannot be told until the end of January. Will wait impatiently for this bit of talk to show up.

Tuesday Jan. 19, 1943

Another beautiful day—last night was as clear and pretty as a Texas night—well, almost. Worked both a.m. + p.m.—worked 30 minute periods but more than before. Three and a half this a.m. + four this p.m. Food today was better than usual—more vegetables and we had liver and heart in the soup tonight. I am commodity officer this month for the 6th Squad and had to put in report this p.m. on property— especially blankets. Mosquito nets were inspected tonight. The hospital is next door to our squad room and Col. [*A. M. L.*] Harrison (British) with his portable is playing records tonight for their entertainment— all classical music. Only news today was remark by Jap Lt. B. to the effect that Japan is being bombed. Trust it is true + in force.

Wednesday Jan. 20, 1943

A feast today—work both a.m. + p.m. Beautiful day—sun. Three Taiwan oranges (more like tangerines) issued at noon. After work 16 of the squad got sacks of cookies (7 each). Had saved bowl of rice from breakfast and lunch so supper was a feast what with the liver in soup, extra rice which I had saved and the cookies. Watered squad garden after work and took bath.

Thursday Jan. 21, 1943

Big day—work both a.m. + p.m. Sunshine—pretty day. Plot almost finished. After work the following news came out. Food to be better. Mizo three times a week—some flour for soup each day—more soy sauce—double sugar issue for cooking. Tonight's rumor—that bill has passed Diet (Japanese legislature) for better treatment of Prisoners of War and that they (Japan) will conform with Geneva Convention Rules. Also again the report that startling news will come out at first of the month. There is certainly something in the air—trust it materializes in some good.

Friday Jan. 22, 1943

Routine—work a.m. + p.m.—Food better. Started strip of land alongside old plot. Rumor that after Feb. 1 no more work started unless direct orders from Tokyo. Something is in the air. Gen. Wainwright very optimistic.

Saturday Jan. 23, 1943

Work this a.m.—p.m. spent cleaning squad room + playing bridge. Got haircut (bowl). Gen. Wainwright notified this afternoon by Jap Lt. that they had received telephone call from Taihoken (Capital of Taiwan) that Domei had heard radio broadcast from states that Gen. Wainwright, 22 other Gens. + other high ranking officers were in prison camp on Taiwan. Hope the folks + Margaret know I am still with the Gen. + that I am OK. Story tonight that Col. Stanley [L.] James, S.C. + Pvt. [*Albert K.*] Walker will soon go to Tokyo for questioning.

Sunday Jan. 24, 1943

Inspection this a.m. and, after that, pay call. Bridge. Bath this p.m. Had cup of coffee with Gen. Wainwright this a.m. Tasted wonderful. Col. James leaves in morn at 7:00 a.m. Food worse today. Rice—less + soup, especially at noon—very, very thin. One of the pigs died last night, but the Vet would not OK it so we can't eat it. Have to bury it. Too bad. Gen. Wainwright is very optimistic about our outlook here. Makes me feel good. Gen. King, as usual, throws cold water on every good outlook we have. Thoughts of home eternally going thru my mind. Everyone convinced there is surely some move or some change imminent. Received word thru sentry that Chile has broken relations or declared war with Germany.

Monday Jan. 25, 1943

Roll call 6:50 a.m. Col. Stanley L. James + orderly (Pvt. Albert K. Walker) left at 7:00 a.m. for Tokyo presumably. Trust he will be all right. Sunshine—work. Have cold. That is very annoying. Weighed this p.m. (official formation)—weight 58.5 K = 128.7#. Weighed this time on spring scales—last time on balance—normal difference about 1.5 K so I am stabilized on weight, I think, I hope no more losses.

Tuesday Jan. 26, 1943

A routine day—work a.m. + p.m. Food—not good. Rain drove us in early by about 5 minutes. Bridge. Had visit last night with Gen. Wainwright, Gen. King + Gen. Luther R. Stevens. Had a few pieces of candy which Sgt. of Guard gave to the Gen. Col. Sage asked by Jap lieutenant if he would like to move into Col. James' place in 3rd Squad. No news this date. Many thoughts of home. How wonderful would be to get back there.

Wednesday Jan. 27, 1943

Routine in a.m. Work. No work in afternoon. p.m.—rearrangement of squads by prison numbers. We are now very crowded. Am now in Sq. 5 with Stu Wood as squad leader. We have 28 in the squad but Lt. Col. Harold [W.] Glattly lives in Hospital + Capt. William H. Wilterdink is now in Hospital. There are 7 in our bay—Col. John P. Horan, Col. Josiah W. Worthington, Col. Theodore Cornell, Stu Wood, myself, Bob Brown, Johnny Pugh. I think Capt. McMillin will probably be asst. Sq. Leader. Col. Donald Curtis + I are permanent soup servers + [Lt.] Col. Earl T. Halstead and Col. Everett C. Williams serve rice. No news.

Thursday Jan. 28, 1943

Work both a.m. + p.m. Plot almost finished. News today of Rommel's withdrawal into Tunisia. Good supper. Beans served separately + curry powder in soup. We are so crowded I dress + undress while standing on my bunk. My cold still hangs on—quite miserable.

Friday Jan. 29, 1943

Weather dull this morn. Announced at roll call that officers would not go to work today. Later found the reason to be that Domei newsmen in camp. Food better today—obviously. I found when I went over for tea water that they had a 3 ration error in our squad. Domei men interviewed Gen. Wainwright and several others—Stu Wood amongst them. They seemed to want personal side not official inquisitions. Report that 51 officers + 24 orderlies (new prisoners) will arrive about Feb. 2. I still think there is something in the air indicating a break for us. Trust there really is. It is cold tonight—how I would love to be at home. Surely one that wants so much to be home with his people will not have to spend the rest of the war here.

Saturday Jan. 30, 1943

Work this a.m.—started extension of garden plot, so it looks like continued work in spite of the rumors. Newsmen still in camp. Understand that some of the British made curt replies in answer to the way we are treated. Crowded + food inadequate in both quality and quantity. British asked why we were being punished instead of being treated as Prisoner of War. Courage admirable but not sure of their judgement. Supper pretty good tonight as Karenko suppers go. Would feed about same to your dog at home only you would give him more of it! Turned cold this p.m. No work. Cleaning of barracks for Sunday morn inspection. Gen. Wainwright ill—trouble with his back. (Sacroiliac out of place). Very painful. Thoughts of home and of good food.

Sunday Jan. 31, 1943

A day of real harassment. Morn roll call ended with long explanation re: saluting. Each corporal of guard on duty making hourly inspections of barracks. Many people slapped including Sir Mark Young—Governor General of Hong Kong. A cold miserable day without all this haranguing. Rain. Baths this afternoon. p.m. spent sitting around squad room talking + smoking, bridge, and reading. *The Mainian*—the Osaka newspaper printed in English.

Monday Feb. 1, 1943

Rumor of news on Feb. 1st blown to bits by Roll call announcement this a.m. Work at 9:00 a.m. No work this p.m. Food very light today. Washed clothes + played bridge this p.m. Announcement tonight that roll call will be at 9:00 p.m. New prisoners arrived about 7:45 p.m. Learned to play cribbage tonight from Col. William H. Braddock. Am extremely hungry tonight. It is terrible to stay hungry all the time. Heat is off little today. Some harassment. Nipponese put announcement of a great victory on Conference Room Bulletin Board this p.m. Claim to have sunk 2 battleships and 3 cruisers and damaged 1 Battleship + 1 cruiser + shot down 3 planes with loss of only 7 planes to themselves. All this near Rennell Island. [*End of Guadalcanal campaign in Solomons.*]

Tuesday Feb. 2, 1943

No work today—harassment in camp. Played bridge all day. Talk with Gen. Wainwright. Discussions of news brought in by new prisoners.

Wednesday Feb. 3, 1943

No work today—rain + cold all day. Played bridge. Heat is still on. This was Stu Woods birthday. Announcement made today requiring all squad chiefs to make roll call report in Japanese. This will probably result in much confusion. Food not so good today. Noon meal quite meager—Breakfast was late. Morale is still high among the prisoners. Many thoughts of home—how wonderful it would be to be there.

Thursday Feb. 4, 1943

Still raining—day dull and damp—roll call still inside. Mizo in soup this morn. Mizo is a soy bean curd—tastes very good. Rumor this a.m. that we will have carabao on the 11th. Trust this comes true.

Friday Feb. 5, 1943

Still raining—cold + damp. Bridge all day. No news.

Saturday Feb. 6, 1943

Work a.m.—Clean barrack p.m.—Routine.

Sunday Feb. 7, 1943

Rain + cold—routine—Food still inadequate.

Mon Feb. 8, 1943

Japanese Holiday—Formation at 9:30. Rescript read. Dutchman bopped by Sgt. Major for being late. Bridge rest of day. Gen. Wainwright told on Sat. that he had a letter at Camp HQ but it has not been delivered yet. Food no good.

Tues Feb. 9, 1943

Cold + damp—worked both a.m. + p.m. Mizo in breakfast soup. Supper soup good—curry. Rummy after supper with Stu Wood + Bob Brown. Gen. Wainwright has not yet received his letter.

Letter from home:

McKinney, Texas
Jan. 27, 1943
My dearest little boy –

We have been informed by the W.D. that we may communicate with you. We are so anxious for you to know that we are all in very good health and everything is the same here in our little town.

Margaret came to see us often until she went to N.Y. where she is working but we are in touch with her all the time—she writes often.

Morris is still here. We believe that we received all your mail. It was wonderful. We hear from many, many of your friends everywhere.

Gerry is still with the show—she is married to her high school sweetheart and he has been away since one month after they were married. We like her very much and hear from her quite often.

You know, I'm sure, that our thoughts are with you constantly, and that we all live for the day you return to us.

Think of us thinking of you always.

We love you so—
Keep Faith—Mother

Wednesday Feb. 10, 1943

Rain a.m.—no work—bridge—p.m. To work at 12:45. Bath for our squad 4:30—4:45. News of Germans withdrawn from Stalingrad area. Rumor of 18 chickens + 60 K. pork + potato cake for tomorrow the 11th—Japanese holiday. 6:30 p.m. Orderly brought in news that [M.] Sgt. James B. Cavanagh died of strep throat at 5:43 p.m. this date. An Iowan—a Master Sgt. and easily the best + best liked NCO in camp. Everyone dreadfully depressed over his death.

We must all be very careful and observant of all commonly known rules for health as we are all so weak from lack of nutriment that there is no resistance to any disease.

Feb. 13, 1943

No news. Johnny got a cockroach in his soup tonight, but of course, removed same before eating soup. Gen. Wainwright received radiogram today from an old friend in Washington. It was dated Dec. 30, 1942.

Feb. 15, 1943

No work today. Group here today to take fingerprints of all of us. Newspapers with good news came in yesterday. Strong wind today—getting colder.

Gristle in soup last 3 days. Food thinnest today for a long time.

Feb. 22, 1943

Washington's Birthday—fire drill—6 men from squad on bucket brigade—turn out at call—barefooted. Col. Samuel L. Howard, Theodore M. Cornell, Hiram Tarkington, [Col.] Melville S. Creusere, [Col.] Albert [F.] Christie, Capt. Robert G. Davis from our squad.

Letter from Home:
McKinney, Tex.
Feb. 25, 1943
My dear sweet child –

We have received your radio message and it was the greatest comfort in the world.

It is marvelous that you were able to send it. We received your address from the War Dept. and notice also that we could write to you through the Red Cross. Margaret, Mary and I have written and sent snapshots, hope you have already received them. We are all well and we are just like you left us. Helen, Gay and I still have breakfast together. Dad is still enjoying your car and Morris is working hard at the office. I pray for you without ceasing. All McKinney joins me in sending love. My darling, keep faith in God.

I love you so much,
Mother
Will send package as soon as War Department notifies us.

March 2, 1943

Worked all day yesterday, but reported to Hospital when I came in and had a fever of 101.4°. Lt. Col. Harold Glattley said he was sorry as he would like to put me to bed at that time, but was not allowed to + I would have to come back at 9:00 AM. This date. Temperature was normal this date, but cold was worse so Nip corporal gave me a permit to be down + remain in from work detail for 3 days.

The heat is about off—I hope—went on about Feb. 28th because of request to Lt. Gen. + Squad Chiefs to write letters to our govt. requesting better treatment to Jap internees in Allied hands. Gen. Wainwright beaten in face on two occasions as was Gen. Lewis M. Heath + several others. Have learned today over 7 month old cup of coffee from Capt. Kenneth Hoeffel (USN) that Gen. Heath distinguished himself early in the war in North Africa by capturing an Italian force at Eritrea. He was knighted for same + made a Lt. Gen. Then he was ordered to Singapore + while enroute Lt. Gen. Percival (at that time junior to Sir Lewis) by some political connection had his date of promotion changed + became senior + then retained command of Singapore. He—Percival—is by talk considered an excellent staff man, but inferior to Heath as commander in field. Easily believed from appearances.

In Daigohan (Squad 5) Stu Wood, Bob Brown, Johnny Pugh + I bunk in a row and we get along very well. Johnny Pugh is peculiar in some ways, but basically of good heart. Bob + Stu are tops. Must in some way upon return to states repay Stu + Bob for kindnesses here.

I have written very little lately of home + those I love but they are uppermost in my thoughts daily. How glorious when we shall return to the States + I shall walk or leap up that small side porch + call for Mother to open the door. I pray incessantly to God that He will keep safely Mother, Dad, Cissy, Morris + Margaret. I realize, more so, as time goes along that I cannot expect Margaret to wait for me. May her happiness come first + if she chooses someone else in this interim may all the happiness possible be hers. She is a wonderful person + the type I want for a wife, but if she chooses otherwise, I shall still love her + look forward to pleasant times with her.

Another thought that I have almost daily are of Jim, Ben + John. May they profit by this war as I know I have and may they come thru safely and untouched by shell or mental unkindness so that we may have more pleasant times together.

Wednesday March 10, 1943

A change has come about—since last Friday night the food has improved immensely. No more rice, but the soup has been thick with more vegetables + a large amount of Irish potatoes. An officer from Tokyo Prisoner of War Bureau is expected today and [*Adm. Hasegawa Kiyoshi*] the Gov. of Taiwan (an admiral in Navy) is expected tomorrow. Hope the better food is continued.

Am reading Henderson's *Stonewall Jackson*. Very interesting + according to Gen. Wainwright, a very good treatise on Jackson's strategy.

Wednesday March 24, 1943

Weight today 54.0 k = 118.8#

Quite a few changes have come about since last writing. On Monday (22nd) the camp commanding officer, Capt. [*Yachasi*] Imamura, + the 2nd in command, 2nd Lt. Nakashima, were relieved + left camp. 2nd Lt. Wakasugi [*Jiro*] remained + the new commanding officer is 1st Lt. Kajuna. The interpreter, Koji, also remained. The sentries are quiet now and no one has been beaten lately. One ruling has been put into effect— All knives had to be turned in + only one pair of shoes per person is allowed.

On Monday, 15 tons of Red Cross supplies arrived in camp, but they are being held until further orders from Tokyo. The supplies are as follows: 1179 pairs heavy shoes; 2 boxes medical supplies; 1722 individual parcels containing a bar of soap + 15 food items; 3000# salt; 16500# sugar; 5809# meat + vegetable stew; 10263# corned beef; + 1456# cocoa. Hope it is issued or part of it soon. [*These supplies were received in camp on March 22, but the individual parcels were not issued until April 9.*]

April 1, 1943

Half-pound of sugar issued this date from Red Cross supplies. Notice received this morn that all officers of Brigadier Gen. or above with a few orderlies will move tomorrow to another camp.

April 2, 1943

Gen. Wainwright left this morning. 117 people in all moved to Taiwan Prison Camp #5 which is said to be about 60 km south of here.

Hated to see Gen. Wainwright + Gen. Moore leave but feel it will be for the better. All civilian officials (including Capt. George McMillin) except Mr. Webb were moved also.

Friday April 9, 1943

Big day—Red Cross parcels issued at 6:30 p.m. Ate chocolate bar immediately and Johnny Pugh, Stu Wood, Bob Brown, + I pooled our common articles and made menu to extend articles over month period.

Saturday April 10, 1943

Stu Wood made administrator for Red Cross supplies. Today we were issued ½# cocoa, 1# sugar, + 1# salt. My Red Cross parcel contained 1 can (12 oz.) apple pudding; 1 can (8 oz.) condensed milk; 1 can (8 oz.) margarine; 1 can (13 cakes) hard biscuit; 1 can (8 oz.) galantine; 1 can (16 oz.) meat and vegetables; 1 can (8 oz.) bacon (the best I have ever tasted); 1 can (2 oz.) creamed cheese; 1 can (8 oz.) syrup; 1 can (8 oz.) creamed rice; 1 can (8 oz.) tomatoes.

On April 2nd, after the Generals left, the squads were re-arranged and new squad leaders appointed. The 5th Squad now consists of 20 men and J. Pugh is squad leader + Capt. Howard, Asst. It is much more comfortable now with only 5 men to a bay. Johnny Pugh, Bob Brown, Stu Wood, + Doc Worth [*probably Col. Josiah W. Worthington, a veterinary officer*] + I are in our bay.

April 14, 1943

Distribution of Corned beef from the Red Cross started today. For first month we will receive 3 oz. corned beef per day; 1# sugar per week. We will get ½# cocoa + 1# salt per month. The Corned beef is Argentine beef and is wonderful. This small amount of Red Cross real food is remarkably raising the morale of everyone.

April 15, 1943

After a.m. banga. Riff between [Col.] Frederick A. Ward + [*Josiah W.*] Worthington. Helped Stu with Red Cross tables.

April 16, 1943

Corned beef + sugar issued today. BP told Bob to kill pig + goat tomorrow. Soup for 4 days has been half + less of previous issues. No more potatoes.

May 11, 1943

Individual parcel issued; cocoa, + sugar; 1—12 oz. corned beef; one Meat + Vegetables (16 oz.).

May 9, 1943

Bob's birthday—gave him my Ray-Ban© glasses—he seemed quite pleased.

May 13, 1943

Orders issued to turn in blanket and sheets and then orders to pack heavy stuff. Many rumors + conjectures. Expected as Bob + I had just planted 71 Kohlrabi plants. Kohlrabi and cabbage doing well in our garden. Treatment now excellent and I am feeling excellent due to added food from Red Cross issues. Stu Wood moved to hospital on 10th as interpreter. Col. Robert J. Hoffman—nervous breakdown. 31 enlisted men moved to work camp. Sgt. [*Alvie L.*] Lairson—one of group. He left with me an affidavit as to service—also his mother's address. He is a good man. The above group moved on May 5, 1943. I think they went to camp at Haito near Tokyo. Not sure. [*Dooley copied Sgt. Lairson's affidavit into the canvas-covered journal that Gen. Wainwright had given him.*]

May 5, 1943

Copy of Affidavit of Sgt. Alvie L. Lairson 6823758 US Army Air Corps

AFFIDAVIT

Personally appeared before me this date, December 25, 1942, Sergeant Alvie L. Lairson, United States Army Air Corps who after being duly sworn deposes and sayeth:

Re-enlisted August 22, 1941, at Fort Douglas, Utah, for Air Corps, Philippine Islands, unassigned in the grade of Private. Reported to Fort McDowell, California on Aug. 25, 1941. Received my first partial payment of $20.00 on or about Sept. 20, 1941; second partial payment of $30.00 on or about October 18, 1941 by the Finance Officer, United States Army, Fort McDowell, California. Sailed for Philippine Islands on October 27, 1941 from Fort McDowell, California. Received partial payment enroute on the *USAT Hugh L. Scott* of $5.00. Was assigned to the Far Eastern Air Force, Nichols Field, Philippine Islands upon arrival. Was promoted to the grade of Private First Class on or about January 6, 1942. Received partial payment from Capt. Shielly in the amount of $10.00 at Headquarters, Fifth Interceptor Command, Little Baguio, Bataan, P.I. on or about January 16, 1942. Was promoted to grade of Sergeant on or about April 8, 1942 S.O. number unknown. Was notified by Field Messenger Tech. Sgt. Keef while on advance patrol.

Further deponent sayeth not to the best of his ability.

A.L. Lairson (signed)

A.L. Lairson,
Sergeant, US Army

Subscribed and sworn before me this 25th day of December, 1942.
J.T. Menzie (signed)

J[*ames*] T. Menzie
Colonel, US Army
Adjutant General's Dept.

Above is True Copy given to me by Sgt. Lairson at Taiwan Prisoner Camp # 4, Karenko, Taiwan on May 5, 1943 upon Sgt. Lairson's transfer by Imperial Japanese authorities to an unknown destination.

Sgt. Lairson's dependent
Mother's name + address
Mrs. Addie Throgmarten
R.F.D.
Lake City, Arkansas USA

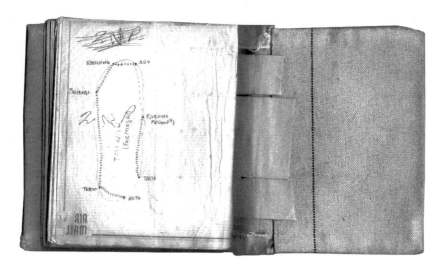

Dooley's sketch of Taiwan showing Karenko Prison Camp and the railroad links that took him to Shirakawa Prison Camp, located where the "i" appears in "Taiwan." Eight months after Dooley's first journal "was flown out of Corregidor . . . on one of the last planes that sneaked away at night from the beleaguered Rock" [from Kenneth Foree Jr series, "Tom Dooley's Bataan-Corregidor Diary," *Dallas News*, 30 September 1945], Dooley received a personal gift made of air-mail stationery sewed to a canvas cover by General Wainwright with the skill that came from repeated patching of the seat and knees of threadbare pants and the elbows of a raveling jacket.

May 20, 1943
Weights taken today. 58.6 kilos—128.92#.

June 6, 1943
On the 13th of last month we were told to pack up all but base essentials in preparation of move. The International Red Cross representative, Dr. Parsvanici visited on the 31st of May. Nothing unusual. On this date, the 6th, the Generals' group returned from Tomasato to join us for the projected move on the 7th. Gen. Wainwright + 13 others were not with them. They [*the fourteen generals not present*] are: Gen. Jonathan Wainwright, George F. Moore, Edward P. King, Arthur E. Percival, Lewis M. Heath, [*Hein*] Ter Poorten, Sir Mark Young, Sir Shentan Thomas, Governor Gen. Tjarda [*van*] Starkenborgh, Mr. Adrian I. Spitz, Sir Percy [*A.*] McElwaine, Sir Harvey Turstad, Dutch Doctor General + Gen. Ian M. McRae, Indian

Red Cross. Each kept an orderly—Sgt. [Hubert] Carroll is with the General.

We presumably move tomorrow to the other side of the island into the vicinity of Tainan. Trust it is all for the best. I feel that the Gen. will now receive treatment commensurate with his rank + position.

June 7, 1943

Got up at 5:00 a. m., had breakfast + prepared to leave. Left Karenko camp at 10:00 a.m. + arrived at dock at 10:55. Went on board *Hozan Maru* (about 1250 tons) and she left dock at 12:00 noon. Up the coast to Suo (only a small fishing village) where we dropped anchor at 4:00 p.m. Were taken ashore in fishing coracles and walked about a kilometer up to the R.R. station. Sat in street about one + half hours and then boarded train. Seats small + cramped (3rd class coaches) and train left Suo station about 10:00 p.m. Stu Wood, Group Capt. [*Gilbert E.*] Nicoletts (British), Bob Brown + I in one set of seats. Traveled all night (napped from time to time) and arrived at station (name unknown) at 10:30 a.m. Transferred to Sugar cane railway + traveled about 1½ hrs at about 8 to 12 mph. Dismounted and walked about 4 km to new camp. New camp—low country—rice paddies. hot—not unlike P.I. Tonight Bob Brown + I in a random room. Squads to be assigned tomorrow.

SEVEN

Moved to Camp Shirakawa, Formosa

June 9, 1943

New squads assigned—*Daigohan* (Sq. 5) Johnny is Sq. Leader— in corner room with Johnny Pugh, Fred Ward, + Lee Vance. Bob + Stu Wood in corner room at opposite end of barrack in 3rd Sq. They have jobs. Col. Donald Curtis + I still serve soup. Capt. William H. Wilterdink and Col. Napoleon Boudreau serve rice.

June 15, 1943

Red Cross issue today. 1 - 12 oz. Corned beef; 1 - 8 oz. Corned beef; 1# sugar; ½ # salt.

June 16, 1943

N.C. newspapers—news in general good. Formation at 1:00 p.m. Capt. Immamura [*Yachashi*] takes command. New interpreter since leaving Karenko. Interpreter + 2nd in command both lived in states prior to war. Bananas.

June 17, 1943

Heavy baggage—bananas—kitchen issued 1000# potatoes.

June 18, 1943

2 bananas—potatoes (good soup).

June 19, 1943

Small piece watermelon + 2 bananas each. Outlook bright.

June 20, 1943

3 bananas each. 1 banana + some cookies from interpreter. Red Cross issue: 3# sugar; 2 - 12 oz. Corned beef; 2 - 8 oz. Corned beef. Red

Cross dividend from Tomosato officers—1 - 8 oz. Corned Beef. Big day. Also newspapers—can read good news between lines.

June 23, 1943

Remainder of Red Cross issued—3 Meat + Vegetables (Stew); 2 - 12 oz. Corned beef; 2 - 8 oz. Corned beef. Tamasato dividend—1 - 12 oz. Corned beef; 1 - 8 oz. Corned beef and approx. 10# sugar. And too, the remainder of individual packages. One issue was 3 packages for 4 people. We divided soap, candy, sugar, etc. and pooled the remaining cans and have prepared schedule to carry us thru Sept. There are several cases of malaria here now. About 9 cases since arriving on the 8th. Many precautions are being taken and I will consider myself lucky if I get out without catching it.

July 30, 1943

Weights taken today—61.4 K = 135#.

Aug. 16, 1943

I am not one to write often. It seems that I cannot keep a day-to-day diary. I have heretofore been terrible at writing letters and this seems peculiar to me but just now I am reading Vera Brittain's *"Testament of Youth"* and she was telling of her saying goodbye to Roland at the station and described his having tears in his eyes and her feeling of "dry-eyedness" and I immediately thought again as I have often in the past of my saying goodbye to Cissy—Mother—Dad—and Margaret at Dallas on my way out here. I have often wondered what Margaret thought of me that night. I had expected Mother to cry and when she came into my arms and so bravely kept back the tears, (I later learned, by sheer determination). I could not help myself and then I kissed Margaret and she must have thought me quite a sentimental lot. I am not one of those except when my family is concerned. Johnny Pugh said the other day that he didn't think he had ever really appreciated his mother until he became a prisoner and I know that I have or think I have—Thank God—I know now that any appreciation for Mother, Dad or Cissy is not enough, but I believe I am more sensible than the usual man. About 50 officers received radiograms from States this PM. How I would like to hear from home.

Aug. 17, 1943

One year ago today we arrived at Karenko. When I think of it all it doesn't really seem like a year.

Excerpt (good thought) from Vera Brittain's *Testament of Youth*: "When you are a soldier, you are one of two things; either at the front or behind the lines. If you are behind the lines, you need not worry. If you are at the front you are one of two things. You are either in a danger zone or in a zone which is not dangerous. If you are in a zone which is not dangerous, you need not worry. If you are in a danger zone you are one of two things; either you are wounded or you are not. If you are not wounded, you need not worry. If you are wounded, you are one of two things; either you are seriously wounded or slightly wounded. If you are slightly wounded, you need not worry. If you are seriously wounded, one of two things is certain; either you get well or you die. If you get well, you needn't worry. If you die, you cannot worry, so there is no need to worry about anything at all."

This would have to be changed a bit to fit this war. To a certain extent World War I could only have 4 fronts in a given sector but this war has brought forth the "5th front" sometimes called "the vertical envelopment." In Bataan there was no rear area with luxuries and rest areas that we heard so much about in the last war. Corregidor had its Malinta Tunnel, but its "rear area" safety was objectionable due to the depressing atmosphere and ultimate "tunnelitis" for a great many.

Sept. 5, 1943

Rumors of peace and cessation of fighting in Europe. Morale (mine) very high lately. Ate a cricket this morn. Prepared by Nip cooks by frying in deep fat and dipping in soy sauce. Beckworth (Enlisted Man) brought it to me. Very tasty. Am reading Alexander [H.] Woollcott's "*While Rome Burns.*" Appreciative of Cpl. Alf Eckles' (Hopkinsville, Ky) many kindnesses and friendship.

Sept. 23, 1943

Received letter from Mother this date. First since Nov. 17, 1941.

Nov. 4, 1943

Five people left camp today—4 Americans + 1 British. Lt. Eric [C.] Marsden, Royal Signals. Americans—Sgt. N[ewton] H. Light, [S. Sgt.] H[enry W.] Hundley, [S. Sgt. Herbert F.] Leemann, Brown—Do not know why or where they are going. Expect 24 new pow's tomorrow night or Sat. morn.

Nov. 8, 1943

About 32 POWs from Java arrived in small hours of the morning. Three Americans in group.

Nov. 13, 1943

Ten new members to Squad 8. I had to move from my comfortable room across the hall into the small room with Johnny. The room is about 6′ x 9′ and is what you might say the least bit crowded.

Dec. 26, 1943

Karenko—1st Song Fest, Numbers. Medley The Souse Family. Thought—

For the first Karenko "Songfest" (Dec. 26, 1942). Gen. Beebe was asked by Gen. Pierce to form an octette for a number on the program. Gen. Beebe directed the efforts of the group formed in following order—

Brigadier Gen. Lewis C. Beebe—Director.

FIRST TENORS
Capt. Wm. Wilterdink (S.C.) US Navy
Colonel Edwin O'Connor (Cavalry)

2ND TENORS (Air)
Brigadier Gen. Charles C. Drake
Colonel Theodore Lilly (Inf)

1ST BASS (Baritone)
Colonel T.M. Cornell (Infantry)
Major T. Dooley (Cavalry—ADC)

2ND BASS
Captain Robert C. Davis (Medical Corps) US Navy
Colonel C. Gordon Sage (National Guard) C.A.C. AA

Music played a major role in the POWs' survival program. In addition to noting the organization of a songfest on 26 December 1942 and holiday caroling, Dooley included in his fourth journal (with a black stripe on the cover) the lyrics for nine original songs, six penned by Col. Gordon Sage between 22 July 1942 and 10 April 1944. Songs ranged from thoughts of home and changes in the weather to loved ones, a tribute to General Wainwright, and a "Prisoner's Prayer."

Jan. I, 1944

Karenko—2nd Songfest

Radio Message—Received March, 1944

Telegraphic Messages For Transmission Via The International Red Cross Committee.

Geneva, Switzerland

Major Thomas Dooley   (Taiwan) 19-1-1

Message: "Birthday greetings family well reply your health

Love always Mother Dooley"

[There are no journal entries for some nine months, from January to September 1944.

In mid-May Dooley copied into his journal the wording of a message signed by the major Dutch, British, and American commanders to the commander of POW Camp #4 near Shirakawa, Formosa (Taiwan). This document notes in great detail the discrepancies between POW treatment as spelled out in the Hague and Geneva Conventions and the treatment meted out by the Japanese.]

May 18, 1944

No. 4   Prisoner of War Camp—Taiwan
To: The Camp Commandant
Thru: The Nippon Duty Officer
Sir.

We understood the Main Camp Commandant to say in his recent speech that prisoners of war would be treated according to International Custom supported by the Code of Bushido. International custom for the treatment of p.o.w.'s is codified in various Hague and Geneva Conventions, which we assumed was to be observed in our treatment.

Under your instructions we now submit our views in writing to you.

TREATMENT UNDER INTERNATIONAL CUSTOM

1. Status of Officers

(a) No P.O.W. may be deprived of his rank. All are entitled to respect for their persons and honor.

(b) Officer P.O.W.s salute only captor officers of equal or higher rank.

(c) P.O.W.s are entitled to respect for their persons and honor. Officer POWs are to be treated with due regard for their rank and age. They are not to be compelled to work; but if they ask for it suitable work should be found, as far as possible, and in accordance

TREATMENT HITHERTO

1. Status of Officers

(a) Rank is not recognized for P.O.W.'s. It is not normally used in addressing P.O.W.s, who have been informed that they are all of one rank level with enlisted men. Senior Dutch, British, and American officers are not recognized as such.

(b) All P.O.W.s, including those of the highest rank, have to salute all Nippon army personnel, including the most junior privates.

(c) Officers are compelled, under threat, to undertake

with their rank and abilities. No POW should be employed on work for which he is physically unsuited.

(d) Soldier POWs should be employed at officers camps in sufficient numbers for the personal services of officers in the camp.

(e) NCOs may be employed on supervisory work only, and in accordance with their rank.

unaccustomed manual labor, in labor gangs, in a tropical climate, and frequently in the strong tropical sun, although most of them are of advanced age. Much of their work, they are told, is essential, in order to produce necessary extra food.

(d) Soldier POWs are almost entirely employed as laborers, and officers have to do nearly all their orderlies' work themselves.

(e) No distinction whatever is made between NCOs and privates. All are employed as manual laborers.

2. Humane Treatment

(a) POWs should at all times be treated with humanity, protected against acts of violence, insult and public curiosity. They are entitled to respect for their persons and honor.

(b) All forms of corporal punishment are prohibited.

(c) Collective penalties for individual acts are prohibited.

(d) Imprisonment is the most severe disciplinary punishment that may be inflicted, and this may not exceed 30 days.

(e) A parole not to attempt to escape may be given voluntarily by a POW; it is forbidden to force it upon them.

2. Humane Treatment

POWs, including officers of the highest rank, have been repeatedly struck with the fist, boot, and rifle butt for offences often most trivial, in many cases they have not understood for what offence.

They have been enforced to perform menial tasks at times in the public highway and in view of the public.

They have been informed that the penalty for attempting to escape is death. They have been forced to sign under threat, an undertaking on their honor as officers not to escape. They have recently been formed into groups and have been told that if one of their members escape, the remainder of the group will be punished.

3. Submission of Petitions
(a) POWs should appoint their own representatives to represent their joint needs to the captor military authorities and their protective powers. At officers camps the senior officer POW should be recognized as this intermediary.
(b) POWs have the right to communicate with Protective Powers about any unsatisfactory conditions of their captivity. Such petitions are to be transmitted immediately and if the complaint is found to be groundless, no punishment is to ensue.

3. Submission of Petitions
(a) Senior officer POWs are not allowed to act as such, and administrative appointments are made by the Nippon authorities without reference to POWs. The submission of petitions through an O.D. who changes daily makes it impractical for POWs as a whole to represent satisfactorily their requirements and grievances, many of which remain unventilated.
(b) An appeal to the Protective Power has been refused, and we are given to understand that such appeals could not be considered.

4. Treatment of Non-Combatants
(a) Medical Personnel and chaplains are not to be treated as POWs. They should be returned to their own nationals.
(b) Clergy should be allowed freely to minister to POWs.

4. Treatment of Non-Combatants
(a) All medical Personnel and Chaplains have been retained and are treated as Prisoners of War.
(b) Clergy may not visit other campuses where there are no clergy of their denominations; they may not hold religious meetings other than church services; communion bread and wine have been refused.

5. Hygiene
(a) Belligerents are to take all necessary hygienic measures to ensure cleanliness of camps:

5. Hygiene
(a) The kitchen, and its facilities are such as to make hygienic preparation of food nearly

POWs are to have, for their use, lavatories maintained in a constant state of cleanliness.
(b) POWs should be provided with sufficient water for bodily cleanliness.

impossible. Latrines frequently overflow for considerable periods. Several barracks are badly illuminated and overcrowded.
(b) The water supply, except in the rainy season, is frequently insufficient.

6. Infirmary

(a) Each camp shall possess an infirmary where POWs shall receive attention of any kind they may be in need of.
(b) POWs who are seriously ill, or in need of important surgical treatment, shall be admitted to a military or civil hospital qualified to treat them.
(c) Sick and wounded unlikely to recover within one year should be repatriated.

6. Infirmary

(a) The camp infirmary cannot provide medical attention at the standards of international custom owing to absence of some necessary drugs and shortages of others; insufficient dressings and absence of surgical apparatus for special cases; shortage of essential dental equipment and supplies, of desirable nursing and laboratory equipment, inadequate supplies of invalid diet and poor facilities for preparing it.

POW medical officers are not allowed, in our opinion, sufficient voice in deciding the fitness or otherwise of patients for return to duty or for manual work.
(b) Opportunities for investigating and treating serious cases by accessory methods and surgical operation in an outside general hospital are not adequate by the standards of international custom.
(c) Not done, though several exchange ships have offered opportunities.

7. Food

(a) Rations of POWs are to be equivalent in quality and quantity to that of captors depot troops.
(b) All collective disciplinary action regarding food is prohibited.

(a) POWs have to work on the farm to get necessary extra food over and above what is allowed by regulations. The authorized ration scale must therefore be less than that allowed for depot troops of the Nippon Army, since otherwise it would not be necessary for POWs to produce extra food for themselves. In spite of repeated assurances that the food produced from the farm is solely for POWs own benefit, so far only a small proportion has been received by POWs. Much has been diverted to other uses. POWs particularly lack proteins and fats.
(b) Collective disciplinary action to reduce food drastically has been threatened if POWs do not work on the farm and at manual labor.

8. Clothing

(a) Clothing is to be supplied to by the captor power, and regular replacement and repair is to be assured.

(a) Many are badly in need of clothing. Articles are normally replaced only if POWs can certify that they have none at all of the article concerned. Repair facilities are still quite inadequate; much clothing is falling to pieces for want of repair and old age.

9. Mails

(a) If POWs are transferred from one place to another all necessary

(a) Prisoners from Java and Hong Kong have, for the most part,

arrangements are to be made for correspondence from former camps to be readdressed without delay.

(b) In cases of urgency, POWs may send telegrams on payment of the usual charges.

received no letters since their arrival in Taiwan, 16, 7, and 9 months ago, respectively.

(b) This has rarely been sanctioned.

10. Transfer of Money

Transfer of money to relatives and other individuals in POW's home countries should be arranged.

10. Transfer of Money

Facilities for transferring money under the arrangement are inadequate. A number of officer POWs have been allowed, only once, to remit a limited sum, but to close relations only and then only to those who were financially dependent upon them before the war.

The above are the chief ways in which we feel that the present treatment falls short of international custom. Many less important items are not mentioned. In order that a comparison may be drawn we attach a report of the treatment of Italians' P.O.W.s in India in British hands, which treatment is in accordance with International Custom.

([*Gustav*] A. Ilgen)   Major General
Senior Dutch Officer

(P.C. Maltby) Air Vice Marshall
Senior British Officer

(Geo. M. Parker, Jr.)   Major General
Senior American Officer

June 12, 1944

On one of the previous occasions when we were allowed to write home, I wrote to Margaret via Mother. Since then (on May 23rd, '44) I received the first word from Margaret (two letters—one Feb.—one

Apr.). The first paragraph of the Apr. letter prompted the letter I wrote to her on June 11th, 1944, although I doubt if it will ever reach her.

Dearest Margaret,

You cannot imagine what a boon your two letters have been which I have just received and your snapshot, received in Cissy's letter, has been a joy. So happy to hear of your fun and enjoyable work in New York. Your saying that nothing has changed has brought about a peace of mind and stability of outlook that makes this separation an inconvenience rather than an unendurable isolation. I think of you constantly and miss you so much, but trust that we can be together soon. My regards to your student, Mother and to Helen.

All my love,
T

Sept. 30, 1944

Received notice about 2 or so p.m. that all American, Dutch, + Australian generals to be ready to leave camp by noon Sunday— Oct. 1st.

Oct. 1, 1944

15 American Generals, 1 American EM, Australian generals. 1 Australian enlisted man, Dutch generals, 1 Dutch enlisted man.

AMERICAN GENERALS
Major Generals
Parker, Geo. M.
Jones, Albert M.
Sharpe, Wm. E.

Brigadier Generals
Beebe, L.C.
Funk, Arnold J.
Weaver, Jas. R.N.
Brougher, Wm. E.
Seals, Carl H.

Lough, Max
Drake, Chas. C.
Vachon, Joseph P.
Pierce, Clinton A.
Stephens, Luther R.
Bluemel, Clifford
Chynoweth, Bradford G.

American Enlisted Men
Sgt. Mullins, Jasper C.

AUSTRALIANS
Maj. Gen. [*Cecil A.*] Callaghan
Brig. [*William A.*] Trott
Brig. [*Duncan S.*] Maxwell
Brig. [*Harold B.*] Taylor
Brig. [*A. S.*] Blackburn
Brig.

Aust. EM
Beatton, [*Cecil N.*] Cess

DUTCH
Maj. Gen. [*Gustav A.*] Ilgin
Statius-Mueller
[*Maj. Gen. Johan H.*] Uhl
[*Maj. Pierre A.*] Cox
[*Maj. Gen. Hans J.*] de Fremery
[*Maj. Gen. Wybrandus*] Schilling
[*Maj. Gen. Jacob J.*] Pesman
[*Gen. Rudolph*] Bakkers

Dutch EM
Private [*J. R. "Rudy"*] Dam

Oct. 2, 1944
Notice received this a.m. that British Generals will leave in 2 groups of 18 each very soon.
They are—

A.V.M.Maltby
Maj. Gen.[*Frank*] Keith Simmons
Maj. Gen.[*Berthold S. W.*] Key
Maj. Gen.[*Hervey D. W.*] Sitwell
Maj. Gen. [*Christopher M.*] Maltby

Brigadier
[*Hubert C.*] Servaes
[*Tristram H.*] Massey-Beresford
[*Wallace R.*] Selby
[*Cecil L. B.*] Duke
[*Edward H. W.*] Backhouse
[*Bernard S.*] Challen
[*George G. R.*] Williams
[*Arthur D.*] Curtis
[*Robert G.*] Moir
[*George C.*] Ballentine
[*Alec W. G.*] Wildey
[*Gordon W. A.*] Painter
[*William O.*] Lay
[*Francis H.*] Fraser
[*Ivan J.*] Simson
[*Arthur E.*] Rusher
[*Eric W.*] Goodman
[*George C.*] Evelegh
[*Charles H.*] Stringer
[*Claude W.*] Richards
[*Herbert F.*] Lucas
[*Thomas K.*] Newbigging
[*Kenneth B. S.*] Crawford

Air Comm.
[*Charles O. F.*] Modin
[*William E.*] Staton

Brig.
[*Samuel R.*] Pearson
[*Cedric*] Wallis

[*Kenneth S.*] Torrance (Canadian)
[*Torquil*] McLeod
[*Andrew*] Peffers

Commodore
[*Alfred C.*] Collinson

Enlisted Men
Guardsman [Cpl. Frederick] Peto
———[Pvt. Graham F.] Tanner
———[Marine George H.] Rogers
———Chester

October 7, 1944
Notification received this date that all Colonels will leave between 10th and 12th.

October 8, 1944
Vic Collier asked me to take Post Exchange job. ok About 7:30 p.m. Cols. notified that they will have Reveille at 3:00 a.m. tomorrow and leave at 4:00 a.m.

Oct. 9, 1944
All Colonels + 3 civilians—Capt. Peterson, Mr. [*Ralph B.*] Webb [*Australian/British Red Cross*] + Mr. Joel (Dutch) had left by 4:45 a.m.

Oct. 10, 1944
Air Raid alarm kept us in all day.

Oct. 11, 1944
All officers moved into old Colonels Barracks. Our room Pugh, [*Capt.*] Thomas A. Dodson, Dooley, [*Lt.*] James P. Ferrey, Brown, Levitt. [*Col.*] Earl T. Halstead, Dean Sherry next door. Dutch—11, Australian—8, New Zealander—1, English—3. All other squads— British. In camp now—141 officers. 55 enlisted men.

[*There are no journal entries from October 1944 to February 1945.*]

Feb. 19, 1945

Left Shirakawa camp at 4:50 p.m.—marched to Kagi—Entrained approx. 10:00 p.m.

Feb. 20, 1945

Taihoku about 9:00 A.M; marched to Camp #1 in rain arrived 4:00 p.m.

Feb. 21, 1945

Left Camp #1 marched again in rain to Station 3–1/2 mi. To Keelung about noon; Marched to Pier and waited about 4 hrs. By crowded lighters to *Melbourne Maru*. Into hold about 6 p.m. Anchor up about midnite.

Feb. 22, 1945

Cleared roads about 4:00 p.m. About 8:30 ran aground sand bar. Turned back to Keelung.

Feb. 23–27, 1945

Laid in hold in harbor.

Feb. 27, 1945

Transshipped to *Winchester Maru*.

Feb. 27–28, 1945

sailed.

Feb. 28, 1945

5:00 p.m. Anchored on China coast—is for—near Foochow?

Mar. 1, 1945

Travel West about 5 hrs.

Mar. 2, 1945

Anchored in fog.

Mar. 3, 1945

Sailed up China coast.

Mar. 4, 1945

Anchored off mouth Yangtze River?

Mar. 5, 1945

Snow—Sailed in early morn—traveling North or Northeast.

Mar. 6, 1945

About 9:30 a.m. took East course—about 11:30a.m.—Southeast.

Mar. 7, 1945

At sea.

Mar. 8, 1945

At sea.

Mar. 9, 1945

Landed at Muji about 5:00 p.m. Taken to theater building. Spent cold night—Glass rod.

Mar. 10, 1945

2:00 p.m.—Entrained at Muji Station—2–1/2 hr. train ride south—walked about 2 kilometers to camp—arrival about 5:30 p.m. Bitter cold—supper delightful—Red Cross Salmon + butter. American coffee (cream + sugar). American cigarettes.

April 25, 1945

11 a.m.—Left Mining Camp #12 (Niata) by train → SE. [*Heading southeast.*] Arrived Fukuoka 3:00 p.m. rest in park. Moved on to Packet ship about 7:00 p.m.

April 26, 1945

Ship moved out 8:45 p.m. Arrived Hosan 4:45 p.m. moved into theatre building for night (Treatment + accommodations much nicer than any before.) Aboard ship met Trapnell, Zero Wilson, Blondy, Burns, Jack Walker, Bill Chandler + others).

April 27, 1945

Train left Hosan Station → N [*traveling northward*] at 8:45 a.m.

Holding the first Aggie Muster on Corregidor since 1942, Marine Lt. Col. Ormond R. Simpson, '36, Major R. N. "Dick" Conolly, '37, and Lt. Tommy G. Martin, '40, gathered at the north dock on 21 April 1945, after the island was retaken. The *Houston Press* reported, "Three Aggies crawled up on the 'Rock' to hold another muster. Jap sharp shooters were still around, and it may have been not too wise a thing to do. But they did it." Photo Courtesy Donald "Buck" Henderson, '62.

[*There are no journal entries between April 27, 1945, and August 18, 1945.*]

August 18, 1945

[*Pfc.*] Howard M. Gilliland
Star Route
Bend, Oregon

Major R.E. Wampler
226 Franklin Ave.
Des Moines, Iowa
(O.SS—Sian, China)

[*Pfc.*] Robert E. Johnson
1467 E. Pierce St.
Phoenix, Ariz.

Col. Samuel L. Myers
Mrs. " " "
Marfa, Texas

[Cpl.] Douglas B. Toone
Del Norte, Colorado

[*Capt.*] A.C. Tisdelle, Jr.
924 Greenleaf Ave.
Wilmette, Illinois

[*M. Sgt.*] Dumont F. Wade
c/o H.J. Nevins
Corona, California

Col. J[*ames*] H. Thyer
Army HQ
Melbourne, Aust.

EIGHT

The War Is Over!

Aug. 16, 1945

The parachutists who dropped near Mukden about noon of the 16th were thought by most to be Japs on maneuvers.

Toward late afternoon the Branch Camp #2 personnel were brought in and they observed a party consisting of 6 men having arrived at Guard House but they were being treated differently. They were still wearing side arms. The camp then buzzed. Later prisoners from the Jap guard house were released, one of them having been in solitary confinement for 121 days and was still awaiting trial when released.

Then the "yardbird" came for roll call and Pfc. Griff asked a Japanese if the war was over—he answered yes and tomorrow you will understand all. I was then convinced. That night poker and bridge were played all night and people sat around smoking with no interference from the guard.

Aug. 17, 1945

Major Gen. George M. Parker, Air Vice Marshal Paul Maltby (British) and Maj. Gen I.A. Ilgen (Dutch) were called to headquarters and, on returning to the P.O.W. compound, Gen. Parker assembled the American group and announced that an Armistice had been signed. p.m. Red Cross food was issued and then was the place gay with plenty of food and coffee + cigarettes. I could not sleep nor could many others.

Aug. 18, 1945

Nothing much out of way. Americans from parachute group were in compound. Maj. Robert F. Lamar (Parachute Surgeon) gave a talk to Generals which I listened to and he told us then that he would leave next a.m. to go and contact Gen. Wainwright. Bob Brown brought in a

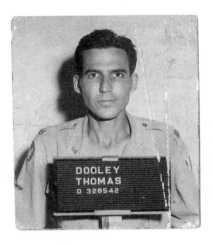

Tom Dooley on release from POW camp 17 August 1945. American parachutists landed outside the Mukden compound, and Russians arrived 20 August and turned the camp over to the POWs. Photo courtesy Tom Dooley family.

note for Lamar to take to Gen. Moore and I added to his a note to Gen. Wainwright.

Aug. 19, 1945

Word that Russians would enter at 10 p.m. Each of these glorious nights were marked with music and coffee + cigarettes with Bob Brown, Cpl. Alfred Eckles + Douglas B. Toone.

Aug. 20, 1945

No word of Gen. Wainwright yet. Programs at 9:00 p.m. interrupted by entrance into camp of Russian representative. The Russian officer (a Major) gave the following speech.

[*The bottom half of the page is blank. The speech is missing.*]

After this the program was resumed + then interrupted again for a formation in which the Japs were aligned in front of POWs and arms were stacked. Then [*the Allied*] POW guards were brought out and presented rifles by the Russian major. Then the Jap garrison marched past under American guard. The [*Japanese*] NCO's + privates placed in guard houses and the [*Japanese*] officers held under guard in conference room of camp headquarters. Stu Wood was helping guard officers, Col. questioned with interpreting and I stood around with him for a while. Japs very low, but if they could only know how differently they have been treated on their first night of surrender as compared with Americans in Philippine Islands.

Aug. 21, 1945

Coffee + saki (from Johnny) for breakfast. Japs working under American guards. American staff taking over offices in Headquarters. Note from Gen. Wainwright to Johnny Pugh and self. Hope we fly home soon. "Hoot" Harrigan, Johnny Pugh, Bob Brown + I had pleasant lunch together. Off now to have hot chocolate with Cpl. Eckles. [*Alfred Eckles was from Hopkinsville, Kentucky. When Dooley visited Eckles after the war, a young Catherine "Kitty" Dade saw Alfred on the sidewalk talking to "a handsome young officer." She told her boss that she was going to the drug store in order to walk past them and possibly meet the young man. Dooley was smitten. They went on a date, had several more, and got married. The wedding caused a great stir in Hopkinsville because General Wainwright walked the groom's mother down the aisle. Tom and Kitty would have a son, Thomas P. "Pete" Dooley II (who provided this anecdote); a daughter, Mary Randolph "Randy" Dooley Peters; and a granddaughter, Kate Dooley.*]

"Rarity in Blue"
"Lawry, Maze, + Sam"
Chorus –

A meeting like this is rare.
The moonbeams softly kiss your hair
You match the beauty above
And this is the night for romance
So, darling, come let us dance
And take our chance.
The lights are turned down low
Your blue eyes shine like glistening snow
So we're in a world of our own
And you will always be the queen on my throne.
I have searched the wide world over
For a girl who looks like you
And when the music started
You were standing there in blue
Your lips so sweet and . . . .

Aug. 21–26, 1945

Felt bad during period with dysentery. Read new magazines, etc.

Aug. 26, 1945

Night of 26th. Gen. Wainwright party arrive in Mukden with Russian party having had long tiresome trip from Hsian, Manchuria, but Johnny and I didn't know he had arrived until later.

Aug. 27, 1945

Johnny Pugh and self called to Headquarters quite early. Messenger said Gen. Wainwright was there but no messages to meet him at airport. Bob Brown, Johnny and I left with others for airport at 9:00 a.m. Met Gen. at airport and soon after we took off. Our group, Generals Jonathan Wainwright, George F. Moore, Edward P. King, William F. Sharp, Albert Jones, James R.N. Weaver, Lewis C. Beebe, Clifford Bluemel, William E. Brougher, [Col.] Newman [R.] Laughinghouse, along with Johnny Pugh, Bob Brown, self. Gen. Arthur E. Percival and Sgts. Hubert Carroll + Crockett, left in C-47 piloted by Lt. Col. Rasmussin, Class of '40 at US Military Academy. Troop carrier of 14th Air (unit).

Took off Mukden Airport approx. 11:00 a.m. Arrive Siam approx. 4:30 p.m. To Office of Strategic Services camp for night. Major Krause—Detachment Commander, Capt. Oats—executive. Beautiful dinner. Sent message home. Major [R. E.] Bob Wampler (Engineer OSS) extremely nice + friendly. Movie in p.m.—Jack Oakie in "That's The Spirit"—Army action pictures all over the world.

Aug. 28, 1945

Drive thru city in early a.m. (Siam), Old Bell Tower. Took off from Siam about 11:00 a.m. Arrive Chungking Airport about 2:00 p.m. Royal reception. Paul Scheidestan and Bob Suggs. Stayed with them at Qtrs 26. Met Annalee [Whitmore] Jacoby of Time + Life. Took her to press interview and to dinner that p.m. Swell person. Gen. Wainwright, Beebe, Maj. Gen. George F. Moore, BG Albert Jones, quartered at Gen. [Albert] Coady Wedemeyer's residence. Sgt. Carroll also. [In the summer of 1941, Gen. George C. Marshall assigned Maj. Albert C. Wedemeyer to develop the Victory Program. Following the attacks on

Pearl Harbor and the Philippines, this became the primary plan for the US military.]

Aug. 29, 1945

Spent in Chungking. a.m. at Army Air Force Headquarters.—Haircut—200.00 Gen. Wainwright pinned Distinguished Service Cross on Brig. Gen. Albert Jones, Gen. Moore, SS Sgt. Carroll. Saw Annalee Jacoby again. Lovely person. Spent evening gathering clothes, pistols, flight bags. Delivered .32 Special to Dutch ambassador from Gen. Wainwright quite late. 4:30 p.m.—to Generalissimo Chiang Kai-shek's country house in mountains near Chungking. Mr. Patrick [*Jay*] Hurley—ambassador. Madame Chiang in US. Rode out with Gen. Wainwright + Wedemeyer.

Aug. 30, 1945

Took off Chungking 8:00 a.m. Short hop to Peishiyi. Changed to Lt. Gen. [*George E.*] Stratemeyer's converted B-17—a luxury craft. About noon passed over Hong Kong—one Jap fighter. Arrive Manila about 5:30 p.m. Philippine time. Mr. Sergio Osmeña (Vice President of the Philippines) met Gen. Wainwright—to admiralty apartments. Processing forms. Identification—physical exams, clothes, decorations, promotion. Ormond [*R.*] Simpson [*A&M Class of 1936*] called. Chas. Stahler. Joe Aston (*A&M Class of 1934*) called from San Fernando, Pampanga. In conversation he told me of Dad's death—date unknown. Cannot say here what I felt. Sam Myers—with 1st Army Headquarters G-3. News of lots of old friends. CBS broadcast. Pack for early take-off.

Aug. 31, 1945

Took off Nichols Field 6:00 AM. Gen. Walter Krueger (6th Army Cmdr), Ike Kampmann (ADC) to Gen. Percival, Gen. [*Sir Thomas*] Blarney, several men in C-54. Beautiful ship. Lunch at Okinawa. Met Gen. John R. Hodge, commanding troops there. Arrived Atsugi Airdrome outside Yokohama about 5:30 p.m. Gen. Wainwright + Gen. King to New Grand Hotel. Wild ride into Yokohama on bus with Jap driver. To Helm house—B. Theilen.

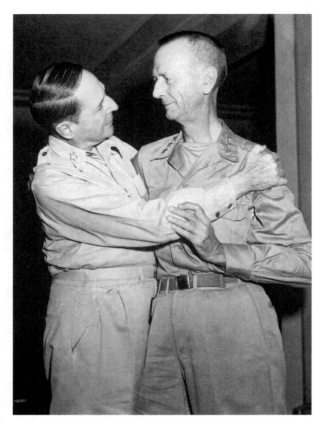

MacArthur greets Wainwright in the dining room of the Hotel New Grand, in Yokohama, Japan, on 31 August 1945, two days before the Japanese surrender aboard the USS *Missouri*. It was the generals' first meeting since MacArthur had turned over command on Corregidor to Wainwright on 10 March 1942, when he left for Australia.

Sept. I, 1945

In Yokohama. Gen. Wainwright—press + radio—Self had interviews with Press. Many famous people about. Old friend Woody Burgess—he thought I was dead long ago. Dinner this p.m. with Lt. Gen. Robert L. Eichelberger, a wonderful personality [*commanded I Corps of the Sixth Army during the campaign on New Guinea, and the US Eighth Army during the invasion of the Philippines.*]—Chief of Staff Maj. Gen. Clovis E. Byers—Brig. Gen. Owens + aides. Back to town—Johnny Pugh + I moved to New Grand Hotel—party at Helm House—Brig. Gen. Frank

Gen. Douglas MacArthur signs the Japanese surrender documents aboard the USS *Missouri* in Tokyo Bay on 2 September 1945. Gen. Wainwright stands behind Gen. MacArthur. Photo courtesy Texas A&M University Archives.

Besson (a swell guy– knows Archie Swank), B. Theilen, Johnny Pugh + self—no geisha. [*In 1940, as a lieutenant on the Army Engineer Board, Besson developed Pierced Steel Planking (PSP), which made it possible to build an airfield in a single day. In early 1945 he became the youngest brigadier general in the ground forces of World War II. After VE Day he assumed control of railroads in the Eighth Army's assigned zone, moving occupation troops throughout northern Japan. After the war MacArthur named him Director of the Civil Transportation Division, responsible for all military water, motor, and rail transportation in Japan, the Philippines, the Marianas, and Korea.*]

Sept. 2, 1945

Up early for memorable day—Upon Col. [*Roger Olaf*] Egeberg's (Gen. MacArthur's personal physician) invitation had breakfast with eggs at General Headquarters Special Table. From New Grand Hotel to docks and boarded Destroyer USS *"Nicholas."* Talked with Gen. [*John R.*] Hodge, Gen. Joseph W. Stilwell, Brig. Gen. Frank Merrill *[transferred to Stilwell's command in Burma and there organized the 5307th Composite Unit (Provisional), which became famous as "Merrill's Marauders.]*, Lt. Gen. Clovis E. Byers, Lt. Gen. Robert L. Eichelberger in route to USS *Missouri* (a beautiful ship). Saw *[Fleet]* Admiral Chester *[W.]* Nimitz + *[Rear Admiral]* William *[F.]* Halsey *[Jr.]*

Surrender impressive with Gen MacArthur's speech splendid.

MacArthur's speech at surrender ceremony on the USS *Missouri* (Source: http://www.pbs.org/wgbh/amex/macarthur/filmmore /reference/primary/macspeech04.html):

[Even his detractors—and the defeated Japanese—recognized the grace with which MacArthur presided over the surrender ceremony aboard the USS Missouri. A few minutes after the Japanese and other delegations were in place, MacArthur, entering with Nimitz and Halsey, strode to the microphone and uttered the following words:]

"We are gathered here, representatives of the major warring powers, to conclude a solemn agreement whereby peace may be restored. The issues, involving divergent ideals and ideologies, have been determined on the battlefields of the world and hence are not for our discussion or debate. Nor is it for us here to meet, representing as we do a majority of the people of the earth, in a spirit of distrust, malice or hatred. But rather it is for us, both victors and vanquished, to rise to that higher dignity which alone befits the sacred purposes we are about to serve, committing all our people unreservedly to faithful compliance with the understanding they are here formally to assume."

It is my earnest hope, and indeed the hope of all mankind, that from this solemn occasion a better world shall emerge out of the blood and carnage of the past—a world dedicated to the dignity of man and the fulfillment of his most cherished wish for freedom, tolerance and justice.

[After the surrender documents were signed and the Japanese delegation had departed, MacArthur went to another microphone and broadcast the following radio message to the world. Note again the ease with which the soldier made the transition to statesman:]

"Today the guns are silent. A great tragedy has ended. A great victory has been won. . . .

As I look back upon the long, tortuous trail from those grim days of Bataan and Corregidor, when an entire world lived in fear, when democracy was on the defensive everywhere, when modern civilization trembled in the balance, I thank a merciful God that he has given us the faith, the courage and the power from which to mold victory. We have known the bitterness of defeat and the exultation of triumph, and from both we have learned there can be no turning back. We must go forward to preserve in peace what we won in war.

A new era is upon us. Even the lesson of victory itself brings with it profound concern, both for our future security and the survival of civilization. The destructiveness of the war potential, through progressive advances in scientific discovery, has in fact now reached a point which revises the traditional concepts of war. Men since the beginning of time have sought peace. . . . Military alliances, balances of power, leagues of nations, all in turn failed, leaving the only path to be by way of the crucible of war. We have had our last chance. If we do not now devise some greater and more equitable system, Armageddon will be at our door. The problem basically is theological and involves a spiritual recrudescence and improvement of human character that will synchronize with our almost matchless advances in science, art, literature and all material and cultural development of the past two thousand years. It must be of the spirit if we are to save the flesh."

[*Dooley's Journal continues*]

September 2, 1945

In ward room after ceremony. Thanked Gen. MacArthur personally for his invitation to attend ceremony. Tears in eyes as I thanked him. He simply exudes personality. Adm. William F. Halsey. Coffee + doughnuts + cinnamon rolls. Return to dock aboard Destroyer [USS] *Buchanan* with select group—Gen. MacArthur. To hotel for bags and then on to Atsugi again. Passed first units of 1st Cavalry Division landing in Yokohama. Word of Ed Treacy from Shore of 5th Cavalry.

At Atsugi—Weather closed in Okinawa. Route changed at Lt. Gen. Ennis C. Whitehead's (Air Corps) suggestion and took off about 2:00 p.m. for Iwo Jima. Landed Iwo about 5:30 p.m. Supper and then took off for Manila about 6:30 p.m. Lt. Gen. Wilhelm D. Styer [*Commander-in-Chief of US Army Forces Western Pacific, who in 1945 chaired the tribunals that convicted Gen. Tomoyuki Yamashita and Lt. Gen. Masaharu for war crimes and ordered their executions*] with aide-

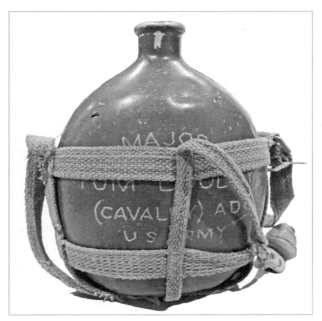

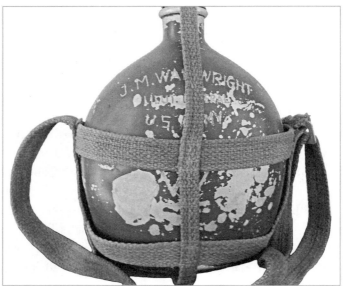

These canteens sustained General Wainwright and Major Dooley throughout their captivity. When Dooley first learned of his fifteen-month-old nephew, on the day of the Japanese surrender aboard the USS *Missouri*, Wainwright gave Dooley his canteen as a present for his nephew. Photos courtesy Tom Dooley family.

Maj. Gen. Edmond H. Leavey, '15, signs the surrender of the Japanese commander in the Philippines on 3 September 1945. Lt. Gen. Jonathan Wainwright, far left, and British Lt. Gen. Sir Arthur Percival suffered for three years at the hands of the Japanese. Second row standing, upper right, is Maj. Tom Dooley, '35. From *A Pictorial History of Texas A&M University*, p. 157.

de-camp Capt. Watson aboard—awfully swell to us. Our rush is due to plans for our party to witness at Baguio (east of Lingayen Gulf) the surrender of Yamashita. No radio's from Mother yet. Arrival in Manila 4 letters from Cissy—news that I am uncle of 15 months standing. Have Gen. Wainwright's canteen for him [*nephew Morris Minton Jr.*]

Sept. 3, 1945

Arrived Manila about 2:00 p.m.—to Admiral Hotel

Up 5:30. Took off from Nielson Airstrip about 8:00 AM. Landed at Luna (Union Province) about 9:30 a.m. By auto up Naguilian Rd. to Baguio. The destruction wrought on Baguio was enough to make you sick. It was such a beautiful place.

Met [*Maj.*] General Edmond H. Leavey (*A&M Class of 1915*), [*Lt.*] Gen. Wilhelm Styer (Chief of Staff) and [*Maj.*] Gen. Percy W. Clarkson [*A&M Class of 1915*], 33rd Division. Lunch at Guest House with fireplace + fire. Surrender ceremony at High Commissioner's Baguio Home at

Camp John Hay. Gen. Wainwright got 1st pen at this ceremony too.

Back to Lima + flight to Manila. Circled Stotsenberg + Clark Field. Dinner this p.m. at Gen. Wilhelm Styer's. Beautiful dinner and private movie (Shirley Temple). Met a [Lt.] Gen. [Sir Frederick Arthur Montague "Boy"] Browning [deputy commander of First Allied Airborne Army during Operation Market Garden in Europe and husband of author Daphne du Maurier] who was awfully nice to me. Johnny Pugh stopped by the Behrenstein's after dinner (Hilda). I went on home. [Col.] Henry [C.] Wendler [A&M Class of 1934] stopped by. Called Joe Aston [A&M Class of 1934].

Sept. 4, 1945

Joe Aston + friend—Maj. Ross came down about 10:00 a.m. Jean DeLong (American Red Cross) + Capt. Reed for breakfast. [Jean Stoy DeLong joined the American Red Cross in her effort to find her husband, Capt. C. W. DeLong, a dentist captured when the Philippines were surrendered to the Japanese and drowned when Americans sank his unmarked prison ship. (Courtesy Susan Robbins Watson, Manager, Historical Programs and Collections, American Red Cross, Washington, DC.)] With Jean to American Red Cross Headquarters for mail. None for me. Johnny Pugh letter with news of death of youngest brother. To lunch with Mrs. MacArthur. Delightful person. [Col. Gerald] Jerry Graham (aide-de-camp [to Gen. MacArthur, responsible for Jean Marie Faircloth, MacArthur's second wife, and their son] very hospitable. Told Mrs. MacArthur about ("Bless Little Arthur"). Talked with Joe most of p.m. Johnny Pugh + I to dinner with Matilde Zóbel [y Montojo] and Sylvia Melian. Saw Lewis Brown. [John] Adams of CBS in room after our return. Must write to Chas. Stahler + Ormond [R.] Simpson '36.

Sept. 5, 1945

Up early—to Nichols. Take off 8 AM. Arrive Guam 5:30 PM. Jimmie Oppenheimer's wife. [Katherine "Kitty" Puening Harrison Oppenheimer] Lt. Gen. [Benjamin F.] Giles (Army Air Force) [Commanding General US Army Forces Africa-Middle East], Mineola, Tex., met up and we stayed at his place. [Lt. Col. Sidney] Sid Huff [aide to MacArthur for nineteen years] and J. Howard Pyle (NBC) on our trip. Sid as personal representative of Gen. MacArthur. Gen.

After the war ended, 127 Texas Aggies still assigned to the Pacific Theatre managed to gather for the Aggie Muster at Malinta Tunnel, Corregidor Island, on 21 April 1946. Photo courtesy Texas A&M University Archives.

Supreme Allied Commander Gen. Dwight D. Eisenhower speaking at the 1946 Aggie Muster in Kyle Field on the Texas A&M campus Easter Sunday. Lt. Col. Tom Dooley stands at far left, next to Col. Olin E. "Tiger" Teague, '32. Eisenhower spoke of "the magnificent contribution made by your college in the gaining of the allied victory of 1945. . . . The ROTC of this one institution furnished the Army seven thousand officers, far more than any other college." Recent estimates place the figure nearer fourteen thousand. Photo courtesy Texas A&M University Archives.

Barney M. Giles [*twin brother of Benjamin Giles, helped develop strategic bombing theory and practice*] + aide Maj. Chesley wonderful hosts. Maj. Cross (Spac) and Billy Large (full colonel) came by.

Sept. 6, 1945

Took off from Guam strip about 8:30 a.m. Cross brought several *Texas Aggie* newspapers to plane. Enjoyed them. Willie Fitzgerald sent donation for me to A&M Fund. Willie is tops. Hope to see Joe McHaney '35 at Pearl Harbor. Arrived Kwajalein about 6:30 p.m. for fuel.

Sept. 6, 1945

At Kwajalein our party was entertained by Commodore Ben Wyatt (the [*Marshall*] Islands commander + a classmate of Capt. Kenneth Hoeffel.) Wonderful steaks and it was while at dinner that the General received radiogram: "President has submitted to the Senate nomination for temporary appointment as General, Army of the United States for Lt. Gen. Jonathan M. Wainwright, 0–2131, US Army." Received at Kwajalein Guest House at 8:00 p.m. Sept. 6. Before plane took off I saw Cavalry Major William R. Manor [*former C Troop—A&M Class of 1944*]. He is enroute to Philippine Islands. Am going to work over M/Sgt. Carroll this a.m.

FLIGHT → Manila—Guam—Kwajalein—Oahu—Hamilton Field [*San Francisco*]—Washington, DC

Perkins, M.M.	Capt	1st Pilot
Stephenson, D.	Capt	Co-Pilot
Collins, H.A.	Capt	Navigator
Smith, W.H.	1st LT	2nd Nav
Prescott, E.H.	Sgt	Radio Oper
Tarbell, G.D.	Sgt	Engineer
Hunter, P.E.	Sgt	2nd Radio Oper
Crosby, L.	Cpt.	Flight Clerk

Postscript

Dooley arrived back in the states after four years of military service during World War II, most of those on the front lines of the battle, and much of it as a Japanese prisoner of war. He remained in service, first being assigned to temporary duty in the Adjutant General's Office in Washington, DC, for POW orientation, and then held assignments at 4th Army Headquarters at Fort Sam Houston, Texas. He commanded the 717th Tank Battalion and the 72nd Heavy Tank Battalion at Ft. Lewis, Washington and was an instructor at the Command and General Staff College at Ft. Leavenworth, Kansas. After language school in Monterey, California and several months of orientation in Washington, DC, he served a two-year assignment as Army Attaché in Czechoslovakia.

In February 1957, he became Asst. Chief of Staff G-3 and headed a Combat Command at Fort Hood, Texas, for two years before serving a year as Chief of Staff at Ft. Stewart, Georgia, followed by a three-year assignment overseeing Automated Fire Support Elements in Naples, Italy. Dooley returned stateside to serve as Director of Instruction at the Armed Forces Staff College in Norfolk, Virginia and Chief of Staff of the Armored Command and Deputy Post Commander at Ft. Knox, Kentucky, retiring on February 28, 1969.

In 1978, Dooley briefly summarized his life and left a message of mission, commitment, and service in his Aggie Muster Address delivered April 21 in the G. Rollie White Coliseum at Texas A&M University:

> Bill, Lisa, Doctor Williams, Doctor Miller and all you people that are too kind.
>
> That's great. Forgive me . . . you start to get overcome when you come back to this school. I have. I want to thank you for asking me, including my wife, to this '78 Muster. Kind of chokes you up a little bit, but I'll simmer down in a minute.

I want to greet the class of '33. I hope you have a nice reunion, and I hope you say sometime during this period, "I wish we'd been nicer to the class of '35."

When I look around on this visit and especially at this group tonight, it reminds me of that commercial—"You've come a long way baby." I recall—I remember it well—that on December 3rd, 1931, a group of us walked up to the old administration building to look at the bulletin board outside the Sgt. Major's office—Sgt. Major King—because that's where they posted the first semester grades. You went up there to learn whether you'd be there next week. But what impressed me—what I'd remembered today—was at the top of the list it said "total enrollment: 1,975 students." I'm sure that's hard for all of you to realize. I'm sorry I didn't go far enough with my research to find out how many were there a week later. But it's a great change, and I'm happy to see the progress made by adding all these beautiful girls too.

People mention these musters as beginning in 1883, or some say in 1903, and that they were held intermittently during those periods from 1883 through the 1920s. But as far as I can ascertain, and I spent four years here during the '30s, none were shown on the records. Perhaps we that attended in that period of the depression couldn't afford a muster. But they're great.

Of course the reason Joe Marshall invited me is because I happened to be in a certain occurrence in World War II, and I'm happy to come here and tell about that because I've wanted to do it ever since I came back during World War II.

A group of us were stationed in the Philippines. Although there were a number of Aggies there, quite a number of Aggies arrived on the ships on November the 28th, 1941, just in time for the war to start on December the 8th for us because we were across the international dateline.

As a result of the Pearl Harbor attack, we were sort of out on a limb there because our resupply was completely cut off. We were immediately rationed—we had to ration ammunition and food because our mission then was to hold on as long as possible to prevent the Japanese from expanding further south, so that the

Lt. Col. Tom Dooley, '35, addressed the 1978 Aggie Muster in G. Rollie White Coliseum on the Texas A&M campus. He told how he managed to send out the report of the Aggie Muster on Corregidor in April 1942, a few weeks before the bastion was surrendered to the Japanese. "Because they [*the Aggies on the Rock*] could not be spared from their positions," he said, "we had a roll call, and a muster is a roll call." Photo by Jerry C. Cooper, '63.

troops back home could take that time to effect a build-up and recoup their losses and then start a successful campaign to end in Tokyo. I might add, to we who were there, it took them an awful long time.

But, early in December the Japanese landed on Luzon Island to the north and moved south. We effected a retrograde movement—US troops and Philippine troops, and did as well as we could—it did take time—and finally the pressure came to bear to the extent that Bataan, the peninsula down there, was forced to surrender on April the 8th, 1942. With that, the Japanese were able to move heavy artillery into positions where they could fire on the last US position, which was Corregidor Island. Having air superiority and heavy artillery to bear, the troops on Corregidor just had to dig in deeper. Naturally, movement was limited and communications were limited.

Along in mid-April, Gen. George F. Moore—who was spoken of earlier—called me in. We were at adjacent headquarters in a tunnel protected by heavy rock. It was mentioned that General Moore was the class of 1908. I'd like to mention also that he was commandant of the Cadets and Professor of Military Science and Tactics in the '30s. At that time he was commanding the harbor defenses of Manila and Subic Bay, and it was the last point that the Japanese had not occupied.

General Moore wanted to discuss the thought of the upcoming April 21st. Of course, he'd heard of past musters, but I didn't. But he knew that I was an Aggie. He said that he wanted to get a list of the Aggies still fighting there. Although the account nowadays says that they gathered on April 21st, it was impossible for that number of people to congregate because they could not be spared from their positions. So, we had a roll call, and a muster is a roll call. We got all of the Aggies listed, and I contacted one of the two correspondents still on the island. I don't remember whether he was UP or AP, but he was willing to use his carefully apportioned time—wire time—
to get a story back to the States. We termed it the "Aggie Story."

At that time it served several purposes. It gave a good plug for the state of Texas, which was a long ways away. It gave a good plug for Texas A&M, and it also served the purpose of notifying parents and wives at home of those that were still living and still fighting, because of the communication limitations there.

So, of that group which included those Aggies, we were unlike those at San Jacinto—we weren't successful in our fight— Corregidor was surrendered about two weeks later. It was May the 6th, 1942. Then came a long wait, and the survivors came back in the summer of '45, and that's when they learned that the Musters had sparked and continued during World War II. I'm sure some of you were here, but I was fortunate enough to attend the one on Kyle Field in 1946. Of course that's when they really got going, and it is a great pleasure to be at this one today.

So, that's my story on the Muster at Corregidor. Let's hope that this tradition, rekindled in the time of war, will long endure in the time of peace.

Thank you.

We, acting by command of and in behalf of the Emperor of Japan, the Japanese Government and the Japanese Imperial General Headquarters, hereby accept the provisions set forth in the declaration issued by the heads of the Governments of the United States, China and Great Britain on 26 July 1945, at Potsdam, and subsequently adhered to by the Union of Soviet Socialist Republics, which four powers are hereafter referred to as the Allied Powers.

We hereby proclaim the unconditional surrender to the Allied Powers of the Japanese Imperial General Headquarters and of all Japanese armed forces and all armed forces under Japanese control wherever situated.

We hereby command all Japanese forces wherever situated and the Japanese people to cease hostilities forthwith, to preserve and save from damage all ships, aircraft, and military and civil property and to comply with all requirements which may be imposed by the Supreme Commander for the Allied Powers or by agencies of the Japanese Government at his direction.

We hereby command the Japanese Imperial General Headquarters to issue at once orders to the Commanders of all Japanese forces and all forces under Japanese control wherever situated to surrender unconditionally themselves and all forces under their control.

We hereby command all civil, military and naval officials to obey and enforce all proclamations, orders and directives deemed by the Supreme Commander for the Allied Powers to be proper to effectuate this surrender and issued by him or under his authority and we direct all such officials to remain at their posts and to continue to perform their non-combatant duties unless specifically relieved by him or under his authority.

We hereby undertake for the Emperor, the Japanese Government and their successors to carry out the provisions of the Potsdam Declaration in good faith, and to issue whatever orders and take whatever action may be required by the Supreme Commander for the Allied Powers or by any other designated representative of the Allied Powers for the purpose of giving effect to that Declaration.

We hereby command the Japanese Imperial Government and the Japanese Imperial General Headquarters at once to liberate all allied prisoners of war and civilian internees now under Japanese control and to provide for their protection, care, maintenance and immediate transportation to places as directed.

The authority of the Emperor and the Japanese Government to rule the state shall be subject to the Supreme Commander for the Allied Powers who will take such steps as he deems proper to effectuate these terms of surrender.

Signed at TOKYO BAY, JAPAN at 0904 on the SECOND day of SEPTEMBER, 1945

> MAMORU SHIGEMITSU
> By Command and in behalf of the Emperor of Japan and the Japanese Government

> YOSHIJIRO UMEZU
> By Command and in behalf of the Japanese Imperial General Headquarters

Accepted at TOKYO BAY, JAPAN at 0908 on the SECOND day of SEPTEMBER, 1945, for the United States, Republic of China, United Kingdom and the Union of Soviet Socialist Republics, and in the interests of the other United Nations at war with Japan.

> DOUGLAS MacARTHUR
> Supreme Commander for the Allied Powers

C. W. NIMITZ
United States Representative

HSU YUNG-CH'ANG
Republic of China Representative

BRUCE FRASER
United Kingdom Representative

KUZMA DEREVYANKO
Union of Soviet Socialist Republics Representative

THOMAS BLAMEY
Commonwealth of Australia Representative

LAWRENCE MOORE COSGRAVE
Dominion of Canada Representative

JACQUES Le CLERC
Provisional Government of the French Republic Representative

C. E. L. HELFRICH
Kingdom of the Netherlands Representative

LEONARD M. ISITT
Dominion of New Zealand Representative

INSTRUMENT OF SURRENDER
of the
**Japanese and Japanese-Controlled Armed Forces
in the Philippine Islands**
to the
**Commanding General
United States Army Forces, Western Pacific.**

Camp John Hay
Baguio, Mountain
Province,
Luzon, Philippine Islands
3 September 1945

Pursuant to and in accordance with the proclamation of the Emperor of Japan accepting the terms set forth in the declaration issued by the heads of the Governments of the United States, Great Britain, and China on 26 July 1945, at Potsdam and subsequently adhered to by the Union of Soviet Socialist Republics; and to the formal instrument of surrender of the Japanese Imperial Government and the Japanese Imperial General Headquarters signed at Tokyo Bay at 0908 on 2 September 1945:

1. Acting by command of and in behalf of the Emperor of Japan, the Japanese Imperial Government and the Japanese Imperial General Headquarters, We hereby surrender unconditionally to the Commanding General, United States Army Forces, Western Pacific, all Japanese and Japanese-controlled armed forces, air, sea, ground and auxiliary, in the Philippine Islands.

2. We hereby command all Japanese forces wherever situated in the Philippine Islands to cease hostilities forthwith, to preserve and save from damage all ships, aircraft, and military and civil property, and to

comply with all requirements which may be imposed by the Commanding General, United States Army Forces, Western Pacific, or his authorized representatives.

3. We hereby direct the commanders of all Japanese forces in the Philippine Islands to issue at once to all forces under their command to surrender unconditionally themselves and all forces under their control, as prisoners of war, to the nearest United States Army Force Commander.

4. We hereby direct the commanders of all Japanese forces in the Philippine Islands to surrender intact and in good order to the nearest United States Army Force Commander, at times and at places directed by him, all equipment and supplies of whatever nature under their control.

5. We hereby direct the commanders of all Japanese forces in the Philippine Islands at once to liberate all Allied prisoners of war and civilian internees under their control, and to provide for their protection, care, maintenance and immediate transportation to places as directed by the nearest United States Army Force Commander.

6. We hereby undertake to transmit the directives as given in Paragraphs 1 through 5, above, to all Japanese forces in the Philippine Islands immediately by all means within our power, and further to furnish to the Commanding General, United States Army Forces, Western Pacific, all necessary Japanese emissaries fully empowered to bring about the surrender of Japanese forces in the Philippine Islands with whom we are not in contact.

7. We hereby undertake to furnish immediately to the Commanding General, United States Army Forces, Western Pacific, a statement of the designation, numbers, location and commanders of all Japanese armed forces, ground, sea, or air, in the Philippine Islands.

8. We hereby undertake faithfully to obey all further proclamation, orders and directives deemed by the Commanding General, United States Armed Forces, Western Pacific, to be proper to effectuate this surrender.

Signed at Camp John Hay, Baguio, Mountain Province, Luzon, Philippine Islands, at 1210 hours 3 September 1945:

TOMOYUKI YAMASHITA,
General,
Imperial Japanese Army
Highest Commander, Imperial
Japanese Army in the Philippines.

DENHICI OKOCHI,
Vice Admiral,
Imperial Japanese Navy,
Highest Commander, Imperial
Japanese Navy in the Philippines.

By command and in behalf
of the Japanese Imperial
General Headquarters

Accepted at Camp John Hay, Baguio, Mountain Province Luzon
Philippine Islands, at 1210 hours 3 September 1945:
For the Commander-in-Chief, United States Army Forces, Pacific:

EDMOND H. LEAVEY,
Major General, USA
Deputy Commander, United States Army Forces
Western Pacific.

In Dooley's third journal he created a listing of 158 American officers held in Prison Camp #4 at Karenko, Taiwan. Details on each individual include rank, military branch, command unit, and location and date of capture.

American Officers Taiwan Prison Camp #4, Karenko, Tom Dooley Aug. 17, 1942–June 7, 1943

Name	Command at Time Rank	Branch	Where + When of Capture	Captured
Aldridge, Edwin E.	COL.	INFANTRY	C. of S. 51st Div. P.A.+ Left Sub-Sector,	BATAAN 4-9-42
Amis, William N.	COL.	AIR CORPS	C.O. Air Ser. Comd.	BATAAN 4-9-42
Atkinson, Edward C.	COL.	INFANTRY	42nd Inf. P.A.	BATAAN 4-9-42
Ausmus, Delbert	COL.	C.A.C.	Beach Def. Ft. Mills	CORREGIDOR
Balsam, Alfred S.	COL.	QMC	I Corps Q.M.	BATAAN 4-9-42
Beebe, Lewis C.	BRIG. GEN.	GSC INFANTRY	CofS USFIP	COR. 5-7-42
Bell, Gilmer M.	COL.	IGD	I.G. Luzon For.	BATAAN 4-9-42
Berry, Karie L.	COL.	INF.	C.O. 1st Reg. Div. P.A.	BATAAN 4-9-42
Bluemel, Clifford	BRIG. GEN.	(INF)	C.G. 31st Div. P.A.	BATAAN 4-9-42
Boatwright, John R.	COL.	INF.	C.O. 53rd Inf. P.A.	BATAAN 4-9-42
Bonham, Roscoe	COL. (P.S.)	ENG.	Asst. Eng. USFIP	BATAAN 4-9-42
Boudreau, Napoleon	COL.	CAC	C.O. Ft. Frank	FT. FRANK 5-8-42
Bowler, Louis J.	COL.	CAC	CofS P.C.A.C. - Act'g G-1 AG - HIDM +	COR. 5-7-42
Braddock, Wm. H.	COL. (ORC)	M.C.	Surg. V-M Force	MIND.
Braly, Wm. C.	COL.	CAC	S-3 HOM + SB	COR. 5-7-42

Name	Rank	Corps	Assignment	Location
Brawner, Pembroke A.	COL.	(INF) GSC	G-4 Ser. Comd.	BATAAN 4-9-42
Brezina, Frank	COL. (P.S. Ret.)	QMC	QM Ser Comd.	BATAAN 4-9-42
Brougher, Wm. E.	BRIG. GEN.	(INF)	C.G. 11th Div. P.A.	BATAAN 4-9-42
Brown, Burton R.	MAJOR	(CAC) ADC	ADC Maj. Gen. Moore	COR. 5-7-42
Browne, Harrison C.	COL.	(INF) GSC	CofS Phil. Div.	BATAAN 4-9-42
Bunker, Paul D.	COL.	CAC	Seaward Defense HDM + SB	COR. 5-7-42
Callahan, James W. Jr.	COL. (P.S.)	INF.	P.M. II Corps	BATAAN 4-9-42
Campbell, Alexander H.	COL.	CAC	Chief - Aircraft Warning Service	BATAAN 4-9-42
Carter, James D.	COL. P.S.	INF.	Ex.O., 92nd INF. P.A.	BATAAN 4-9-42
Chase, Theodore M.	COL.		C.O. 60th C.A. (AA) C.O. AA DEF.	COR. 5-7-42
Chastaine, Ben Hur	COL.		C.O. AGUSAN SECT.	MIND.
Christie, Albert E.	COL.		C.O. 61st Div.	
Churchill, Lawrence S.	BRIG. GEN.		C.O. F.E.A.F.	BATAAN 4-9-42
Chenoweth, Bradford G.	COL.	(INF)	C.G. VISAYAN FOR.	CEBU
Collier, James V.	COL. P.S.	(FA) G.S.C.	G-3 LUZON FOR.	BATAAN 4-9-42
Cook, John D.	COL.	QMC	C.O. CEBU PORT ADV. DEP.	CEBU
Cooper, Webb E.	COL.	M.C.	SURG - USFIP	COR. 5-7-42
Cordero, Virgil N.	COL.	INF	C.O. 72ND INF. P.A.	BATAAN 4-9-42

Name	Rank	Branch	Command at Time of Capture	Where + When Captured
Corkill, Wm. E.	COL.	FA	EXEC. TO CofS LUZON FOR. F.A.	BATAAN 4-9-42
Cornel, Theodore M.	COL.	INF	C.O. SAMAR-LEYTE SEC.	LEYTE 5-26-42
Cottrell, Joseph F.	COL.	CAC	EX.O. (CofS) HDM +SB	COR. 5-7-42
Creusere, Melville S.	COL.	F.A.	Q.M. V-M FORCE	
Crews, Leonard R.	COL.	CAC	G-4 HDM +SB	COR. 5-7-42
Dalton, Wm. F.	COL.	INF.	C.O. RESERVE - V.M. FOR.	
DeCarre, Octave	COL.	CAC	C.O. 92ND C.A. (T.D.) P.S.	COR. 5-7-42
Doane, Irvin E.	COL.	INF.	C.O. PROV. A.C. REGT.	BATAAN 4-9-42
Dooley Thomas	MAJOR (ORC)	(CAV) ADC.	AIDE-DE-CAMP TO LT. GEN.	COR. 5-7-42
Dougherty, Louis R.	COL.	F.A.	II CORPS ART. OFF.	BATAAN 4-9-42
Drake, Charles C.	BRIG. GEN.	(QMC)	QM - USFIP	COR. 5-7-42
Dumas, Albert H.	COL.	INF.	3rd INF. 1stRES. DIV. P.A.	BATAAN 4-9-42
Elmes, Chester H.	COL.	QMC	Q.M. HDM +SB	COR. 5-7-42
Enos, Wm. A.	COL.	F.D.	F.O. V-M. FORCE	MIND.
Fortier, Malcolm V.	COL.	INF.	SR. INST. 41st DIV. P.A.	BATAAN 4-9-42
Foster, Valentine P.	COL.	CAC	C.O. FT. HUGHES	FT. HUGHES 5-8-42
Frissell, Howard N.	COL.	INF	C.O. COM. ZONE -V-M-FOR	MIND.
Fry, Philip T.	COL.	INF	C.O. REF. CAMP SER. COMD.	BATAAN 4-9-42
Funk, Arnold J.	BRIG. GEN.	(INF)	CofS LUZON FORCE	BATAAN 4-9-42

Name	Rank	Branch	Assignment	Location
Galbraith, Nicoll F.	COL.	(FA) G.S.C.	G-4 USFIP	COR. 5-7-42
Garfinkel, Abraham	COL. (P.S.)	INF.	IG + JAG - II CORPS	BATAAN 4-9-42
Gillespie, James O.	COL.	M.C.	C.O. GEN. HOSP #2 BATAAN	BATAAN 4-9-42
Glattley, Harold W.	LT. COL.	M.C.	SURG. - LUZON FORCE	BATAAN 4-9-42
Halstead, Earl T.	LT. COL.	AGD (ORC)	A.G. - LUZON FORCE	BATAAN 4-9-42
Hamilton, Stuart A.	COL.	CWS	CHEM. OFF. - USFIP	COR. 5-7-42
Hilton Roy C.	COL.	(INF) GSC	G-4 LUZON FORCE	BATAAN 4-9-42
Hilsman, Roger	COL.	INF.	C.O. NEGROS I. V-M FOR	
Hilton, Donald B.	COL.	INF.	IN HOSP #2 AT TIME OF	BATAAN 4-9-42
Hirsch, George W.	COL.	O.D.	ORD. OFF. USFIP	COR. 5-7-42
Hoffman, Robert G.	COL.	(INF) GSC	G-3-PHIL. DIV.	BATAAN 4-9-42
Hughes, James C.	COL.	FA	C.O. 11th F.A. P.A.	BATAAN 4-9-42
Ives, Albert R.	COL.	FA	C.O. PROV. F.A. BRIG.	BATAAN 4-9-42
James, Stanley L.	COL.	S.C.	SIG. OFF. SER. COMD.	BATAAN 4-9-42
Johnson, Edwin H.	COL.	INF.	C.O. 32nd INF. P.A.	BATAAN 4-9-42
Jones, Albert M.	MAJ. GEN.	(INF)	CG - I CORPS	BATAAN 4-9-42
Keltner, Edgar H.	COL.	INF	CofS 91st DIV. P.A.	BATAAN 4-9-42
Killen, Wade D.	COL.	INF	CofS 101st DIV. P.A.	MIND.
King, Edward P. Jr.	MAJ. GEN.	(F.A.)	C.G. LUZON FORCE	BATAAN 4-9-42
Kohn, Joseph P.	COL.	CAC	C.O. 91st CA (PS)	COR. 5-7-42
Laughinghouse, Newman	COL.	AIR CORPS	AIR OFF. USFIP	COR. 5-7-42

Name	Rank	Branch	Command at Time of Capture	Where + When Captured
Lathrop, Leslie T.	COL.	INF.	C.O. INF. 1st REG. DIV. P.A.	BATAAN 4-9-42
Lawrence, Charles S.	COL.	QMC	QM LUZON FORCE	BATAAN 4-9-42
Lilly, Edmund J.	COL.	INF.	C.O. 57th INF. (PS)	BATAAN 4-9-42
Lough, Maxon S.	BRIG. GEN.	(INF)	C.G. PHIL. DIV.	BATAAN 4-9-42
Lynch, Thomas A.	COL.	JAGD (RET)	JAG USFIP	COR. 5-7-42
MacDonald, Stuart C.	COL.	INF.	C.O. 91st DIV. P.A.	BATAAN 4-9-42
Maher, Wm. F.	COL.	(FA) G.S.C.	CofS I CORPS	BATAAN 4-9-42
Mallonee, Richard C.	COL.	F.A.	SR. INST. 21st FA.. P.A.	BATAAN 4-9-42
Manees, James R.	COL.	(INF) IGD	P.M. SER. COMD.	BATAAN 4-9-42
Marshall, Floyd	COL.	(INF) G.S.C.	G-1 LUZON FORCE	BATAAN 4-9-42
McBride, Allan C.	BRIG. GEN.	(FA) (GSC)	C.G. SER. COM'D.	BATAAN 4-9-42
McCafferty, Grattan H.	COL.	INF.	G 1-3, SER. COM'D.	BATAAN 4-9-42
McLennon, Carter R.	COL.	CAV.	EX. O. NEGROS, V-M	
Mead, Wallace A.	COL.	INF.	SR. INST. 23rd INF. P.A.	BATAAN 4-9-42
Menzie, James T.	COL.	AGD	AG USFIP	COR. 5-7-42
Mielenz, Lloyd E.	COL.	C.E.	EX. OFF. TO ENG. OFF USFIP	COR. 5-7-42
Mixon, Archibald M.	COL.	INF.	DEP. CofS V-M FORCE	MIND.
Monihan, James G.	COL.	(CAV) GSC	CofS SOUTH SUB-SEC. - I CORPS	BATAAN 4-9-42
Moore, Arthur P.	COL.	FA	ART. OFF. SOUTH SUB-SECT. I	BATAAN 4-9-42

Name	Rank	Branch	Assignment	Location/Date
Moore, George F.	MAJ. GEN.	(CAC)	CG-PCAC + HDM + SB.	COR. 5-7-42
Morse, Wm. P.	COL.	INF.	C.O. 101st DIV. P.A.	MIND.
Murphy, Dennis P.	COL.	INF.	C.O. 1st INF 1st R. DIV. P.A.	BATAAN 4-9-42
Nelson, Frank	COL.	(CAV) GSC	G-3 I CORPS	BATAAN 4-9-42
O'Connor, Edwin	COL.	CAV.	SR. INST. 2nd REG. DIV. P.A.	BATAAN 4-9-42
O'Day, Ray M.	COL.	INF.	SR. INST. 21st DIV. P.a.	BATAAN 4-9-42
Parker, Geo. M. Jr.	MAJ. GEN.	(INF)	C.G. II CORPS	BATAAN 4-9-42
Peck, Harry M.	COL. (NG)	CAC	C.O. 515th CAC	BATAAN 4-9-42
Penrose, Arthur W.	COL.	(INF) GSC	G-2 PHIL. DIV.	BATAAN 4-9-42
Pierce, Clinton A.	BRIG. GEN.	(CAV)	C.G. SOUTH SUB-SECT. I CORPS	BATAAN 4-9-42
Pilet, Nunez C.	COL.	(INF) GSC	G-1 USFIP	COR. 5-7-42
Pugh, John R.	LT. COL.	(CAV) ADC	G-2 USFIP + ADC TO LT. GEN. WAIN.	COR. 5-7-42
Quesenberry, Marshall H.	COL.	(INF) GSC	G-4 PHIL. DIV.	BATAAN 4-9-42
Quinn, Michael A.	COL.	QMC	CHIEF - MOTOR TRANSP. LUZON	BATAAN 4-9-42
Quintard, Alexander S.	COL.	FA	C.O. 301st F.A. P.A.	BATAAN 4-9-42
Rawitser, Emil C.	COL.	JAGD	ASST. JAG - USFIP	COR. 5-7-42
Richards, Harrison H.C.	COL.	A.C.	C.O. A.C. DET. SIG. HILL	BATAAN 4-9-42
Rodman, John H.	COL.	INF.	C.O. 92nd INF. P.A.	BATAAN 4-9-42
Rogers, Richard G.	COL.	QMC	TRAFFIC CONTROL OFF. LUZON	BATAAN 4-9-42
Rutherford, Dorsey J.	COL.	CAC	C.O. PROV. REGT. HDM+SB	COR. 5-7-42

Name	Rank	Branch	Command at Time of Capture	Where + When Captured
Sage, Charles G.	COL. (NG)	CAC	C.O. PRO. PHIL. C.A.C. BRIG.	BATAAN 4-9-42
Scudder, Irvin C.	COL.	INF.	CofS VISAYAN FOR. C.O. CEBU	
Seals, Carl H.	BRIG. GEN.	(AGD)	AG-USFIP (ENROUTE TO AUSTRALIA)	MIND.
Selleck, Clyde A.	COL.	F.A.	CofS SER. COM'D	BATAAN 4-9-42
Sharp, Wm. E.	MAJ. GEN.	(F.A.)	C.G. V-M FORCE	MIND.
Sherry, Dean	MAJ. (ORC)	INF.	HQ 71st DIV. P.A.	BATAAN 4-9-42
Skerry, Harry A.	COL.	CE	ENG. OFF. I CORPS	BATAAN 4-9-42
Sledge, Theodore J.	COL.	INF.	ADM. EX. TO CofS USFIP	COR. 5-7-42
Stansell, Joshua A.	COL.	S.C.	SIG. OFF. LUZON FORCE	BATAAN 4-9-42
Steele, Charles L.	COL.	INF.	CofS II CORPS	BATAAN 4-9-42
Stickney, Henry H.	COL.	CE	ENG. OFF. USFIP	COR. 5-7-42
Stowell, Allen L.	COL.	S.C.	SIG. OFF. II CORPS	BATAAN 4-9-42
Swanton, Donavon	COL.	INF.	ST. INST. PROV. REGT. 2nd REG. DIV.	BATAAN 4-9-42
Teague, Theodore T.	COL.	S.C.	SIG. OFF. USFIP	COR. 5-7-42
Thompson, John W.	COL.	INF.	CofS V-M FORCE	MIND.
Townsend, Glenn R.	COL.	INF.	C.O. 11th INF. P.A.	BATAAN 4-9-42
Traywick, Jesse T. Jr.	COL.	(INF) GSC	G-3 - USFIP	COR. 5-7-42

Name	Rank	Branch	Position	Location/Date
Uhrig, Jacob E.	COL.	INF.	SR. INST. 22 INF. P.A.	BATAAN 4-9-42
Vachon, Joseph P.	BRIG. GEN.	(INF)	C.O. 101st DIV. P.A.	MIND.
Vance, Lee C.	COL.	CAV	C.O. 26th CAV. (PS)	BATAAN 4-9-42
Vance, John R.	COL.	FD	F.O. USFIP	COR. 5-7-42
Wainwright, Jonathan M.	LT. GEN.	(CAV)	C.G. USFIP	COR. 5-7-42
Ward, Frederick A.	COL.	P.S.	SUPT. ATS - USFIP	COR. 5-7-42
Weaver, James R.N.	BRIG. GEN.	(INF.)	C.G. PROV. TK GRP.	BATAAN 4-9-42
Wetherby, Loren A.	COL.	INF.	SR. INST. 41st INF. P.A.	BATAAN 4-9-42
Williams, Everett C.	COL.	F.A.	CH. Of ART - LUZON FOR.	BATAAN 4-9-42
Wilson, Albert T.	COL.	INF	C.O. ZAMBOANGA SEC.	MIND.
Wood, Stuart	COL.	F.A.	G-2 USFIP	MIND. (ENROUTE
Worthington, Josiah W.	COL.	V.C.	VET. OFF. LUZON FOR.	AT SEA
Young, Adlai C.	COL.	INF.	C.O. 51st DIV. P.A.	BATAAN 4-9-42

--NAVY--

Name	Rank	Branch	Position	Location/Date
Curtis, Donald	COL.	USMC	EX. OFF. 4th MARINES + BEACH DEF.	COR. 5-7-42
Davis, Robert G.	CAPT.	(M.C.) USN	C.O. NAVAL HOSP. MANILA	MANILA 1-2-42
Hoeffel, Kenneth M.	CAPT.	USN	COMDT. 16th NAVAL DIST. COR.	COR. 5-7-42
Howard, Samuel L.	COL.	USMC	C.O. 4th MARINES	COR. 5-7-42
Lowman, Kenneth E.	CAPT.	(MC) USN	CHIEF SURGEON - NAVAL HOSP.	MANILA 1-2-42

Name	Rank	Branch	Command at Time of Capture	Where + When Captured
McMillin, George J.	CAPT.	USN	GOVERNOR OF GUAM	GUAM 12-10-41
Roberts, Lyle J.	CAPT.	(MC) USN	EX. OFF. NAVAL HOSP. MANILA	MANILA 1-2-42
Wilterdink, Wm. H.	CAPT.	(SUPPLY) USN	ATTCHD - US NAVAL HOSP. MANILA	MANILA 1-2-42
Stevens, Luther	BR. GEN.	(P.C.)	WEST SUB-SECTOR 1 CORPS -	BATAAN 4-9-42
Horan, John P.	COL.	INF.		
Mitchell, Eugene	COL.	INF.	C.O. 61 INF. (P.A.)	MIND. 5-2-42
Tarkington, Hiram	COL.	F.A.	C.O. 61 F.A. (PA)	MIND. 5-2-42
Dodson, Thomas A.	CAPT.	131st F.A. (NE)	C.O. BAT. E, 131st F.A.	MADURA N.E.I. MAR.
Ferrey, James P.	1st. LT.	A.C.		
Levitt, Herbert A.	ENSIGN	U.S.N.	COMMUNICATIONS OFF. USS	

Throughout his journals Tom Dooley refers to books he is reading, beginning with William Shirer's Berlin Diary *on 12 January 1942. In his third journal he lists books he has read or talked about with other prisoners, and he expands the list in his fourth and sixth journals. The list includes just over two hundred entries ranging from a sixteenth-century autobiography to contemporary novels. It paints Dooley as a man of letters and suggests his perspective on the events surrounding him.*

The bracketed question mark following some titles indicates that the editor was unable to identify those titles independently. The numbers preceding several titles early in this list likely are call numbers for the library in the Manila Club, where Dooley was first confined.

Third (Red Band) Journal

F485 *Reading I've Liked: A Personal Selection Drawn from Two Decades of Reading and Reviewing*—Clifton Fadiman, 1941

B229 *The Saint in Miami*—Leslie Charteris, 1940

Chivalry—Rafael Sabatini, 1935

A13 *Sick Heart River*—John Buchan, 1941

A12 *Mr. Standfast*—John Buchan, 1919

F425 *Two Years before the Mast*—Richard Henry Dana Jr., 1840

A86 *Under Capricorn*—Helen de Guerry Simpson, 1937

A111 *A Passage to India*—E. M. Forster, 1924

A19 *A Tale of Two Cities*—Charles Dickens, 1859

Bomber Command—Brig. Simpson [?]

A34 *Tom Brown's School Days*—Thomas Hughes, 1857

A2 *The Crowthers of Bankdam*—Thomas Armstrong, 1940

A1 *Anthony Adverse*—Hervey Allen, 1933

A182 *Lost Horizon*—James Hilton, 1933

A130 *The Scarlet Pimpernel*—Baroness Orczy, 1905

A169 *The Sword of Islam*—Rafael Sabatini, 1939

The Doctor: A Novel—Mary Roberts Rinehart, 1936
The Silver Bride—Ethel M. Dell, 1932

Fourth (Black Band) Journal

Stars on the Sea—F. Van Wyck Mason, 1940
The Legion Book—Captain H. Cotton Minchin, ed., 1929
Psychology and Leadership—J. H. Burns, 1934
A Short History of the World—H. G. Wells, 1922
Berlin Diary—William L. Shirer, 1941
Soldiers in the Sun: An Adventure in Imperialism—
    William Thaddeus Sexton, 1939 (read in Bataan)
Reader's Digest magazine
Fortune magazine—May 1939 issue
Esquire magazine
The Story of San Michele—Axel Munthe, 1929
The Rosary—Florence L. Barclay, 1909
Padlocked—Rex Beach, 1925
Away from It All: An Escapologist's Notebook—Cedric Belfrage, 1937
The Longhorn Feud—Max Brand, 1941
Four-Part Setting: A Novel—Ann Bridge, 1938
Wuthering Heights—Emily Brontë, 1847
The Rains Came—Louis Bromfield, 1937
The Jury—Gerald Bullett, 1935
Night in the Hotel—Eliot Crawshay-Williams, 1931
A Christmas Carol—Charles Dickens, 1843
The Three Musketeers—Alexandre Dumas, 1844
Silas Marner—George Eliot, 1861
Give Me Liberty: The Story of an Innocent Bystander—John Erskine, 1940
    (for Cissy)
Galahad: Enough of His Life to Explain His Reputation—John Erskine, 1926
Pylon—William Faulkner, 1935
Don Desperado—L. L. Foreman, 1941
The Captain from Connecticut—C. S. Forester, 1941
The Earthly Paradise—C. S. Forester, 1940
Show Boat—Edna Ferber, 1926
Girl on His Hands—Maysie Greig, 1939
The Four Million—O. Henry, 1906
The Voice of the City—O. Henry, 1919
Cabbages and Kings—O. Henry, 1917

The Trimmed Lamp and Other Stories of the Four Million—O. Henry, 1907

The Passionate Year—James Hilton, 1924

Green Mansions—William Henry Hudson, 1904

If Winter Comes—A. S. M. Hutchinson, 1921

Fiesta in Manhattan: A Novel—Charles Kaufman, 1939

Soldiers Three and Other Stories—Rudyard Kipling, 1899

Puck of Pooks Hill—Rudyard Kipling, 1906

Walking the Whirlwind—Brigid Knight, 1941 (for Cissy and Margaret)

Something of a Hero—I. J. Kapstein, 1941

And Tell of Time—Laura Krey, 1938

The Job—Sinclair Lewis, 1917

The Impregnable Women—Eric Linklater, 1938

Autobiography of a Cad—A. G. Macdonnell, 1938

Ah King—W. Somerset Maugham, 1933

We Forget Because We Must—W. B. Maxwell, 1928

Royals Free—Mordanat [?]

The Fountain—Charles Morgan, 1932

Hira Singh: When India Came to Fight in Flanders—Talbot Mundy, 1918

The Bounty Trilogy—Charles B. Nordhoff and James N. Hall, 1932–34

Scarlet Sister Mary—Julia Peterkin, 1928

The Rocklitz—George R. Preedy, 1930

K—Mary Roberts Rinehart, 1915

Don't Think It Hasn't Been Fun—Quentin Reynolds, 1941

Northwest Passage—Kenneth Roberts, 1937

Oliver Wiswell—Kenneth Roberts, 1940

His Official Fiancée—Berta Ruck, 1914

Master-at-Arms—Rafael Sabatini, 1940

Guy Mannering—Sir Walter Scott, 1815

The Little French Girl—Anne Douglas Sedgwick, 1924

"The Shepherd Boy's Song in the Valley of Humiliation"
    [from *The Pilgrim's Progress*]—John Bunyan, 1678

The Grapes of Wrath—John Steinbeck, 1939

The Temple of Costly Experience—Daniele Varè, 1939

The Maker of Heavenly Trousers—Daniele Varè, 1935

The Gate of Happy Sparrows—Daniele Varè, 1937

The Woodcarver of 'Lympus—Mary Ella Waller, 1907

Dear Enemy—Jean Webster, 1915

The Puritan Strain—Faith Baldwin, 1935

Cotton: A Novel—Bethea, 1928

The Jasmine Farm—Elizabeth Von Arnim, 1934

Invitation to the Waltz—Rosamond Lehmann, 1932

A Warning to Wantons—Mary Mitchell, 1934

The Man in Lower Ten—Mary Roberts Rinehart, 1909

The Best Time Ever—Berta Ruck, 1934

Of Mice and Men—John Steinbeck, 1937

The Red Pony—John Steinbeck, 1933

Beau Geste—P. C. Wren, 1924

The General Died at Dawn—Charles Boothe, 1941

Murder in College—J. Y. Dane, 1935

The Circular Staircase—Mary Roberts Rinehart, 1908

Busman's Honeymoon—Dorothy L. Sayers, 1937

Collected Verse—Rudyard Kipling, 1927

Evangeline: A Tale of Acadie—Henry Wadsworth Longfellow, 1847

"The White Cliffs"—Alice Duer Miller, 1940

Not So Deep as a Well: Collected Poems—Dorothy Parker, 1936

Great Fights in Literature—C. James, ed., 1931

Fifty Amazing Secret Service Dramas—Anonymous, *1937*

Dry Pickwick and Other Incongruities, The—Stephen Leacock

Great Short Stories of Guy de Maupassant, The—Guy de Maupassant, 1939

Great Tales and Poems of Edgar Allan Poe, The—Edgar Allan Poe, 1940

Little Gods, The: A Masque of the Far East—Rowland Thomas, 1909

The Heart of a Goof—P. G. Wodehouse, 1926

While Rome Burns—Alexander Woollcott, 1934

Glimpses of the Last [?]

Testament of Youth—Vera Brittain, 1933

Days to Remember: The British Empire in the Great War—John Buchan
        and Henry Newbolt, 1923

Last Flight—Amelia Earhart, 1937

My Four Years in Germany—James W. Gerard, 1917

Return via Dunkirk—Gun Buster, 1945

Stonewall Jackson and the American Civil War—G. F. R. Henderson, 1898

Mein Kampf [English-language edition]—Adolph Hitler, 1939

Captain Lee Hall of Texas—Dora Neill Raymond, 1940

I Find Treason: The Story of an American Anti-Nazi Agent—
        Richard Rollins, 1941

Generals and Generalship—General Sir Archibald Wavell, 1941

Guilty Men—Cato [Michael Foot, Frank Owen, and Peter Howard], 1940

With Love and Irony—Lin Yutang, 1934

Microbe Hunters—Paul de Kruif, 1926

The Autobiography of Benvenuto Cellini, 1558; J. A. Symonds trans., 1927

The Life of Arthur Duke of Wellington—G. R. Gleig, 1911

*Richard Halliburton: His Story of His Life's Adventure as Told in Letters
     to His Mother and Father*—Richard Halliburton, 1940

Autobiography—Benjamin Franklin, 1791

The Innocence of Father Brown—G. K. Chesterton, 1910

"Dead Man's Plack" and "An Old Thorn"—William Henry Hudson, 1920

"Markheim" [1885] and "The Body Snatcher" [1884]—Robert Louis
     Stevenson [sources unknown]

The Portrait of Angela [?]

The Rough Riders—Theodore Roosevelt, 1899

When Adam Wept—Alan Robert Craig, 1933

The Naulahka: A Story of West and East—Rudyard Kipling and
     Wolcott Balestier, 1892

R.A.F.—H. E. Bates, 1942 [?]

Sabotage—Cleve F. Adams, 1940

Trail Smoke—Ernest Haycox, 1936

I Was a Nazi Flier—Gottfried Leske, 1941

The World's 100 Best Short Stories, 10 vols.—Grant M. Overton, ed., 1927 [?]

"The Snows of Kilimanjaro"—Ernest Hemingway (in *The Bedside Esquire,*
     Arnold Gingrich, ed., 1940)

"The Seven Men of Rouen"—G. Slocombe (in *The Bedside Esquire,*
     Arnold Gingrich, ed., 1940)

Black Tobias and the Empire—Heinz Werner, 1938

Duel by Candlelight [?]

I Mix the Drinks [?]

Arrowsmith—Sinclair Lewis, 1925 [*Erskine Caldwell listed and then
     scratched out*]

Stately Timber—Rupert Hughes, 1939

The Thin Man—Dashiell Hammett, 1934

The Nutmeg Tree—Margery Sharp, 1937

Captain Caution: A Chronicle of Arundel—Kenneth Roberts, 1934

The Case of the Curious Bride, The—Erle Stanley Gardner, 1934

Drums—James Boyd, 1928

Short Stories of War (1914–18) [?]

My Ten Years in a Quandary, and How They Grew—Robert Benchley, 1936

The Idiot—Fyodor Dostoevsky, 1869

The Citadel—A. J. Cronin, 1937

Spanish Grammar Self-Taught—Andrés Garcia, 1931 (Marlborough's
    Self-taught Series) [?]
Babes in the Wood—Michael Arlen, 1929
Hatter's Castle—A. J. Cronin, 1931
Restless Is the River—August Derleth, 1939
Death Lights a Candle: An Asey Mayo Mystery of Cape Cod—
    Phoebe Atwood Taylor, 1932
A Pocket Book of Short Stories—M Edmund Speare, ed., 1941
The Door Between: A Problem in Deduction—Ellery Queen, 1936
Elizabeth and Essex: A Tragic History—Lytton Strachey, 1928
*The Gentleman in the Parlour: A Record of a Journey from Rangoon
    to Haiphong*—W. Somerset Maugham, 1930
The Case of the Howling Dog—Erle Stanley Gardner, 1934
Disgrace Abounding—Douglas Reed, 1939 (unfinished)
The Tree of Liberty—Elizabeth Page, 1939
Bedside Book of American Short Stories—Modern Library Edition [?]
The Singapore Exile Murders—F. Van Wyck Mason, 1939
Three Harbours—F. Van Wyck Mason, 1938

Sixth (Canvas) Journal

My Early Life: A Roving Commission—Winston Churchill, 1930
Forty-One Years in India: From Subaltern to Commander-in-Chief—
    Field-Marshal Lord Roberts of Kandahar, 1900
"You Are National Guard," by J. P. McEvoy, *Reader's Digest*, September 1940
    (Have Cissy read.)
All This and Heaven Too—Rachel Field, 1938
This above All—Eric Knight, 1940
Rabble in Arms—Kenneth Roberts, 1933
*The Lively Lady: A Chronicle of Certain Men of Arundel in Maine,
    of Privateering during the War of Impressments, and of the Circular
    Prison on Dartmoor*—Kenneth Roberts, 1931
Arundel—Kenneth Roberts, 1930
March to Quebec: Journals of the Members of Arnold's Expedition—
    Kenneth Roberts, ed., 1938
Trending into Maine—Kenneth Roberts, 1938
From Private to Field Marshal—by Field-Marshal Sir William
    Robertson, 1921
Old Soldier Sahib—Private Frank Richards, 1936
Gallipoli Diary—by General Sir Ian Hamilton, 1920

Sergeant Lamb of the Ninth—Robert Graves, 1940 (and sequel) [*Proceed, Sergeant Lamb,* 1941]

Jungle Patrol: The Story of the Philippine Constabulary—Victor Hurley, 1938

Bullets and Bolos—Col. J. R. White (PC set [?])

Roving and Fighting: Adventures under Four Flags—Edward S. O'Reilly, 1918

"The Irish Guards"—Rudyard Kipling, 1918

Chasing Villa: The Story behind the Story of Pershing's Expedition into Mexico—Colonel Frank Tompkins, 1934

With Malice toward Some—Margaret Halsey, 1938 (American poet pokes fun at English customs)

The Coming Struggle for Latin America—Carleton Beals

An American Doctor's Odyssey—Victor Heiser, 1936

The Boston Cook Book—Fannie M. Farmer, 1918

Black Is My Truelove's Hair—Elizabeth Madox Roberts, 1938

Lady Chatterley's Lover—D. H. Lawrence, 1928

The Works of Edgar Allen Poe—Edgar Allan Poe, 1849

Some Experiences of an Irish R. M.—Edith Somerville and Martin Ross, 1899

Frozen Inlet Post—James B. Hendryx, 1927

APPENDIX E:
TEXAS AGGIE DEFENDERS OF CORREGIDOR, 1942

Maj. Gen. George F. Moore	'08
Maj. John V. King	'22**
Maj. Paul Brown	'29**
Lt. John L. Lester	'29*
Capt. Graham M. Hatch	'31**
Capt. William M. Curtis	'32**
Capt. Jerome A. McDavitt	'33
Capt. Chester A. Peyton	'33**
Capt. Hervey H. Whitfield	'34***
Capt. Stockton D. Bruns	'35
Maj. Tom Dooley	'35
Capt. Roy M. Vick Jr.	'35**
Lt. John McCluskey	'36**
Capt. Willis A. Scrivener	'37**
Lt. David Snell	'37
Capt. Wilbert A. Calvert	'38**
Sgt. Hugh Hunt	'38
Lt. Andy James	'38**
Lt. William Boyd	'39**
Lt. Lewis B. Chevaillier	'39
Lt. Carl Pipkin	'39**
Capt. Henry A. Schutte Jr.	'39**
Lt. Clifton Chamberlain	'40
Lt. Stanley Friedline	'40*

Lt. William A. Hamilton	'40
Lt. Urban C. Hopmann	'40
Lt. Charlton Wimer	'40

*	Killed in action (2)
**	Killed while Japanese POW (13)
***	Ordered to pilot the last supply plane mission off Corregidor, May 5

From *The Fightin' Texas Aggie Defenders of Bataan and Corregidor* (2016), courtesy of John A. Adams.w

ADC Aide-de-camp

Admiral Hotel Built in 1939, the hotel was occupied by the Japanese during World War II. After the liberation of Manila, the American High Command rented the building for use as its headquarters.

ANC Army and Navy Club

A.R.C. American Red Cross

Banca Native canoe

Banga A popular or enjoyable song

Bantam (See also Peep.) American Bantam Car Company built a 1/4-ton 4×4 that, in a 1/2-ton version, would be known as a jeep.

Bejuca Simple style of Philippine furniture

Baluga Part of the Negritos Tribe

Binta Slap on the face

Bolo A common harvesting tool of Filipino origin similar to the machete. Because of its availability, the bolo became a common choice of weapon for the peasants.

Bongo POW roll call by the numbers

Calesse (Italian noun, pl. Calessi) Two-wheeled horse-drawn carriage

Carabao a swamp-type domestic water buffalo found in the Philippines.

CAST Station CAST was the US Navy signals monitoring and cryptographic intelligence fleet radio unit at Cavite Navy Yard in the Philippines until Cavite was captured by the Japanese in 1942. It was an important part of the Allied intelligence effort, addressing Japanese communications as the war expanded into the Pacific theatre. As Japanese advances threatened CAST, its staff and services were transferred to Corregidor and, eventually, Australia.

Chesterfield Cigarette brand widely recognized in early and mid-twentieth century

C.G. Commanding general

C. of S. Chief of Staff

Cocomalt Cocoa and malt drink provided with field rations during World War II

Coracle Small, round boat

Corn-willie Hash whose main ingredient is corned beef.

Cow-tow Low Oriental bow, sign of subservience

Dapecol Davao Penal Colony (POW camp on Mindanao)

Domei (Dōmei Tsūshinsha, "Federated News Agency") Official Japanese news service from 1936 to 1945.

DSC Distinguished Service Cross

Eight Ball 8th Naval Construction Battalion

FEAF Far East Air Force

G-1 Administration and Personnel

G-2 Intelligence and Security

G-3 Operations

G-4 Logistics

Gen. W. Gen. Jonathan M. Wainwright.

Getta Wooden clogs worn by POWs

Gabi Taro

Galantine Boneless stuffed poultry or fish poached and served cold with coating of aspic.

Garand The M1 Garand, a semiautomatic rifle chambered for the .30-06 Springfield rifle cartridge, was used by the US Army from 1936 to 1957. Named after its designer, John Garand, it was the first standard-issue semiautomatic military rifle. George S. Patton called it "the greatest battle implement ever devised."

Helm House A five-story, reinforced-concrete building constructed in 1938. It contained thirty-one modern, fully furnished apartments. During the US Occupation it was used by officers of the Eighth Army.

Hospital #1 See Limay General Hospital.

Hotel New Grand A historic hotel in Yokohama, Japan. Opened in 1927, it was used by American troops following World War II. One suite is maintained just as it was when General MacArthur stayed there on his first night in Japan during the Occupation.

Imperial Rescript The Imperial Rescript was the official code of ethics for Japanese military personnel. Issued by Emperor Meiji in January 1882, the Rescript was considered the most important document in the development of the Japanese army and the Japanese navy.

Karo Corn syrup, used as a substitute for sugar during World War II

KGEI Before the Japanese occupation of Manila, on 2 January 1942, many radio stations were on the air throughout the Philippines. The US Army had removed the shortwave transmitter from KZRH in Manila, and on 5 January they reactivated it as the Voice of Freedom on Corregidor Island. A few days later they activated a shortwave station on the Bataan Peninsula as a part-time relay for the California station KGEI. On 14 January the Japanese relaunched shortwave KZRH. On 6 May, in a series of three broadcasts over the Voice of Freedom, General Wainwright addressed the Japanese general Masaharu Homma, offering to surrender. The next day he made a broadcast over KZRH stating that the American forces had surrendered.

KP (Kilometer Post) Marker indicating distance from Manila.

KZRH See KGEI.

Limay General Hospital (also Hospital #1) The first hospital for American and Filipino forces.

Lugao Water gruel of rice soup

Luzon Force See USAFFE.

Mizo Seasoning from fermented soybean

Momoyama Pipe tobacco produced by Japan Monopoly Corporation and packaged in 50g tins.

Moro Indigenous Philippine Muslim

N.C.O. Noncommissioned officer

New Grand Hotel See Hotel New Grand.

North Luzon Force See USAFFE.

NG No good

Nipa hut Bamboo-framed structure covered with palm branches

P-40 (Curtiss P-40 Warhawk) An American single-engine, single-seat, all-metal fighter and ground-attack aircraft, it first flew in 1938, and it remained in service until the end of the war.

Peep (See also Bantam.) Because the name Jeep had been applied to the ½-ton 4×4, many called the new 1/4-ton reconnaissance vehicle a Peep to differentiate them.

Prisoner of War Bureau In 1941 the POW Information Bureau was established in the Japanese Army Ministry in Tokyo to deal with POWs captured in Southeast Asia.

Prisoner of War Camps (Taiwan) In 1942 the Japanese established fourteen camps on Taiwan for prisoners captured in Southeast Asia. All the highest-ranking American, Australian, British, and Dutch military officers from Singapore, the Philippines, and the Dutch East Indies, along with the governors of the Dutch East Indies, Guam, Hong

Kong, Malaya, and Singapore, were held on the island in camps at Karenko, Shirakawa, and Taihoku.

PX An exchange—called a Post Exchange (PX) in the US Army and a Base Exchange (BX) in the US Air Force—is a retail outlet resembling a department store. Exchanges are found on US military installations worldwide

Rock Nickname for Corregidor Island

Sakied up Intoxicated on rice wine

SNAFU Situation normal, all fouled up

Souse Family, The A traditional drinking and marching song that became popular during the First World War and was sung across the United States throughout the twentieth century.

South Luzon Force See USAFFE.

Speedo Japanese army slang meaning "to move faster"

Tripe The first or second stomach of a cow or other ruminant used as food.

USAAF United States Army Air Force

USAFFE In December 1941, Gen. Douglas MacArthur organized the United States Armed Forces Far East into four tactical commands:

> 1. The *North Luzon Force*, under Maj. Gen. Jonathan M. Wainwright, defended the most likely sites for amphibious attacks and the central plains of Luzon. Wainwright's forces included the 11th, 21st and, 31st Infantry Divisions (Philippine Army); the US 26th Cavalry Regiment (Philippine Scouts); a battalion of the 45th Infantry (PS); and the 1st Provisional Artillery Group.

> 2. The *South Luzon Force*, under Brig. Gen. George M. Parker Jr., controlled a zone east and south of Manila. Parker had the 41st and 51st Infantry Divisions (PA) and the 2nd Provisional Artillery Group of two batteries of the US 86th Field Artillery Regiment (PS).

3. The *Visayan-Mindanao Force* under Brig. Gen. William F. Sharp comprised the 61st, 81st, and 101st Infantry Divisions (PA), reinforced after the start of the war by the newly inducted 73rd and 93rd Infantry Regiments. The 61st Division was located on Panay, the 81st on Cebu and Negros, and the 101st on Mindanao.

4. The *Reserve Force*, under MacArthur's direct control, comprised the Philippine Division, the 91st Division (PA), and headquarters units from the PA and Philippine Department, positioned just north of Manila. The 192nd and 194th Tank Battalions formed the separate Provisional Tank Group, also under MacArthur's direct command, at Clark Field/Fort Stotsenburg.

USFIP United States Forces in Philippines

Victory Program US program to mobilize industry, build up American armed forces, and create a strategy to defeat any enemies

Visayan-Mindanao Force See USAFFE.

Voice of Freedom See KGEI.

W.D. War Department

Zero High-performance Japanese fighter plane

SUGGESTED READING

Adams, John A. Jr. *Give 'em Hell, Son: The Fightin' Texas Aggie Defenders of Bataan and Corregidor, 1941–1945* (College Station: Texas A&M University Press, 2016).

———. *Keepers of the Spirit: The Corps of Cadets at Texas A&M University, 1876–2001* (College Station: Texas A&M University Press, 2001).

———. *Softly Call the Muster* (College Station: Texas A&M University Press, 1994).

———. *We Are the Aggies: The Texas A&M University Association of Former Students* (College Station: Texas A&M University Press, 1979).

Bart, Barry. *A Book of Battles: From Troy to Bataan* (N.Y.: Garden City Publishing, 1942).

Bartsch, William H. *Doomed at the Start: American Pursuit Pilots in the Philippines, 1941–1942* (College Station: Texas A&M University Press, 1995).

———. *December 8, 1941: MacArthur's Pearl Harbor* (College Station: Texas A&M University Press, 2012).

Beck, John J. *MacArthur and Wainwright: Sacrifice of the Philippines* (Albuquerque: University of New Mexico Press, 1974).

Beebe, Lewis. *Prisoner of the Rising Sun: The Lost Diary of Brig. Gen. Lewis Beebe* (College Station: Texas A&M University Press, 2006).

Bond, Charles R. Jr., and Terry Anderson. *Flying Tiger's Diary* (College Station: Texas A&M University Press, 1984).

Brereton, Lewis H. *The Brereton Diaries: The War in the Air in Pacific, Middle East and Europe, 3 October 1941–8 May 1945* (NY: William Morrow, 1946).

Calvocoressi, Peter, and Guy Wint. *Total War: Causes and Courses of the Second World War* (NY: Pantheon Books, 1989).

Coleman, John S. *Bataan and Beyond: Memories of an American POW* (College Station: Texas A&M University Press, 1978).

Dethloff, Henry C. *A Centennial History of Texas A&M University: 1876–1976* (College Station: Texas A&M University Press, 1975).

———. *A Pictorial History of Texas A&M University: 1876–1976*, 2nd ed. (College Station: Texas A&M University Press, 1996).

221

———— with John A. Adams, Jr. *Texas Aggies Go to War: In Service of Their Country* (College Station: Texas A&M University Press, 2006).

Drea, Edward J. *Japan's Imperial Army: Its Rise and Fall, 1853–1945* (Lawrence: University Press of Kansas, 2009).

Edmonds, Walter D. *They Fought with What They Had: The Story of the Army Air Forces in the Southwest Pacific, 1931–1942* (Boston: Little, Brown, 1951).

Esposito, Vincent J., ed. *West Point Atlas of American Wars.* 2 vols. (NY: Frederick A. Praeger, 1959).

Hohenberg, John. *Foreign Correspondence: The Great Reporters and Their Times* (NY: Columbia University Press, 1964).

Gailey, Harry A. *The War in the Pacific: From Pearl Harbor to Tokyo Bay* (Novato, CA: Presidio Press, 1995).

Knox, Donald. *Death March: The Survivors of Bataan* (NY: Harcourt Brace Jovanovich, 1981).

Lea, Tom. *The Two Thousand Yard Stare: Tom Lea's World War II* (College Station: Texas A&M University Press, 2008).

MacArthur, Douglas. *Reminiscences* (NY: McGraw-Hill, 1964).

Mallonee, Col. Richard C. *The Naked Flagpole: Battle for Bataan* (Novato, CA: Presidio Press, 1980).

Manchester, William. *American Caesar: Douglas MacArthur 1880–1964* (Boston: Little, Brown, 1978).

Miller, Edward S. *War Plan Orange: The US Strategy to defeat Japan, 1897–1945* (Annapolis, MD: Naval Institute Press, 1991).

Morton, Louis. *War in the Pacific: The Fall of the Philippines* (Washington, DC: Center for Military History, 1989).

Nelson, Jack Adolph. *The Disabled, the Media, and the Information Age* (Westport, CT.: Greenwood Press, 1994).

O'Donnell, Patrick K. *Into the Rising Sun* (NY: Free Press, 2002).

O'Neill, Richard. *Suicide Squads W.W. II* (NY: Dorset Press, 1989).

Owens, William A. *Eye-Deep in Hell: A Memoir of the Liberation of the Philippines, 1944–1945* (Dallas, TX: Southern Methodist University Press, 1989).

Perret, Geoffrey. *Winged Victory: The Army Air Forces in World War II* (Westminster, MD: Random House, 1993)

Perry, George Sessions. *The Story of Texas A&M* (NY: McGraw-Hill, 1951).

Redmond, Juanita. *I Served on Bataan* (Philadelphia, PA: J. B. Lippincott, 1943).

Reiss, Curt, ed. *They Were There: The Story of World War II and How It Came about by America's Foremost Correspondents* (NY: G. P. Putnams Sons, 1944).

Shortal, John Francis. *Forged by Fire: Robert L. Eichelberger and the Pacific War* (Columbia: University of South Carolina Press, 1987).

Sloan, Bill. *Undefeated: America's Heroic Fight for Bataan and Corregidor.* (NY: Simon & Schuster, 2012).

Spector, Ronald H. *Eagle against the Sun: The American War with Japan* (NY: Free Press, 1984).

Wainwright, Jonathan M. *General Wainwright's Story: The Account of Four Years of Humiliating Defeat, Surrender, and Captivity* (NY: Modern Library, 1945).

White, William Lindsay. *They Were Expendable* (NY: Harcourt, Brace, 1942).

Woodall, James R. *Texas Aggie Medals of Honor* (College Station: Texas A&M University Press, 2010).

———. *Twelve Texas Aggie Heroes* (College Station: Texas A&M University Press, 2015).

Wright, B. C. *The First Cavalry Division in World War II* (Tokyo: Toppan, 1947).
[\\Store1\mac_share\EDITORIAL\10S\Charles--Allies at Odds\4Final]